Healing God's Creation

THE GLOBAL ANGLICAN CONGRESS
ON THE
STEWARDSHIP OF CREATION

THE GOOD SHEPHERD RETREAT CENTER
HARTEBEESPORT, SOUTH AFRICA

AUGUST 18–23, 2002

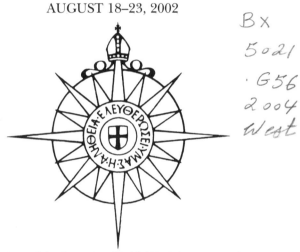

SUBMITTED TO THE ANGLICAN COMMUNION BY

Archdeacon Taimalelagi Fagamalama Tuatagaloa-Matalavea
The Anglican Observer at the United Nations
New York

EDITED BY

The Revd Canon Jeffrey Mark Golliher, Ph.D.
Program Assistant for the Environment and Sustainable Development
The Office of the Anglican Observer at the United Nations

2004

MOREHOUSE PUBLISHING
A Continuum imprint
HARRISBURG • LONDON • NEW YORK

In Memory of
Darrell Addison Posey, Ph.D.

Dedicated anthropologist, devoted Anglican,
courageous defender of God's creation.

His efforts to organize the Earth Parliament
of indigenous peoples at the 1992 Earth Summit in Rio
and his 30-year friendship with Canon Golliher
inspired the vision for this Anglican Congress.

Published for the Anglican Communion Office
Saint Andrew's House
16 Tavistock Crescent
London W11 1AP
England

Morehouse Publishing
P.O. Box 1321
Harrisburg, PA 17105

Morehouse Publishing is a Continuum imprint.

© 2004 The Secretary General of the Anglican Consultative Council

Photo credits: Ethan Flad, Asha Golliher
Cover design: Corey Kent

Library of Congress Cataloging-in-Publication Data

A record of this book is available from the Library of Congress.

ISBN 0-8192-2159-7

Contents

Section II: Homilies

Section III: Provincial and Country Reports

Section IV: Biographical Sketches of Congress Speakers

The Compass Rose

The emblem of the Anglican Communion, the Compass Rose, was originally designed by the late Canon Edward West of New York. The modern design is that of Giles Bloomfield. The symbol, set in the nave of Canterbury Cathedral, was dedicated by the Archbishop of Canterbury at the final Eucharist of the Lambeth Conference in 1988. The Archbishop dedicated a similar symbol in Washington Cathedral in 1990, and one in the original design in New York Cathedral in 1992, demonstrating that its use has become increasingly widespread. The centre of the Compass Rose holds the Cross of St. George, reminding Anglicans of their origins. The Greek inscription "The Truth Shall Make You Free" (John 8:32) surrounds the cross, and the compass recalls the spread of Anglican Christianity throughout the world. The mitre at the top emphasises the role of the episcopacy and apostolic order that is at the core of the churches of the Communion. The Compass Rose is used widely by the family of Anglican-Episcopal churches. It is the logo of the Inter-Anglican Secretariat, and it is used as the Communion's identifying symbol.

Message from the Archbishop of Canterbury to the Anglican Congress on the Stewardship of Creation

—THE MOST REVD. AND RT. HON. DR. GEORGE L. CAREY,
ARCHBISHOP OF CANTERBURY

I am delighted that so many representatives from around the Communion have been able to attend this timely Congress on the Stewardship of Creation. By your presence you are ensuring that any discussions and work that the Communion undertakes on sustainable development are informed by a truly international perspective. By meeting immediately before the UN World Summit on Sustainable Development, your presence is an important reminder that all must take seriously the spiritual dimension to the ecological and humanitarian crises facing our planet.

I have every confidence that our Congress will be diligent in considering the full complexity of sustainable development, so that environmental, economic, social and spiritual concerns will be addressed with equal care. I believe we can set the world's leaders an example in this, as we look beyond our immediate experience to God's saving purpose for Creation. We have an inescapable obligation to cherish the living planet that has been entrusted to us by our Creator.

I know that you will not only pray together about these matters, you will also bring practical skills and suggestions for projects around the Communion that will demonstrate our fundamental care for creation.

I welcome the recent declaration signed by His Holiness Pope John Paul II and His Holiness the Ecumenical Patriarch Bartholomew I. This is an historic statement, testifying to our common concern for all humanity and creation. May this Congress bear further witness to such shared commitment.

Archdeacon Tai and Canon Golliher leading a discussion on the Congress Declarations.

Participants from the Province of Southern Africa, the Scottish Episcopal Church and the Church of England.

INTRODUCTION

Reflections on the Global Anglican Congress

Declarations of the Global Anglican Congress on the Stewardship of Creation

Resolutions

> On Creation; On Ecology (1998 Lambeth Conference)

> On UN Observer and Environmental Network (Anglican Consultative Council Twelfth Meeting, Hong Kong, 2002)

Global Anglican Congress Delegates and Participants

Reflections on the Global Anglican Congress

—ARCHDEACON TAIMALELAGI FAGAMALAMA TUATAGALOA-MATALAVEA,
THE ANGLICAN OBSERVER AT THE UNITED NATIONS

Greetings in the mighty name of Jesus Christ! It is my greatest pleasure, and hope for the future, that I present to my sisters and brothers in the Communion these Proceedings of the Global Anglican Congress on the Stewardship of Creation. The Congress was held in August of 2002 in South Africa, organized by my office, the Anglican Office at the United Nations (AUNO), and was hosted locally by The Rt. Revd Geoff Davies, Bishop of Umzimvubu.

This was a first of its kind event that brought together over eighty Anglican leaders (lay and ordained) representing twenty of the Communion's Provinces. They were chosen and sponsored by the Provinces as their official representatives, and the Province of Southern Africa, as host Province, sent a substantial delegation as well. Our purpose in convening the Congress was to learn more about the ecological crisis and to nurture a more organized Anglican response. The Congress was held immediately before the United Nations Summit on Sustainable Development in Johannesburg, where the nations of the world reviewed progress made towards reaching the goals of Agenda 21, the comprehensive plan for sustainable development set forth by the 1992 Earth Summit.

The outcome of the UN Summit was mixed. On the one hand, it affirmed the basic assumptions and goals of the Earth Summit, which say that the ongoing impoverishment of the majority of the Earth's people and its ecosystems calls us to thoroughly transform how we understand and pursue economic development. On the other, we found many of our governments stuck in entrenched positions about many issues and unable to move forward, despite the unprecedented, urgent crisis due to humankind's destruction of God's creation. Having worked with the United Nations Development Program in the Pacific for many years, I know first-hand that the successes and shortcomings of the work of the UN are a reflection of the energy and commitment brought to it by the member States and the people of many NGOs who work tirelessly to make their voices heard. We are obviously at a turning point and the stakes are very high.

The Global Anglican Congress, I'm happy to say, demonstrated how we can come together, with love and respect, as one people, in response to the challenges before us. We understood that those challenges are really spiritual and moral at their heart. God and all God's creation need us now to act with commitment and perseverance. I feel confident that the many seeds planted at the Congress will take root and flourish in the years ahead, and our churches throughout the Communion will take up the responsibilities of stewardship and caring for creation that faith so clearly calls us to do.

As a step toward that goal, the Congress issued two formal Declarations—one submitted to the United Nations, and the other, to the Anglican Communion—which are included in these Proceedings. Soon after the Congress, in September of 2002, the ACC-12 meeting in Hong Kong, having received the Anglican Observer's report, which also covered the Congress, passed four resolutions by which the Council:

(a) asks all churches of the Anglican Communion to place environmental care on their agenda;

(b) asks all Anglicans to make their own personal commitments to care for God's world, respecting all life, for "the Earth is the Lord's and all that is in it" (Psalm 24);

(c) establishes the Anglican Environmental Network as an official network of the Anglican Communion;

(d) endorses for immediate action the Declarations of the Anglican Congress to the United Nations and to the Anglican Communion.

There are a great many people I would like to thank for making the Congress such a successful event in the life of the Anglican Communion. In addition to The Rt. Revd Geoff Davies, I would also like to thank The Rt. Revd Simon Chiwanga, former President of the Anglican Consultative Council who delivered the opening address on behalf of the Communion, and The Most Revd Njongonkulu Ndungane, Archbishop of the Province of Southern Africa, not only for attending and participating in the Congress, but for showing enthusiastic support. Our planning team was indispensable in their dedication: The Revd Canon Jeff Golliher, Ph.D., who coordinated the Congress, David Shreeve of the Conservation Foundation in London, who organized press and publicity; Claire Foster of the Church of England who did our morning meditations; The Rt. Revd George Browning, Bishop of Canberra & Goulburn who graciously assisted the team in drafting initial versions of the Declarations prior to the event; Mrs. Kate Davies who assisted our host and the team; Joe and Katie McGervey, who, working as environmental missionaries for Bishop Davies in the Diocese of Umzimvubu, tirelessly helped with local arrangements; and the Revd Canon Eric Beresford of the ACC staff and Convener of the Anglican Environmental Network. Dr. Jan Loubser, who participated in the Congress, provided invaluable assistance in the planning process. I would also like to add my sincere thanks to my former Secretary Mrs. Yasmeen Granville-Anderson, Holly A. Weber for her assistance with transcriptions and to Mrs. Asha Golliher, for her cheerful encouragement, genuine participation, and for photographing some of the events. I want to thank Brother William Jones, BSG, my administrative assistant, for his enthusiasm and perseverance in the layout and production of these Proceedings. The many parishioners in the province of Southern Africa who attended the Congress were a blessing. In addition to their active involvement in the sessions and workshops, they enriched and enlivened our worship services. All of us owe a lot of gratitude and inspiration for the fruitful sharing of our stories and values and to the comfort of our accommodations and services provided by the Sisters and staff of the Good Shepherd Retreat Center in Hartebeesport—*danke* and many thanks.

Lastly, I want to gratefully acknowledge and thank our several funding sources: The Most Revd and Rt. Hon. George L. Carey former Archbishop of Canterbury, The Most Revd Frank Griswold, Presiding Bishop of the Episcopal Church of the United States (ECUSA) who provided the main funding for the Congress, The Compass Rose Society, the Anglican Communion Fund of the Archbishop of Canterbury, The ECUSA Peace and Justice Ministries through The Revd Canon Brian Grieves, The ECUSA Anglican and Global Relations Division through The Revd Canon Patrick Mauney, The Rt. Revd Mark Sisk and the Diocese of New York, and Mrs. Nancy E. W. Colton, a friend of the Observer's office and Secretary to many UN-NGO commissions. The Revd Canon John Peterson's moral support and assistance in finding the necessary funding is very much appreciated. Without these contributions, the Anglican Congress and its success would not have been possible.

In closing, I wish it known that the ministry of the Anglican Observer at the United Nations was established in 1987 to share the God-given gifts of our 75 million members in advocating for justice and peace in the world. AUNO is required by the Anglican Communion to bring to the conscience of the United Nations the full commitment of the Church to its Faith and God's mission prompting us to:

Walk with love and care on God's earth;
Walk with vital awareness of God's comprehensive vision and purpose for creation; and,
Walk with awe and gratitude to ensure justice to the trees and rivers and the persons next to you.

The Congress was organized with that commitment in mind.

Declarations of the Global Anglican Congress on the Stewardship of Creation

Declaration to the Anglican Communion

The Good Shepherd Retreat Center, South Africa, August 18–23, 2002

Brothers and Sisters in Christ, we greet you and speak to you in the name of our Trinitarian God, Father, Son, and Holy Spirit: Creator, Redeemer, and Life Giver.

We write as representatives of the provinces of the Anglican Communion gathered in response to the planetary crisis and immediately prior to the World Summit on Sustainable Development. With the blessing of the Archbishop of Canterbury, the General Secretary of the Anglican Consultative Council, and the chair of the Anglican Consultative Council, our purpose is to consider the Communion's responsibilities to God and God's creation at this critical time. At the last Lambeth Conference in 1998 our Bishops again identified the environment as one of the key moral and religious issues of our time and their principles have been part of our reflection.

We have come together as a community of faith. Creation calls us, our vocation as God's redeemed drives us, the Spirit in our midst enlivens us, scripture compels us.

> *Where were you when I laid the foundations of the earth? Tell me if you have understanding. Job 38:4*

> *All things came into being through him, and without him not one thing came into being. John 1:3*

> *We know the whole creation has been groaning in labour pains until now. Romans 8:22*

Our planetary crisis is environmental, but it is more than that. It is a crisis of the Spirit and the Body, which runs to the core of all that we hold sacred. It is characterized by deep poverty: impoverished people, an impoverished Earth. As people of faith, Christ draws us together to share responsibility for this crisis with all humanity.

In the twentieth century, the human impact on the earth increased enormously. In the last thirty years alone, human activity has destroyed many of the planet's natural resources. Climate change, flooding, habitat destruction, desertification, pollution, urban expansion, and famine have all played their part. A third of all fish species and a quarter of all mammal species are in danger of extinction. One billion people now suffer from a shortage of fresh water. Scientists have said the web of life is unraveling.

People must be willing to face change and participate actively in the decisions before us all. Unjust economic structures have taken from people and the land without giving in return, putting at risk all life that is sustained by the planet. Greed and over-consumption, which have dictated so much of economic development in the past, must be transformed into generosity and compassion. Transformation is, at its heart, a spiritual matter; it includes every aspect of our lives. As members of the Anglican Communion, at all levels of its life, we must play our part in bringing about this transformation toward a just, sustainable future. Now is the time for prayerful action based on the foundation of our faith.

In 1998, the Bishops of the Anglican Communion resolved to face these challenges and provided the scriptural and theological justification for the involvement of the Church in caring for creation. We recognize this and other ongoing work of people in the communion. Such work needs our support. However, it is not enough.

We urge you to acknowledge the gravity of our call to prayer and action. Both individuals and decision-making bodies of the Church at all levels need to be actively involved in addressing these problems. As brothers and sisters in Christ's Body and as fellow Anglicans seeking to fulfill our baptismal covenant and witness to the power of the Holy Spirit in Christ, we ask you, in your parishes, dioceses, or provinces, acting at the most appropriate level, and in cooperation with ecumenical and interfaith partners wherever possible to undertake the following:

• To acknowledge that the Church's mission must now take place in the context of a life and death planetary crisis whose impact affects all aspects of the Church's life and mission.

• To bring prayers and actions concerning ecology, environmental justice, human rights, and sustainable development to the forefront of public worship as well as private and corporate reflections on the Holy Scriptures.

• To support the struggle of indigenous peoples to maintain their cultural heritage, natural heritage, and human rights.

• To encourage all members of our congregations to understand that God calls us to care for the creation by making our communities and environments better places for the next generation than they were in our lifetime.

- To actively support initiatives in all Churches and communities that are concerned with the planetary crisis.

- To help publicize and network information, developments, events, publications and all sources of knowledge among our friends, neighbours, congregation members, Church leaders, and government officials.

- To encourage links among our provinces, dioceses, and parishes worldwide to increase understanding of the many issues involved and how they are interrelated.

- To support opportunities for younger people to experience first-hand how people in their own and other congregations and communities are affected by the planetary crisis and how they can work to change the world in which they live.

- To promote training and educational programs in all aspects of the planetary crisis even as they relate to our worship and community life.

- To encourage diligently our secular and Church leaders, lay and ordained, in all parts of the Anglican Communion to place the planetary crisis at the highest level of their concerns.

- To encourage and support public policies that reflect the principles of sustainable community.

- To request all bodies within the communion to undertake an environmental audit and take appropriate action on the basis of the results. To commit ourselves both to energy conservation and the use of sustainable energy sources.

- To demonstrate simplicity of lifestyle in our patterns of consumption to counteract greed and over-consumption. Such greed dictates so much of our economic past that it must be transformed into generosity and compassion.

Christ has no hands but ours, and he calls us to offer ourselves to share in his work of healing and reconciliation so that all creation may know that "The truth shall set you free."

Respectfully submitted on behalf of the Global Anglican Congress,

Archdeacon Taimalelagi Fagamalama Tuatagaloa-Matalavea
Anglican Observer at the United Nation

Declaration to the United Nations World Summit on Sustainable Development

The Good Shepherd Retreat Center, South Africa, August 18–23, 2002

We desperately need a change of spirit. The environmental debate is as much about religion and morality as it is about science. Sustainable development is one of the most urgent moral issues of our time. It begins in sustainable values that recognize the interrelatedness of all life. Sustainable development cannot be defined in economic terms alone, but must begin in a commitment to care for the poor, the marginalized, and the voiceless. Therefore it is sustainable community that we seek. The ecological systems that support life, the qualities that sustain local communities, and the voices of women, indigenous peoples and all who are marginalized and disempowered must be approached from this perspective.

As we move into the third millennium, it becomes increasingly obvious that human beings are set on a path of unprecedented environmental destruction and unsustainable development. A profound moral and spiritual change is needed. Human exploitation of the environment has yielded not only benefit, but also appalling poverty, pollution, land degradation, habitat loss, and species extinction. Despite political and scientific debates in some quarters, it is clear that human behaviour has overwhelmingly contributed to ozone depletion and global warming. We desperately need to change.

We write as representatives of the Anglican Communion. Our 70 million members are present in 165 countries across the globe. They speak from their experience of the problems of development in both urban and rural communities. At all levels of the life of the communion the environment has repeatedly been identified as one of the key moral and religious challenges before us.

Religious faith properly understood can and should be a major force for change towards sustainable development, sustainable communities, and a healthy environment. Anglicans accept the need to oppose all forms of exploitation. Specifically, we believe that a better, more holistic, and religiously informed understanding of Creation, which recognizes that human beings are part of the created order not separate from it, will make a major contribution to the transforming change of spirit that is essential in the third millennium. We are committed to putting our faith into action.

Many different religious traditions start from the belief that the world primarily belongs to God and not to human beings. Land, sea and air belong first and foremost to God. At most they are entrusted to human beings who are expected, in turn, to respond with gratitude and to hand them on faithfully and intact to generations to come. As stewards of the environment human beings are required by God to act faithfully and responsibly. Other theological perspectives within the Christian faith also support a renewed ethics of caring for the whole creation.

All religious traditions call their believers to disciplines of life that show respect for the environment that we inhabit. We value life more than possessions. We value people more than profits. Based on this shared commitment this Anglican Congress calls on people of all faiths to act together by:

- understanding that humanity is a part of the created order, not separate from it;

- evolving a new relationship with the created order founded on stewardship and service, with production and consumption restrained by genuine need and not simply governed by desire;

- locating our unity in the Spirit that breathes life into all things;

- celebrating the glorious God-given diversity that is everywhere.

We therefore call upon Governments of all nations to support sustainable communities, by

- working together for peace, justice and economic prosperity within a context of ecological stability;

- refusing to subordinate the good of all for the good of some;

- recognizing the intrinsic worth of non-human forms of life, and committing ourselves to strengthen and enforce the protection of endangered species;

- recognizing the intrinsic worth of the diversity of life, as well as the inextricable link between biodiversity and cultural diversity on which the survival of indigenous peoples, indeed all humankind, depends;

- rejecting the destructiveness of the culture of militarism, that spends disproportionate amounts of money on armaments when so many people in the world are still hungry, and stockpiles nuclear weapons and materials at great cost to the environment and to human well-being;

- recognizing that environmental degradation constitutes a violation of the universal declaration of human rights. Poverty and environmental degradation are interwoven and it is the poor, and the exploited, often on the basis of race and gender, who suffer most from this degradation;

- recognizing that development is not sustainable if it steals from present and future generations. The security of future generations can only be attained by addressing the urgent questions posed by the intolerable burden of un-payable debt, the challenges of unsustainable agricultural practices, and by the reduction of greenhouse gas emissions to ecologically stable levels. To this end we recommend serious consideration of the principle of contraction and convergence;

- affirming that the rivers and the land, the sea and the air are a global commons, entrusted to human beings to be handed on faithfully and intact to generations to come.

- defining the rules of international trade in ways that demand greater corporate responsibility in promoting greater inclusion of the marginalized and more sustainable environmental practices.

- recognizing that current rates of HIV/AIDS present a profound challenge to sustainable community, which must be met by adequate and equitable access to education and treatment.

Respectfully submitted on behalf of the Global Anglican Congress,

Archdeacon Taimalelagi Fagamalama Tuatagaloa-Matalavea
Anglican Observer at the United Nations

Resolutions on Creation and Ecology at the 1998 Lambeth Conference

Resolution 1.8: Creation

This Conference:

(a) reaffirms the Biblical vision of Creation according to which: Creation is a web of inter-dependent relationships bound together in the Covenant which God, the Holy Trinity has established the whole earth and every living being.

    (i) the divine Spirit is sacramentally present in Creation, which is therefore to be treated with reverence, respect and gratitude;

    (ii) human beings are both co-partners with the rest of Creation and living bridges between heaven and earth, with responsibliltiy to make personal and corporate sacrifices for the common good of all Creation;

    (iii) the redemptive purpose of God in Jesus Christ extends to the whole Creation.

(b) recognises

    (i) that unless human beings take responsibility for caring for the earth, the consequences will be catastrophic because of:

        — overpopulation
        — unsustainable levels of consumption by the rich
        — poor quality and shortage of water
        — air pollution
        — eroded and impoverished soil
        — forest destruction
        — plant and animal extinction;

    (ii) that the loss of natural habitats is a direct cause of genocide amongst millions of indigenous peoples and is causing the extinction of thousands of plant and animal species. Unbridled capitalism, selfishness and greed cannot continue to be allowed to pollute, exploit, and destroy what remains of the earth's indigenous habitats;

(iii) that the future of human beings and all life on earth hangs in balance as a consequence of the present unjust economic structures, the injustice existing between the rich and the poor, the continuing exploitation of the natural environment and the threat of nuclear self-destruction;

(iv) that the servant-hood to God's creation is becoming the most important responsibility facing humankind and that we should work together with people of all faiths in the implementation of our responsibilities;

(v) that we as Christians have a God given mandate to care for, look after and protect God's creation.

(c) prays in the Spirit of Jesus Christ:

(i) for widespread conversion and spiritual renewal in order that human beings will be restored to a relationship and harmony with the rest of Creation and that this relationship may be informed by the principles of justice and the integrity of ever living being, so that self centred greed is overcome; and

(ii) for the recovery of Sabbath principle, as part of the redemption of time and the restoration of the divinely intended rhythms of life.

Resolution 1.9 Ecology

This Conference:

(a) calls upon all ecumenical partners and other faith communities, governments and transnational companies:

(i) to work for sustainable society in a sustainable world;

(ii) to recognise the dignity and rights of all people and the sanctity of all life, especially the rights of future generations;

(iii) to ensure the responsible use of and re-cycling of natural resources;

(iv) to bring about economic reforms which will establish a just and fair trading system both for people and the environment.

(b) calls upon the United Nations to incorporate the right of future generations to a sustainable future in the Universal Declaration of Human Rights.

(c) asks the Joint Standing Committee of the ACC and the Primates to consider the appointment of a co-ordinator of an international ecological network within the Anglican Communion, who would:

    (i) work in co-operation with other ecumenical and interfaith agencies;

    (ii) be funded thorough and responsible to the Anglican Consultative Council;

    (iii) support those engaged in grass-roots environmental initiatives;

    (iv) gather and disseminate data and information on environmental issues so that the Church can play an informed role in lobbying for ecological justice in both the public and private sectors; and

    (v) contribute to the development of environmental educational programmes for use in the training of Christian leaders.

Resolution of the Twelfth Meeting of the Anglican Consultative Council

15–26 September 2002, Hong Kong

11. UN Observer and Environmental Network

This Anglican Consultative Council:

1. receives the UN Observer's report presented to the Council;

2. adopts the resolutions suggested in the report and letter (Annex IV) as its own, namely:

   a) asks all churches of the Anglican Communion to place environment care on their agenda;

   b) asks all Anglicans to make their own personal commitments to care for God's world, respecting all life, for "the Earth is the Lord's and all that is in it" (Psalm 24:1);

   c) establishes the Anglican Environmental Network as an official network of the Anglican Communion; and,

   d) endorses for immediate action, the declarations of the Anglican Congress to the United Nations and to the Anglican Communion.

Global Anglican Congress
Delegates and Participants

Name	Province of the Church or Organization represented
Mr. Gerald Billings	The Church of Aotearoa, New Zealand and Polynesia
The Revd Advent Dlamini	The Church of the Province of Southern Africa
The Very Revd Bernard Duma	The Church of the Province of Southern Africa
Mr. Fiu Elisara-Laula	Representing Least Developed Countries in the Pacific
Mr. Ethan Flad	The Episcopal Church in the United States
Ms. Claire Foster	The Church of England
Dr. Richard Fuggle	The University of Cape Town
The Revd Chad Gandiya	The Anglican Urban Network
Mrs. Martha Gardner	The Episcopal Church in the United States
Mr. Miles Giljam	The Church of the Province of Southern Africa
The Revd Canon Jeff Golliher, Ph.D.	The Episcopal Church in the United States/ Anglican Observer's Office at the United Nations
Mrs. Asha Golliher (Volunteer)	The Episcopal Church in the United States/ Anglican Observer's Office at the United Nations
The Revd Canon Ernle Patrick Gordon	The Province of the West Indies
The Revd Canon Kenneth J. Gray	The Anglican Church of Canada
The Revd Canon Thamsanqa Marshall Guma	The Church of the Province of Southern Africa
The Ven. Lewis E. S. Gumede	The Church of the Province of Southern Africa
Dr. Graham Humphrys	The Church in Wales
Mr. Pratyush Kumar Jena	The Church of North India
Mr. Willis Jenkins	The Episcopal Church of the United States
Mrs. Jessie Jeyakaran	The Church of South India
Mr. Lau Yan Kin	Hong Kong Anglican Church
The Revd David Kiviet	The Church of the Province of Southern Africa
Dr. Jan Loubser	Consultant with the United Nations and Member States
Mrs. Noluthando Lucas	The Church of the Province of Southern Africa
Mr. Peter Mann	World Hunger Year
Mr. David Lalmohon Mazumder	Church of Bangladesh
Mr. Joe McGervey	The Church of the Province of Southern Africa
Mrs. Katie McGervey	The Church of the Province of Southern Africa
Ms. Helen Meintjes	The Church of the Province of Southern Africa
Mr. Terry Miller	The Church of England
The Ven. Keith Muller	The Church of the Province of Southern Africa

Mr. Musa Mkunda	The Anglican Church of Tanzania
Mr. Teboho Mokau	The Church of the Province of Southern Africa
The Rt. Revd John Wesley Nduwayo	Episcopal Church of Burundi
Mr. Joseph Ngereza	Anglican Church of Tanzania
The Revd Mlibo Ngewu	The Church of the Province of Southern Africa
The Rt. Revd John Oliver	The Church of England
The Revd George Pitt	The Church of Ireland
Mrs. Janice Proud	The Episcopal Church in Jerusalem and the Middle East
Mr. Lucas Raphela	The Church of the Province of Southern Africa
The Revd Mario Ribas	Church of Brazil
Ms. Baruna Roy	The Church of North India
The Rt. Revd William Rukirande	The Church of the Province of Uganda/ Solar Light for Churches in Africa
Mr. Bruno Sengulane	The Church of the Province of Southern Africa
Mr. David Shreeve	The Conservation Foundation
The Revd Don Stephen	The Church of the Province of Southern Africa
Ms. Noami Thaele	The Church of the Province of Southern Africa
Dr. Anthony Turton	University of Pretoria
Ms. Vanya Walker-Leigh	Sunday *Times*
The Revd Andrew E. Warmback	The Church of the Province of Southern Africa
Professor Alan Werrity	The Scottish Episcopal Church
Mrs. Rose Wiltshire	Barbados
Dr. Rosina Wiltshire	UN Development Program, Barbados
The Revd Peter Sikelela Zumgu	The Church of the Province of Southern Africa
The Ven. Ignatius C. M. Zwane	The Church of the Province of Southern Africa

SECTION I

The Purpose of the Anglican Congress:
The Stewardship of Creation and Sustainable Development

Plenary Presentations

>   Community Empowerment
>   Water
>   Food and Agriculture
>   Energy and Climate Change
>   HIV/AIDS
>   Biodiversity
>   Eco-Justice
>   Gender and Human Development
>   The Beauty of Empowerment

The Purpose of the Anglican Congress: The Stewardship of Creation and Sustainable Development

—THE REV. CANON JEFF GOLLIHER, PH.D.

The Anglican Observer at the UN convened the Global Anglican Congress for obvious reasons. Examine any part of the Earth's ecosystems—freshwater, oceans, the atmosphere and climate, food and agriculture, forests, cities, or rural settlements. What do we find? The web of life is under so much destructive pressure that it may be unraveling. In some places, the web of life has already been unraveling for many years. If the onslaught continues, there will not be adequate resources, clean water, food, or a stable enough climate to support human life. Scientists may debate the degree or rate of destruction, but evidence that the ecological crisis exists is overwhelming. This is virtually inconceivable, but true. Perhaps equally inconceivable is that while "it happens" some of the world's more politically powerful governments persist in their inaction and denial. Our goal at the Congress was to energize the Anglican Communion around this urgent situation and to deliver a clear message to the United Nations Conference on Sustainable Development, which would be addressing many of the same issues. My purpose here is to discuss the rationale and underlying assumptions of the Congress, hoping to clarify one kind of response the Anglican Communion can make to this unprecedented ecological crisis.

In planning the Anglican Congress, as in organizing any response to the ecological crisis, we faced some crucial strategic issues. The way we addressed those issues shaped, to a large extent, the content and organization of the Congress. First, the reality of the ecological crisis and its spiritual and moral roots may be self-evident to those of us who are already involved, yet the whole Anglican Communion does not necessarily share this perspective. Every delegate to the Congress expressed genuine concern about the lack of appropriate action and commitment in many of our churches. The fact is that the destruction affects everyone, regardless of our points of view; and for that reason, we are all very deeply involved. Nevertheless, the question of whether we should respond to the ecological crisis must still be addressed positively, persistently and persuasively on all levels of the Anglican Communion. Second, we must recognize that it is not enough simply to say that we must do something. Our responses must engage the heart of the crisis as effectively as possible. The more difficult question is: "How can we best respond?" That was the principal strategic question of the Congress.

A good starting point in answering this question is to recognize that the ecological crisis takes different forms in different places, and the practical dimension of our responses can vary widely, depending on local circumstances. In other words, there are many ways to do environmental ministry and to pursue sustainable development. Also, it is important to understand that, in a very real sense, this is not a new ministry. The large-scale, systematic destruction of ecosystems has been taking place for generations, and people in the church have been involved with this issue for many years. However, the scale of the crisis today and the gravity of the threat to the whole web of life are unprecedented in human history. The point is that many grass-roots leaders in this area of ministry, working in local communities, have been isolated and without helpful resources. We need to know each other; we need more involved people; and if anyone needs support in any way, we should make every effort to provide it. For the Anglican Communion, this may necessitate new levels of communication, cooperation and collaboration across the diverse ecological and cultural regions of our Provinces. In some places, it will require closer relationships among our parishes and dioceses and the communities of which they are a part. In every part of the Anglican Communion, we will hopefully discover or rediscover more about our common humanity as brothers and sisters in Christ and as members of a global "communion" which finds a large part of its identity through the stewardship of God's creation.

Archdeacon Matalavea's vision of sharing stories about stewardship from the Anglican Communion and making commitments in our lives and work was pivotal in the planning process. How can we best hear the voice of the Spirit speaking through the Holy Scriptures, in the lives and words of our sisters and brothers, through rivers, mountains, endangered species, and even whole ecosystems across the Anglican Communion? How can this be done in ways that nurture existing ministries and foster the development of new ones? An appreciation of the sacred power of speaking and listening is required to unlock the meaning hidden within stories about our own experience. This involves discernment as well as empowerment (of individuals, small groups, and communities), and an understanding that spirituality and justice are inseparable. In a number of settings at the Congress, we shared personal stories and reports about the stewardship of creation from all parts of the Anglican Communion. It was our hope that this strategy would nurture an empowered community that would be more capable of empowering other communities and congregations as a result of the Congress. **We believe the best way to achieve sustainable development is to empower communities to be sustainable.** These communities and congregations can be anywhere, in the city or countryside, in villages and city councils. Although Dr. Jan Loubser, one of our participants with international expertise in community empowerment, was not officially on the planning team, his guidance and experience in this area was particularly helpful in planning the Congress. The community that eventually gathered in South Africa, the collegial bonds and friendships formed there, and the willingness of delegates to share their experiences openly and candidly were crucial—both as signs of a working Congress and (primarily) as raw material of and for the practice of stewardship and sustainable development wherever we live.

The "stewardship of creation" was chosen as the unifying theme for the Congress, rather than as a theological position. We had no desire to promote a particular creation theology or to stage a general debate about it in which there would be the appearance of winners and losers. Everyone there already agreed that the stewardship of creation is integral to faith, in part, because we asked the Provinces to select delegates on that basis. As the theme of the Congress, its general usage was broad and inclusive enough to encourage people with diverse theological backgrounds and interests to speak openly about any number of theological perspectives, including eco-justice, "deep ecology", environmental ethics, and eco-feminism. More importantly, this approach would bring to the surface those practices and programs that are working in different ecological regions of the Anglican Communion, as well as specific problem areas and obstacles that arise. It also helped us avoid long discussions about the meanings of "stewardship", a subject which has been a traditional concern of the Church, and the more recent focus on "sustainable development", first brought to public attention by the United Nations. The language of stewardship and of sustainability both point in the direction of the soul's desire to care for the earth with practical action taken by empowered communities. We were looking for insights and guidance from people who are actually doing the ministry in academic and community settings, recognizing that people often work in both. Interestingly, just one month before the Congress, Secretary-General Kofi Annan gave an address about the UN Conference on Sustainable Development in which he spoke in terms of stewardship, for much the same reason.

By focusing on personal stories and testimonies about actual experience, we were hoping to go beyond the modern assumption, common in so-called "developed" nations, that human life is somehow separate from the "environment". The web of life, which existed before humankind, makes our lives possible. We are part of it. Without it, we would not exist. Their conceptual separation contradicts the interdependence of ecological systems; and, one might argue, it works as a weapon in the ongoing war against God's creation. This is a major problem currently for those who want environmental considerations to be a required part of international trade agreements. The issue goes much deeper. To separate the environment from almost any part of our lives is a strategy of colonial domination. It rationalizes the theft of land from indigenous and traditional peoples, perpetuates economic and political exploitation, disempowers communities, and disembodies experience.

The impact of economic colonialism is critical to our understanding of sustainable development, sustainable communities, and our efforts to create them. Resistance to economic colonialism is one reason why many people in developing countries have had justified negative reactions to North American environmental groups who seem to separate people from the environment in their strategies for action. This is also why developing countries often insist on a "pro-people" approach. Such an approach does not imply insensitivity to the environmental crisis, as is suggested sometimes by North Americans. Instead, groups advocating sustainable development in the developing "South" are resisting new forms of colonialism that would preserve the environment, while ignoring or destroying local knowledge, human rights, and the needs of indigenous peoples and traditional communities. People and the land go together. Since the Earth Summit, the United Nations has placed a great deal of emphasis on this linkage in the context of the community. Put in another way, biological diversity is inseparable from cultural diversity. To preserve one is to preserve the other. The human community is inseparable from the environment, which is, after all, the whole community of life.

Our decision to focus on experience and community at the Congress had at least one additional implication. The many different manifestations of the ecological crisis are interrelated, whether we are considering economics, decision-making processes in small communities, urban growth and mega-cities, health, gender inequality, forests, water, climate change and energy, or agriculture, just to name a few of areas of critical importance. Well-intended programs, designed to deal with one issue without taking other factors into account, can be a recipe for failure. For many years, the United Nations Development Program has been wrestling with these dynamic relationships and several contributors to these Proceedings address them too. The holistic integration of the web of life must be a guiding principle for programs in sustainable development and stewardship, which necessarily include local knowledge, community-based decisions, and equitable partnerships with large institutions. This guiding principle shaped the purpose and content of the Anglican Congress, including the concrete goal of helping to create the Anglican Environmental Network. Every delegate enthusiastically supported this goal, recognizing that ongoing threats to ecosystems in all parts of the Anglican Communion need immediate and urgent action. At the same time, the crisis we face involves every aspect of life and relates to the concerns of all the Anglican Networks. Fortunately, several networks were able to send representatives to the Congress. **Future collaboration among the Networks may provide a valuable key to an effective Anglican response to the ecological crisis.**

As a final note, these Proceedings can only provide a taste of what actually happened at the Global Anglican Congress. The informal, open-minded, open-hearted, often spontaneous nature of our discussions was a gift given to each participant by the others, and it made all the difference. We believe this record, as partial as it must be, will still be helpful as we take many more steps together in faith and love for God and God's creation.

Congress participants gathered at the Good Shepherd Retreat Center.

Local Community Empowerment

—DR. JAN LOUBSER

For just as the body is one and has many members, and all the members of the body, though many, are one body, so it is with Christ.

—1 Corinthians 12:12

I realized this morning very clearly that the problems we face in the world and in our communities are so formidable that they require responses beyond those of individuals and institutions. What I'd like to suggest this afternoon is that we not look at local community empowerment just in the abstract, but that we actually practice a bit of it and try to understand how it works in reality.

When I say "local community", I don't mean community-based organizations like environmental groups and women's groups and youth groups. They are there, and they are very important. Instead, I'm talking about a local community as the village or neighbourhood as a whole. Primarily, in most societies the village has been the fundamental unit of human habitation and organisation. After the family, the clan, and the extended family, the village is one of the earliest forms of human organization and government. It is one that has served humanity through the centuries better than any other human structure invented. Yet, if you look at what we do today in most societies, we've put the local community aside in our thinking about and practice of development process.

In most developing countries, donor organizations are very fond of working with community-based organizations. The World Bank, for example, has big projects that support so called "community-driven projects". But if you look at them, it all has to do with Non-Government Organizations (NGOs) and Civil Society Organizations (CSOs), not with local communities. CSOs and NGOs in many ways are organizations that tend to step into the vacuum that we've created in governance at the local level by sidestepping the local community as a self-governing unit.

There are countries that are laudable exceptions to this—take the example of India. India amended its constitution in 1992 to empower the village within a decentralized government structure. All the adults in the village are members of the village assembly; they elect a council, and that council is accountable to the village. Anyone who comes and wants to work in the village is accountable through the council and eventually to the village community as a whole. Uganda has a decentralized government system that works very much the same way. The village council is the basic unit of administration. That's what I'm talking about. I'm not talking about the usual community empowerment that says, let's get some community-based organizations, even some church groups, to do some work in the villages. We are talking about empowering the village as a whole to manage its own development. Now what I suggest to you is that for this to work effectively, one needs to help the village to develop a participatory culture.

Just thinking back over the topics that we looked at this morning, for example, HIV-AIDS and genetically modified foods, we can see how local communities can deal effectively with these issues. In Senegal, for example, there are now more than 200 villages that have banned female genital mutilation (FGM) in their villages. They call themselves "human rights villages", as they have become concerned with a broader range of human rights issues. Think of the cultural practice that we have talked about of inheritance of the wife of a deceased brother in certain African communities. In Zambia, some villages have proceeded to ban that practice. Although the practice was culturally significant to them, once they understood the link to HIV-AIDS and the risks of infection, they decided by themselves that they do not want to do this anymore. Now nobody, but nobody, else could do that for them. You and I can advocate it; we can provide information, but we could not decide for them. Individuals alone can't decide it, but the community, a cohesive community, can make those decisions, especially when endorsed by their traditional leaders.

In Tanzania, village councils have passed bylaws to control the risk-taking behavior of their members with regard to visiting places seen as presenting high risks of infection with HIV, especially for vulnerable groups such as women and children. We can say that this might not be effective. But there are many, many examples, especially in the area of environmental protection and natural resource management and many other fields, where communities have demonstrated that they can, and do, take effective action if they are so empowered by the governing system of the country. Therein lies the key.

So that is the topic I would like us to work on this afternoon: participatory decision making as a community. Perhaps I can start by suggesting that what we might work on specifically is something we began to debate earlier—the debate between eco-centric and human-centric or people-centric ethics, but in the context of stewardship. Is that not what we're here for, ultimately to organize ourselves around?

I was involved in the development of the program of action of the World Summit for Social Development in 1995, the first WSSD in Copenhagen. Afterwards, I worked on making it operational in a number of countries.

I called it "Holistic People-Centered Development." There is no need for a reference to sustainability anymore because people at the local community level in particular don't think of their lives in sectoral terms. They don't think about their economy, their society and their environment. To them, life is immediate and whole and they relate to it that way. If one empowers them with their own development, they take a holistic approach that has been sustainable in the past, as we all know. With the proper decision-making process, building on their own knowledge, they and we can be sustainable in the future too. So the issues debated earlier of eco-centric or human-centric ethics is resolved by embracing a holistic approach.

Local community empowerment within enabling environments is a fundamental formula, I believe, for ensuring that development is balanced and indeed holistic. People's interests, people's concerns, and people's values are taken into account, and the well-being of the environment and future generations are taken into account. Also there are no contradictions and conflicts between them in a holistic approach that respects their inextricable inter-relatedness.

Now we might have a bit of a time problem and I don't know exactly how to handle it, but what I had in mind was for us to do a little participatory exercise in small groups this afternoon. Let me briefly suggest this to you, and see whether you like to do that or not. It may mean that we have to work till about 6:30. Is that OK? What I would suggest is that we do two things. First, what I'd like to do, is introduce you to the methodology, a very simple and basic way of practicing participatory decision making. In doing this, I would suggest that we focus on a very personal question.

The question I would suggest we work on is this: "What does stewardship mean to me personally?" Not as a church, but me as a person. Then we share our answers with each other in small groups and report back to the plenary on the profiles of stewardship that emerged as we worked together in our groups. Let's discover the notions of stewardship, the commitments of stewardship that are in the room, in our hearts. Then after the coffee break, I would suggest that we imagine ourselves as a village community that has come together to plan its own development, its own vision.

Perhaps you feel that this is impossible here; we can't do that, it's too complex. But I want to reassure you that we can demonstrate the power of this very simple method of helping people to refocus their values and their hearts and their minds on things that really matter most to them. That, to me, is a practical definition of ethics, holistic ethics.

Let's break into six groups so that the circles are small enough. I would really like you to know how easy it is to do this. Of course, it is not for me to decide that we all have to do this, but I would urge you to do it. I still want to know if you are comfortable this afternoon doing this? Yes? Great! I can promise you that I'm not going to talk much. You all are going to talk and listen to each other, share your thoughts and work together to produce a shared vision of stewardship. And you are going to produce something that is your own, that you can internalize for the rest of the week and maybe for the future. You have the notes on the participatory workshop process in your materials, so let's organize ourselves into our groups and get started.

Notes on the Participatory Workshop Process and Local Community Empowerment Guiding Principles

1. Respect and empower each other
2. Participate actively, but patiently
3. Listen and seek to understand
4. Be mindful of time; share it equitably
5. Be frank, open and transparent
6. Build on each other's ideas, seeking synergy
7. Forget about positions; interact as equal people
8. Enable each other's learning
9. Seek new insights, be creative, relaxed
10. Build trust and common ground

The Participatory Group Process

As described below, the process involves participants, who are all those present, including "lead facilitators" (members of the planning team and or others appointed, who introduce the workshops and guide the process), "plenary speakers" (who make presentations for each workshop), "small group facilitators" (who guide the small group discussions), and "reporters" (who assist small group facilitators and report back to the plenary on behalf of the small group).

This is not a controlled but a principled process that relies on self-discipline by participants and groups. Everyone should understand, accept, and abide by the Guiding Principles.

After the introduction and plenary presentations which begin each workshop, participants divide into small groups for discussion and then come together again to complete the session.

Each small group selects a facilitator to guide the process and a reporter who will report on behalf of the group to the plenary. The participatory process may involve the use of cards to record, share, sort, organize and summarize thoughts, ideas and conclusions about the purpose of the group work. Participants are provided with a pen or marker and an adequate supply of cards on which to write down their ideas, usually one idea per card. Ideas are best expressed in three or four words in which adjectives or adverbs bring precision to a noun and/or verb. If they prefer, participants may draw pictures of their ideas: a good picture is worth a thousand words.

The process begins with the facilitator asking group participants to reflect for three minutes on the content of the plenary presentation before recording on a card their most important thought or idea they want to share. Participants are then involved to present their ideas quickly, without comment or discussion by the other members. All ideas are captured and taken into account. This can be done by placing the card(s) with the idea(s) in front of the group for all to see. The reporter assists with this process.

When all ideas are posted, the group facilitator and the reporter lead the group in ordering and naming the ideas into a coherent set of statements on the subject under consideration.

Led by the group facilitator and the reporter, the group reviews the whole outcome of its work and reflects on the collective product.

Participants are then invited to share more fully their personal experiences and responses (which are noted by the reporter) with regard to the subject matter of the initial presentations and the small group discussion.

The reporter collects all the cards and summary materials and presents the group results to the plenary.

The Role of Participants

Group participants are the owners and active "movers and shakers" of the programme of the workshop itself. They are encouraged to become fully involved, participate actively and make suggestions for any improvements they consider desirable in the programme to optimize learning. Such suggestions will be discussed and incorporated where there is agreement that they would improve the effectiveness of the learning and discovering processes.

The primary role of the participants is to have an open spirit and mind for learning and developing deeper insights into the purposes that the workshop is designed to achieve.

Participants are encouraged to internalize the Guiding Principles, to envision themselves as co-facilitators of the group process and to set for themselves specific learning goals that they wish to achieve during the workshop.

The Role of Facilitators

Small group and lead facilitators will facilitate all the sessions, plenary and small groups.

In the plenary, a lead facilitator:

- presents the purpose of the exercise and ensures that these are understood by all

- fosters observance of the Guiding Principles

- assists the participants in shaping their shared views and products

In the small groups, facilitators selected by the groups:

- read the guidance provided for the group work and ensure that it is understood

- moderate the group work process ensuring that the ground rules are observed, that conflicts are avoided and that synergy is generated

- keep the group work focused within the time available and inform the lead facilitator if more time is needed

- ensure that each participant has equal opportunity to contribute

- ensure that materials are available for the group

- ensure that the physical space and amenities are conducive to group comfort and effectiveness assist reporters in preparing group reports.

The Role of Reporters

Reporters are volunteers selected or endorsed by the small group to report on its behalf to the plenary.

In the groups, the reporters:

- ensure that a recording process is followed that ensures that all contributions are considered for inclusion in the report

- keep track of the flow of ideas, propose ordering them into different categories and assist the group in naming the categories

- prepare a creative and succinct presentation of the resulting group product to present to the plenary, ensuring that it reflects the group's congruent views

- safeguard the raw material of the group work for later consideration and analysis.

In the plenary, the reporters:

- make a clear and concise presentation to the plenary

- work with the principal reporter to consolidate the group presentations into a plenary product where this is required

- assist in keeping the plenary on schedule by not taking more than the time allotted.

(After meeting in six small groups for a few hours, delegates from the Communion's Provinces produced the following summary statements reflecting their collective and personal understanding of stewardship. These statements and subsequent involvement in the participatory workshop process after other plenary sessions led to the "commitments" reproduced in a later section of this report.)

Small Group Conclusions on the Theme of "Stewardship"

The groups came up with the following conclusions about what
stewardship meant to them.
Perhaps the virtual similarity of
these concepts is not surprising
given the relative homogeneity
of the participants as members of
the same faith community.

Group 1

Looking after all that has been
entrusted to us: carefully, responsibly, lovingly and joyfully.

A youth volunteer shares his views.

Group 2

Our commitment to stewardship comprises leading by example, reducing our ecological footprints to a level that is sustainable and accountable
to the common good, and encouraging the same in others.

Group 3

Our commitment to stewardship is valuing and caring what God has given.
Using resources sustainably; recycling and waste prevention; educating,
modeling for, and empowering the younger generation and the whole village to take action to deal with environmental and social problems.

Group 4

Stewardship is the reverent, loving and responsible relationship with and
care for all God's Creation. Our commitment is to endeavor to discern
and fulfil God's will for us, the rest of Creation, and future generations.

Group 5

Stewardship begins with God's love and is fulfilled in a committed human
response to the whole-created order as we celebrate the gift of life.

Group 6

We accept a responsibility for the sustainable use of God's Creation for present and future generations. We will use our talents to educate about and advocate for the well-being of all our fellow creatures and other living organisms.

Group discussion on community empowerment.

What is Happening to Water?

—Dr. Anthony Turton

As a deer longs for flowing streams, so my soul longs for you, O God.

—Psalm 42:1

As we have the World Summit coming upon us, it's time to ponder a couple of questions. So, just to give us a formal structure, it's interesting to think a few minutes about where it came from? What it is about? Should we take it seriously? How does it impact on us? And I think this is very important given the fact that all you good folk out there have a rather huge constituency that you interface with on a daily basis. Ultimately my purpose here is to present a couple of provocative questions because this event is going to open up a number of questions that need to be answered.

Let's start off by asking where does it come from? There is a particular view of a well-known philosopher that I love to mention. It's a quotation by a well-known philosopher from the seventeenth century. This philosophy is powerful stuff because this is the philosophy on which the natural sciences are based. I'm not going to read it. The important part is the piece that I'm emphasizing which is the desire to make ourselves masters and owners of nature and that is really the foundation of modern engineering. Hydraulic engineering, for example—there is a big dam here and the engineers that design that dam were schooled in this kind of natural science. They envisioned it when they cast the concrete plug in that natural riverbed that had taken millions of years to form. In a blink of an eye, really, in terms of geological time, they cast the concrete plug that changed the stream flow forever. They were, in fact, making themselves masters and owners of nature.

On top of this, in the 1960's we had that testosterone froth thing called the space race, when the United States of America and Russia decided that they had to get the first man on the moon. Of course it was a huge event. This was also part of making ourselves masters and owners of nature. NASA started beaming back imagery, powerful imagery, of space. Ordinary people like you and me could actually see, firsthand, what it is like up there. One of the powerful images that came back was this notion of earth as a fragile oasis, floating in a seeming likeness in space. One of the astronauts at the time was asked what he saw when he looked back down at earth and the astronaut said, "I see no political boundaries . . . I see one planet, one ecosystem". If you look at the atmosphere that protects us, if you compare the earth to an orange, that veil of atmosphere is as thick as an orange peel. It's a relatively thin atmosphere that is enshrouding us from all of those hostile things out there in space.

So this brings us to the notion of development. What is development? What do we mean by development? There are many, many definitions of development and this is a definition that I chose because it captures some of the essential elements and it's a condition that guarantees some of the functioning of an interconnected ecosystem. That is important. We are part of ecosystems, and up until now the discourse has been about making ourselves masters and owners of nature, which would mean we are outside of the ecosystem. We've created, as it were, those environments around us, which has enabled human beings to inhabit the most inhospitable parts of planet earth. We are the one species that has inhabited every conceivable ecological lease on this planet earth because we've tried to make ourselves masters and owners of nature. So, if we're talking about development, we need to put people back into ecosystems, rather than have people standing away from ecosystems and looking at them as if they are something sick.

This whole process has spawned a powerful literature called Political Ecology. I'm not going to go into the whole Political Ecology literature, but just basically say that it started out with some early NASA imagery, where people started asking some fundamental questions about where we are. For example, do trees have moral standing? There were two very significant bits of literature published about this. One was called *The Limits to Growth* and the other one was called *Blueprint for Survival.* You may have heard about them. They posed the very daunting question of unsustainability. How do we start making ourselves sustainable? This became highly politicized because it started asking the developing South, essentially, to stop developing. The developed North had already reached the stage of development where you could, supposedly, ignore the consequences of development, while the developing South was using dirty technologies, wasteful techniques, etc. So we immediately got this international tension between North and South, "the developing world" versus "the developed world". And now, we have this discourse between anthropocentrists saying that nature is there to serve our needs, we can exploit nature because we are humans, and the eco-centrists, the deep ecologists, the more radical people. They feel the ecosystem actually matters and that human beings should not be seen outside of the ecosystem.

Now let me give you a bit of background about the global context because you are not all from South Africa, or from Africa. About 40 percent of the total global food production comes from irrigated agriculture. That's a significant amount of production. This includes approximately eighteen million people per year at the current growth rate, so I'm talking about a substantial figure here. Yet, many of the world's major rivers are running dry. We've started seeing this in the last century. The Colorado River is the most litigated river in the world. It now seeps across the border into Mexico and is the subject of major international litigation. Some of the most fundamental international water law, in fact, goes back to the original Colorado case studies. Or the Nile River, which has sustained civilization for thousands of years—it was one of the first sources of early human civilization. What sustained civilization was the natural flooding and ebbing of the Nile River. Because humankind has sought to become the master and owner of nature in that region, the Nile doesn't flood anymore. Flooding is being controlled, so the natural process has stopped. The delta is dying; the delta is receding. It's not getting the sediment that it needs.

The Ganges River is also a very, very well-known case, and, of course, the Yellow River in China in 1972 started running dry. It flows only a few days of the year. During half of the year, it simply doesn't flow; it's just dry. So, what is this all about? If you plotted the time line of human ingenuity, particularly on the basis of when water has been mobilized to serve human interests, you get a grasp of what I'm talking about. The important thing to know is that from about the industrial revolution until now, we've mobilized a significant amount of water and that can be broken down into two distinct phases. The first phase is the period of modern industry that is the period of time from the industrial revolution that enabled new technologies to be developed. This received particular impetus during World War II, when engineering specifications and knowledge about steel-reinforced concrete became well known. Large dams were being built in the Colorado River for the first time during World War II at the end of the Great Depression.

But we reached our peak in that phase and a new phase kicked in, which we call "reflexivity and modernity". "Reflexivity" is a very important notion in the whole discourse on sustainable development, because reflexivity happens when a society becomes concerned about the unintended consequences of their actions and seeks to do something about it. Humankind becomes reflexive and sees that all these things aren't such good ideas. It takes about fifty to one hundred years after you've built a dam to see the ecological impact of that dam. It's interesting that around the 1970's, there was the birth of the green environmental movement in America, specifically around the issues of water and greenhouse gases and the desire of the American authorities to build dams in the Grand Canyon. This touched a sensitive nerve and the Sierra Club mobilized its efforts. Their work really began at the onset of the period of reflexivity.

This is a global picture, and what's interesting is that the World's Commission on Dams decided to audit the impact of dams worldwide, trying to get some scientific background on this growing large-dam effect. Some very, very interesting things came out of it. One of them is that of the top twenty countries in the world for dams, South Africa is in the top twenty—not only is South Africa in the top twenty, Zimbabwe is also. It is quite significant for two developing countries to be up there with the big ones. We are a nation of dam builders here and we have all kinds of issues that go with it. So what are some of the river-related issues? One of the classic river-related issues—the upstream/downstream relationship— is a very complex debate, but basically, it means that if you're downstream, you take what the people upstream give you.

Let's think of the South Africa scenario as we stand today. Under apartheid, water was unevenly distributed in society. The rich people had more water than the underprivileged people. So we've taken that from apartheid and extrapolated it forward in order to redress the imbalances of the past. When apartheid collapsed, the government brought out a new policy called the RDP Policy, and the RDP Policy was about redressing the imbalances of the past. It was about giving to people that didn't have before. That has now caused an upsurge in demand for water. So we are now reaching a point when, literally in the next two or three years, we are going to start reaching these theoretical figures when we run out of fresh water. We've happened to have had ten wet years, so maybe we've afforded ourselves a couple of years. The important thing is that we are reaching the limit. Whether it's now, whether it's the next decade, it's not that important. We are reaching the finite limit of our surface water.

In Namibia, the higher your income, the more water you consume. As we are trying to develop our economies, we are trying to move people out of low income categories, moving them up into higher income categories. What automatically happens is that there is a major upsurge in the demand for water.

We are talking about development, and development is about poverty. There is a project that I'm doing at the moment, and those of you who live in or near Zambia will probably recognize what I'm talking about. You get limestone in Zambia, very close to the surface. People, in this case women, derive livelihood from it. Women break rocks—big rocks and stones about three meters in diameter. They are used to make concrete. Now, what does this mean? Well, a number of things from the environmental perspective. First, we may quarry the stuff and dig down into the ground, very close to the surface. That's dangerous as the many mining laws and regulations suggest. Then you get these great big rocks, the size of this room, so what they then do is cover the rocks with tires and set these tires alight, in order to break up the rocks. So, the result is black, burning tires polluting the environment; the smoke is carcinogenic. Once the rock is hot, then buckets of water are thrown on the rocks and the rocks shrink and now you get rocks of a smaller size. A human being can handle a rock that size. Then a man handles those rocks, carries them away, and they usually end up on the side of the road.

So, a woman can take the rocks of that size and break them down even smaller. Now, let's give a monetary value to it—a woman has to crush six bags of stones and sell it, to earn one US dollar. And that US dollar is what that woman has to pay for her water every month. That water is subsistence water, survival water.

Running parallel to the Johannesburg Conference is something called the Dublin Conference and the Dublin Conference determined that water has an economic value and it must be charged in order to be sustained. In keeping with the Dublin principle, people have to pay for water, so there is what they call a "tap meter". Most of those taps are only open for one hour a day and people have to come and draw their water and take it back to their house. A young girl comes from a family that can't afford it, so what do they do now? They dig a "stoop hole", a very shallow little well, in a high-density population area. There is no sewage in the area. They just dig sewage pits and all this stuff seeps into the stoop holes. There is high rate of cholera in this area, which is what happens when you have no option—it is one of the unintended consequences.

For those of you who come from the Swaziland, think of the Logos Dam. This dam is actually in South Africa; it is an obscene dam in my view. It was built at the height of apartheid and it was built so that Mozambique could not get water. The sole purpose was to catch water, in terms of the international law principle of "prior appropriation". The irony is that it has never been used, and downstream it is the most beautiful ecosystem. The flood plain has a wide meandering river and it's an incredibly intricate ecosystem that has been developed over millions of years. The ecosystem is now being reduced to nothing. The idea was to settle farmers there, so they could live, but now their lives have been reduced to drawing tap water, which causes all kinds of other diseases in an area like this. And now, there is a big debate between the local communities and the dam managers about when they are going to release the floodwater. The flood rejuvenates the ecosystem; the flood recharges the wetlands. There's a debate because the farmers want a flood on this date and not that date. And the other guy wants a flood on another date, not this date. So we've become masters and owners of nature, we are trying to emulate that and we are not doing a very good job.

There are other problems. In order to get the energy from coal you need water. We have to manage our water resources and capture water from other river basins and pump it into power stations. One particular river basin uses something like eighty percent of the energy of South Africa, which is more than fifty percent of the energy of the entire African continent. It's a huge, huge amount of energy. Also, coming out of this is, of course, acid rain. The continent now has the highest sulfur content and that's the problem.

In my view, this is a moral question. We can talk as much as we want about numbers and figures, but behind all of this are human beings. What is man's relationship with nature? Have we truly become masters and owners of nature? We emulate it and try to become it. Sustainable development, as we know it, is a lie, I think. It's not sustainable. Is there a biblical basis for sustaining us? I ask this question, in part, because of work I did in Yemen in 1998. It is very interesting because in Islamic culture, there are scholars who are now looking at their own scriptures to determine a new basis for interpreting the Koran in such a way that sustainability becomes a key issue.

At the center of this whole thing is the question of whether we are really playing God. We need to strip away all this emotional rhetoric and ultimately start asking questions. What do we mean by equity? Are we all worshipping at the altar of profit, as seen in the United States with the Enron debacle? It's all about CEOs who are lying and cheating. They lie to their own shareholders; they really don't care two whits about the environment or what they do, as long as they are chasing a short-term profit.

Do trees and rivers have rights? Do they have moral standing? What sort of tolerance table do we have? International equities are very important issues because it's going to come up at the World Summit. Do we have the right to take from future generations? Or do we have the responsibility to be good stewards, leaving for our children that which we have found? At the moment we are not doing that. Just because we can do something doesn't mean to say we should. This is the classic Frankenstein movie kind of story. If you look at the countries that are exporting terror at the moment, they are all resource poor, water poor, and they are absolutely in the depths of poverty. So they've got nothing left to lose. It's about equity; it's about sharing the resource pipeline.

And with that I thank you very much, and God Bless!

Sacred Meals and the Global Food System

—PETER MANN

. . . for I was hungry and you gave me food . . .

—Matthew 25:35

The World Summit on Sustainable Development challenges the faith communities. We all share deep hopes and fears about the Earth and the prospects for the future. Kofi Annan recently warned the world community that we are entering the third millennium through a gate of fire. He was referring, first, to September 11th and the threat of terrorism, but also to the dangers of social and ecological collapse—the twofold threat of widespread poverty and environmental devastation with billions of people facing food and water shortages.

I want to share some thoughts with you on the deepening crisis in our food system. It's not only an economic and social and political crisis. In its depth, in its most radical form, it's an ethical and spiritual crisis, which can only be overcome by a different way of thinking, new strategies for action, and changed patterns of living. That's why it's so important that we now contemplate this challenge to the experience of the sacred meal that we shared yesterday and we'll share today. The Eucharist, which is a sacred meal, can change fear into hope.

So first, let's look at the food system from field to plate and in its most basic elements: the food, the meal, the local and global community, the seed, the soil, the farm and the land. Also, let's look at it in terms of what Thomas Berry has called "The Great Work." The Great Work is a new, mutually enhancing, no longer destructive relationship between humans and the earth community, shaped by values such as diversity, sustainability, democracy and justice. We must begin to articulate our vision of a world without hunger and of regional food systems that provide high quality food and sustainable livelihoods, while enhancing the natural resources and biodiversity on which sustainable agriculture is based.

As we begin to translate this vision into action, we challenge the food system as it's now constituted and build on the many alternatives emerging in communities around the world. There is a global threat. Hunger and poverty are a global reality. More than eight hundred million people in the world are persistently hungry. More than one billion people live in extreme poverty on less than one dollar a day, and another one and a half billion live on less than two dollars a day. Last year alone, hunger and disease related to malnutrition, a direct consequence of poverty, silently claimed the lives of ten to twelve million children under the age of five. Yet the world produces an abundance of food. Paradoxically, hunger is the most widespread where food is produced—in rural areas, the home of the vast majority of the world's poor and often the source of the abundance which we know in the cities and supermarkets of the global North or sometimes in the global South. This is built upon the dispossession of the rural poor largely in the South, who are forced to grow cash crops for export. Hundreds of millions of peasant farmers, small farmers, and fisherfolk in the North and South are threatened with the loss of their land, as corporate agribusiness strengthens its grip on the world's food system.

Just a couple of facts: In my state of New York, which is still a farming state in many ways, one thousand farms a year are disappearing. Farmers in the United States are no longer even counted in the census, being less than two percent. Why? Because farmers cannot cover the cost of the production of their crops. They are being squeezed in the middle between the inputs, which are more and more expensive, and the output, that is, retailing and marketing. The amount of money that farmers are getting is not enough to make a living. Someone is making a lot of money out of the food system. Therefore, one of the persistent cries heard among many of us who are fighting this kind of situation is "take back the middle." Give the farmer in the middle more of the food dollar, more support in all ways.

In the South, millions of farmers are losing their land by the dumping of cheap food by the United States and Europe. Anti-hunger groups around the world look at the scandal of hunger in the midst of abundance and ask what's wrong with the world, with the food system? How can it be fixed? I think they are coming up with the same answer. They see poverty as the root cause of hunger. And poverty is rooted in the powerlessness, or better yet, the dis-empowerment of the poor.

So one of the challenges for us as we go into the World Summit is now spearheaded by a coalition that has been forming over many years. They go into the Summit around the human right to food. We are going to get behind the right to food as a basic human right. Another coalition is emerging around farm workers' rights for a just wage and better living conditions. These are the priorities of an initiative that I'm very involved in called the SARD Initiative—Sustainable Agriculture and Rural Development—and it's working with coalitions of farmers, fisherfolk, indigenous peoples, women, United Nations agencies like FAO (the Food and Agriculture Organization), and governments. Basically the major areas we are working on are: access to land, water credit, technology, seeds, best practices and model programs, sustainable agriculture, and farm workers' rights.

So from an anti-poverty perspective, groups fighting hunger in the North and in the South have a common vision of justice—solidarity with the poor and the moral imperative of social change. They see hunger as part and parcel of a global economic system that's driving inequity, exploitation, waste and poverty. Often they (we) are inspired by our own faith traditions in this struggle for justice. How can the Christian tradition challenge us to bring hope where there is fear? I believe a large part of this empowerment comes through the power of sacred meals, symbolizing the fullness of the earth belonging to the Lord.

Let's look at the power of sacred meals. The ministry of Jesus is shaped by meals. As a companion at the table, his dealings with people liberate them and bring them joy. It's like a wedding feast. It's impossible to fast in his presence (Mark 2:18–22). As host at the miraculous meal of the multiplication of loaves and fishes, his presence reveals the sheer abundance of God's blessings. It's revealed as the bread of life, the true vine, the life-giving water. He's the host at the table; he takes and blesses the food and he is the servant who breaks and gives it to those at the table (Mark 6:41).

So the reign of God is coming to us in the form of food and drink as a sacred meal. The problem for us is that it's easy to miss the transforming power of these meals, both in the gospel stories and potentially in our own lives and ministries. It is open table fellowship not based on spiritual or political hierarchy, prestige or power. It represents and enacts a radical form of sharing God's out-flowing love, justice, and reconciliation. Therefore, table fellowship in Jesus' ministry can be seen as undermining political power and religious law.

This leads to the Last Supper, in which the Pascal Mystery was made present in the breaking of the bread and the sharing of the cup. It has always been difficult to retain this transformative power of the Eucharist as a sacred meal, one which looks back to those original meals of the early Christian communities, made present in the Lord's Supper, and looks forward to the messianic banquet where everyone will be full. We might say that the sacramental passing of the cup and breaking of the bread became separated from the everyday meal, which is sacred too. The social and spiritual transformation, inherent in the sacred meal, its power to heal and bring us together, were endangered early on, as seen in 1 Corinthians 11, and they still are endangered. Where is the church today in this struggle for justice?

Of course, the church is already deeply involved in the struggle for economic and social justice and the transformation of society. Many churches feed the hungry through soup kitchens and food pantries, and they see this rightly as following Christ—"I was hungry and you gave me to eat" (Matthew 25)—and living out the meaning of the Eucharist by sharing resources.

In New York City, where I live, in the 1980's there were something like 50 soup kitchens and food pantries, but there are now something like 1,300. They are overflowing and turning people away and very many of them, perhaps most of them, are in church communities.

So it's heroic, admirable, and it's not enough. The danger is that emergency feeding will stay at the level of charity, and it will not reach the root causes of hunger and poverty and may even leave the structural causes intact, as governments and corporations retreat from their responsibilities to help create a just society. They leave it to the churches, to the faith community, or the community groups. Emergency feeding can replace social policy; it can take the energy, the action, and the power that we could put into changing the reason why people don't have enough to eat. Why don't people have jobs? Tragically, charity can replace advocacy, policy, and building real community food security. There is enough food, which can be accessible to everyone.

In my view, the big challenge of the World Summit on Sustainable Development is to move us beyond charity alone and into justice. If we go to the meetings and really listen, the stories we'll hear from peasant farmers, fisherfolk, farm workers and food workers, women and indigenous peoples will confront us with the global scale of the problem. They are not asking for charity, but for food sovereignty, for control over their own land and water and forests and livelihoods. Their struggles are contagious once we know about them, but unfortunately few people know and they also face enormous obstacles.

I look at the Global Food System and I see a kind of values, or a lack of values, that undermines the value of local diversity and sustainability. These are being threatened by the spread of the monoculture of fast foods. McDonalds is saying that in the twenty-first century no one should be more than four minutes away, by foot or by car, from a McDonalds. In cities where I've been, Moscow and Beijing, I think they are on the way there. It's a monoculture driven by global advertising and corporate power within the food system. I think this is really an ethical and a spiritual question because the diversity of cultures and communities is central to life itself.

Thomas Berry in his book *The Dream of the Earth* argues that the threefold pattern of diversity, interiority and communion are intrinsic to the created universe as a manifestation of divine mystery. With respect to diversity and interiority—the inwardness within the diversity and the ability to commune together—Berry suggests that the ecological age, which we are in now, is leading us to a new awareness of the sacred presence within each and every part of the universe. One expression of this is the food system.

It would be a new awareness of a shift away from monocultures and high energy petrochemical agriculture to organic processes, mixed crops, local markets, diverse cultures, and subsistence gardening within bioregions as well as more generous assistance to countries all over the world—not to feed them, but to help them grow their own food. There is a huge difference between feeding the world and helping the world feed itself, which is what the divine mystery demands, it seems to me. And in each place, each situation, people will know their ecosystem, and on that basis, they will be able to grow their own food.

You will encounter two other forms of agriculture at the WSSD: industrial, concentrated ownership, based on pesticides and insecticides and all that and small farmer agriculture, the agro-ecological model. They'll both be there and

Example of community based agriculture.

we'll look at what the problems are and where we want to go. When I look at this dilemma of the two forms of agriculture, I'm helped by another spiritual tradition and that is of indigenous peoples. Whenever I've been at the UN and I've listened to the indigenous peoples speak, it seems to me that they are the ones who most adequately and persuasively show us the sacredness of food, the land, and meals. Here is a prayer from their traditions: "I'm an Indian, I think about common things like the bubbling water that comes from the rain cloud; it represents the sky. The fire comes from the sun, which warms us all, men and women, animals, trees. The meat stands for the four-legged creatures, our animal brothers who gave of themselves so that we shall live. The steam is living breath; it is water as it goes up in the sky and becomes a cloud again. These things are sacred; looking at that pot full of good soup, I'm thinking how, in this simple manner, the Great Spirit takes care of me."

This text and many other texts from other spiritual traditions express a vision, imaged by a spiritual meal representing society, where the separation of ourselves—from each other and the earth—has been overcome. Such a vision can inspire us to build a food system that meets the needs of the poor, the overwhelming survival needs of farmers, and the long term needs of all people for healthy food, a clean environment and healthy families and communities. This work begins with a common eco-justice framework for a society free of hunger and full of healthy, fulfilled people. So we can grow some of our own food and we can buy locally and we can build solidarity with the farmers and food producers of the world. And we can get to know farmers and share some of this research on how small farmers, peasant farmers with their traditional knowledge, are helped by modern knowledge to feed themselves and their communities.

Finally, I would like to share some thoughts about other elements in the food system: seeds, soil, and farmland. Ethical and spiritual principles underlie the strategies we will encounter at the WSSD to rebuild our local, regional and global food system. I've mentioned networks I'm working with at the WSSD that are forming partnerships around access to resources and land. These partnerships involve different positions on land reform because it's very region specific, and it includes some very powerful initiatives, which we hope will be funded. In traditional farming systems, peasant farmers are the custodians of the planet's genetic wealth. They treat seeds as sacred, as the critical element in the great chain of being, and this is the theme, the "great work" we are involved with. In the model based on a great chain of being, seeds were not bought or sold—they were exchanged as a free gift of nature.

Corporate agribusiness, by contrast, treats seed as private property protected by patent and intellectual property rights. Contrast the corporate centralization of research about seeds in the North with the decentralized approach of local cultivators and plant breeders and the diversity of thousands of locally cultivated plants in the agricultural system, built up over generations on the basis of local knowledge, generated over centuries. It's a completely different model for the sharing of seeds.

Marakele National Park.

There is a growing movement, which I would like the churches to get behind, in the South and in the North, to recover the sacred meaning of seeds, to restore biodiversity, and to revolutionize the way we think about food. There is a revolution happening now as people become scared about the problems of food safety, as they begin to long for the well-being of their youth, or the taste they remember. So, they want to buy local food and have contact with local farmers. I'm part of the CSA, Community Supported Agriculture, movement. When we began in 1996 in New York City, we had one CSA group, which had been there for a number of years. We now have twenty-six and the last ten of them have been low income CSAs. Just before I came here, to South Africa, I heard that the Kellogg Foundation has given a large grant to the Community Resource Center, Just Food, and other organizations to get CSAs into Harlem and to get institutions in Harlem to start buying local and regional food. That's really how things begin—when institutions, schools, colleges, defense departments, and government agencies start buying local food and get others to do the same.

So there is a growing movement in the global North and in the global South. In Fred Kirshenmann's words, sustainable agriculture is more than an alternative farming system; it's part of the ecological revolution that many now believe to be essential to our survival. If agriculture is to be truly sustainable, it must encompass this larger vision. One of the ways to bring about this revolution is to become lovers of the soil, which means learning to see the soil, see its life and beauty, sense its rich aroma, and hear its voice.

I'm with you here as a Catholic, of the Roman Catholic persuasion, and I lived many years in a Benedictine monastery. As I remember it in England, our lives were centered around worship, the sacred meal, and prayer and work. Work was very often work in the fields. I'd really forgotten that tradition till I started working on a local farm, a biodynamic farm, in upstate New York. It really became clear to me that the soil is not just material in which you put plants, which it's becoming now actually. In the Central Valley of California, someone told me that he has never seen an earthworm in three years of digging and farming. It's becoming a place where you can put stuff which will help plants to grow, but what I saw in the farm on the monastery was soil that really is a mystery: the micro-organisms, the way that animals know what's good for them when they see the plants in the field, the way the fertility of that soil, its organic matter, increases year by year in a small kind of agro-ecological experiment. It is a divine mystery and one of the quickest ways to see this is to grow and prepare your own food. Wendell Berry, who follows a similar path, suggested that we relocate the farm economy within the "great economy," as he calls it—the "great work," the "great chain of being,"—which connects us to human virtues, human scale, and to an order, which, like the Kingdom of God, is both visible and invisible, comprehensible and mysterious. We are being called to recover the sacred traditions: land as a gift for the whole community to be treasured and its produce shared among everyone.

Finally, there are two ways forward. One of them is the industrial agriculture model, which has produced enormous amounts of food. Many would say it has brought food cheaply to many people around the world. But we are seeing huge problems with it, ecological problems of the topsoil, the pollution of ground water, and many other problems. Now the next stage in this model is genetic engineering. We're seeing problems in terms of people's health and we are seeing problems in terms of the destruction of the family farms around the world. But there's another way, which is the way of agro-ecology, in which people can help each other, as we have already seen in Latin America and Africa. Agricultural movements which are more sustainable, which look at the whole community, the food, the farm, the land and the seeds in terms of the regenerative processes. It's a challenge to faith communities to decide where we will put our energies. I am going to put my energy in this new, but ancient, form of agriculture which is being renewed again through modern ecological knowledge and which I think is the way forward.

I would like to end with an indigenous prayer from North America, a blessing litany, as an appropriate way to reaffirm our respect for the dignity of all beings and to reconnect, renew, and revitalize the food system with a world free of hunger and despair. I would like you to repeat at the end of it this phrase, "Teach us and show us the way." Can you say that? "Teach us and show us the way."

"We call upon the land, which grows our food, the nurturing soil, and the fertile fields, the abundant gardens and orchards, and we ask that they teach us and show us the way. We call upon the creatures of the fields and forests and seeds, our brothers and sisters, the wolves and deer. The eagle and dove, the great whales and the dolphin, the beautiful orca and salmon who share our northwest home. We ask them to teach us and show us the way. And lastly, we call upon all that we hold most sacred. The presence and power of the Great Spirit, of love and truth, which flows through the entire universe to be with us to teach us and show us the way. Amen."

Food Security in India

—Jessie Jeyakaran

India today is not only self-sufficient in grain production, but also has a substantial reserve. The progress made by agriculture in the last four decades has been one of the biggest success stories of free India. Agriculture and allied activities constitute the single largest contributor (almost 33%) to the Gross Domestic Product. About two-thirds of the work force in the country depends on agriculture as a means of livelihood. Despite these impressive gains, India, at present, finds itself in the midst of a paradoxical situation: on the one hand, there are record food grain stocks standing at an all-time high (62 million tons against an annual requirement of around 20 million tons for assuring food security); on the other hand, over 200 million of India's population is underfed, and millions are undernourished. The challenge is to bridge this gap.

Food security is defined as the situation in which all people have physical and economical access to sufficient, safe, and nutritious food at all times to meet dietary requirements and food preferences for an active and healthy life. Food security has to be about people and resources, not commodities, and it has to be about access, rather than availability. Food security and sustainable development can be assured, only if every individual has the physical, economic, social, and environmental access to a balanced diet that includes necessary macro- and micro-nutrients, safe drinking water, sanitation, environmental health, primary health care, hygiene, and education to lead a healthy and productive life.

Sustainable land and water management are directly linked to food security. Population growth, environmental sustainability, poverty reduction, agricultural production, distribution, marketing, credit and many other factors also need to be recognized as a part of this whole. The major challenge is not only to produce additional food. It is also to provide physical, economic and ecological access to food and nutrition security for the household.

Food security must focus on a diversified food system. Food security must not be based on markets, but rather on self-reliance and sufficiency. Nutritional security must be given integrated attention by emphasizing horticulture, animal husbandry, fishery, millets, pulses and several other resources for which India is traditionally known. There is a need for investment in science and technology that will promote diversification.

The problem in India today is not necessarily access and affordability. It is one of meeting the three challenges of producing enough to meet the demands of a growing population, ensuring sufficient purchasing power through livelihood security, and an alternatively proactive development paradigm that is pro-poor, pro-woman and pro-nature. We need on-farm and off-farm jobs and livelihoods backed by good economic practices, which will counter the bottom-line thinking of all our economic and developmental policies. What India needs today is a genuine green revolution in the whole food system. So it expects an "Ever Green Revolution" through a blending of traditional and frontier technologies.

The impoverishment of God's Creation.

Assessing the Promise of Genetically Modified Food

—THE REV. CANON ERIC BERESFORD,
THE ANGLICAN COMMUNION ENVIRONMENTAL NETWORK

It's an odd fact for believers in a tradition whose central and most defini-
tive act of worship is a meal, yet it's very easy not to think carefully about
food. Most of us were probably shocked yesterday to hear how much
water is used up in food production. Even if we do not take food for
granted, most of us rarely think about the farm practices that go into the
production of our food, or of the impact of those farming practices on
the environment, on local ecosystems, even on weather systems. We
rarely think about the economic systems that enable the delivery of food
to our tables and affect quite dramatically both the kinds of food available to us and its cost.

The situation is made more complex by the advent of genetically modified (GM) foods. Now, let me be clear that I am not interested in engaging in some fundamental critique of the scientific principles that lie
behind GM. Even though I've actually been a practicing geneticist, I have
some concerns about the way that science is being practiced.
Nonetheless, I want to say that in principle I find the science neither
immoral nor threatening. I remember once being told that if God had
meant to put human genes into a mouse, God would have found a way
of doing so. I answered that God has, through human ingenuity. We need
to remember that we too are part of the natural world, and therefore to
call what we do unnatural is both oddly anthropocentric and rarely helpful in clarifying why something is right or wrong. There are problems in
this area, but I think we need to be careful about getting ourselves
involved in the language of natural and unnatural types of behavior here.
I don't think it leads us in the right direction. What I want to focus on
this morning is the way that the social and economic context within
which GM is being developed is affecting the production of genetically
modified foods, the shape of the food system, and the problems associated with food security.

One of the key tools used by the biotechnology companies to ensure the
profitability of their investment is the patenting of genetic materials
including both gene sequences and even whole organisms. Patents are
applied for on either the basis of modification of an organism or on the
basis of discovery. When a company modifies a plant or an animal to
make it more useful, whatever that means, it will take out a patent. That

means that everyone who wants to grow wheat, for example, that has been modified by Monsanto, has to pay Monsanto a license fee. They probably also have to buy from Monsanto the chemicals, the fertilizers and the pesticides with which that particular form of wheat has been designed to work. It's a very profitable system, but often farmers become locked into the production method of the particular biotechnology company they decide to do business with. This can be profitable for farmers too, if yields are high and of good quality. But the high "up-front" costs of this approach to agriculture and the costs that must be borne long before any harvest is ready can lead to a dramatic rise in both debt and bankruptcy if crops fail or yields become low. One of the interesting phenomena here is that GM crops do not give higher yields than non-modified corps. It's one of the things we are finding in the Canadian context. The yields are often 10% or 15% lower, so genetically modified crops do not necessarily give high yields. They are simply less susceptible to certain types of problem, certain pests.

Obtaining a patent by discovery is another interesting area in my view and basically this is the practice of some biotechnology companies that has been called "bio-prospecting". What it boils down to is that the company sends staff into a region, into a country, most often a developing nation, to identify any biological resources that might provide the basis for a new product. They then take out patents on all the natural genetic and biological resources of that county which may have commercial value. The patents are applied for on the basis of so-called "discovery". In my view, this is a little problematic. Recently Monsanto applied for a very wide-ranging patent on basmati rice. As I said in a newspaper article I wrote in response to that, basmati rice can be discovered on any super-market shelf. It's not clear to me why that discovery makes it worthy of a patent in any clear sense.

The most famous example of patenting on the basis of discovery is the so-called neem patent. The bark of the neem tree contains a natural occurring fungicide that has been used for millennia in India. The US Department of Agriculture in partnership with a biotechnology company called W. C. Grace took out a patent on neem. It took eight years before the European patent court eventually overturned that patent. The court agreed that this was a clear case of piracy of traditional indigenous knowledge. Unfortunately, indigenous peoples are not as well placed as large organizations such as transnational corporations to fight legal battles such as this one. Therefore most such patents are applied for and granted without opposition.

The great promise of GM is "food for a hungry world", and we should not minimize the pressures that continuing population growth will place on food production in the foreseeable future. However, at present the problem is not food production but food distribution. We are currently producing enough food to feed everybody; it is just distributed very unevenly. In the light of this, what I really do not understand is how concentrating both the ownership of the genetic resources of the developing world and the control of the food production systems of the developed world into the hands of a half dozen or so large multinational biotechnology companies is going to improve the distribution of food.

What theological resources might we bring to bear on these problems? I do not have much time so what I say must be suggestive rather than complete and worked out, although I have addressed these issues elsewhere. In the first place, we must start with the doctrine of creation and with the fundamental Judeo-Christian assertion that the whole of creation belongs to God the creator. This assertion leads us to question the claim that any individual or company might claim ownership not only over an individual animal, but also over a species, or even over all the members of a species that possess a particular gene that has been modified or introduced. We need to remember that the concepts of ownership that are at work in patent laws today are not self-evident trans-cultural concepts. They have a particular source and are, in fact, traceable to the English philosopher John Locke. Writing in a treatise on government, Locke set out to explain how something could pass from being in a state of nature, part of the global commons, something not owned by anyone, to a state of being privately owned, the property of some particular individual or corporation. The concept of property that he developed was the product of particular historical, social and economic conditions. In particular, Locke developed his arguments in the context of European colonial expansion and used his arguments quite explicitly to justify the land grab that was going on in the Americas at the time. Locke presented his argument as an attempt to show why the British could claim that the land that we now understand as the United States and Canada didn't belong to anyone, so they could claim it for themselves. That was the purpose, the explicit purpose of Locke's argument. I think nothing has changed. As Vandana Shiva has pointed out, the vacancy of target lands has been replaced by the vacancy of target life forms[1]. Bio-prospecting is better named "bio-piracy" and in my view what we are witnessing is simply a more sophisticated form of economic colonialism.

Another resource we might turn to, with some profit, is the biblical call to Jubilee. We have been reminded repeatedly over recent years that the Jubilee vision offers the promise of freedom from bondage, including bondage from debt. In the context of social realities that are exclusive, it offers a call to inclusion and it promises a Sabbath rest not only for the people of God, but also for the land. Indeed, if we turn back to that most cited Jubilee text, Leviticus 25, it becomes clear that without the Sabbath rest for the land, without the seven cycles of fallow land, there can be no Sabbath rest for people or the land. How do the promises offered in the new biotechnologies stand up to such a vision?

A view of the experimental Gardens.

"The earth is the Lord's," declares the psalmist[2], and the Jubilee text echoes that in a social practice that concretely reminds God's people that the land belongs to God and not to them. In the provisions that demand that everyone can gather the produce from the land left fallow, the Jubilee provisions insist that what the land produces of itself, apart from any planted crops, belongs to everyone. This is a far cry from the bio-prospecting that I described earlier. Of course, biotechnology companies need some means of protecting their investment in research and the development that they undertake, but the Jubilee vision sets strict limits to that, limits that begin with the assumption that the natural world is a commons, available to all and belonging to none. By contrast, what we are dealing with today is the steady erosion of that global commons as the biological and genetic resources of the world slip quietly into the posses-sion of a handful of biotechnology companies. I'm reminded of a Calvin & Hobbes cartoon that I saw recently that's now on the door of my office. Hobbes says, "When I grow up I'm going to be a scientist. I'll dedicate my career to the proposition that human beings can reshape the universe according to their own whims. I'll probably go into genetic engineering and create new life forms." Calvin asks, "You want to play God?" Hobbes responds, "Not exactly, God never bothered to patent his stuff!"

A second observation that I would make is that if we think about the new technologies in the light of the Jubilee, then we will need a more focused critique based on greater social concreteness than most analyses offer. When we talk about risk and benefits, we need to be specific. We need to ask ourselves about risks for whom and benefits for whom? The trouble is they are not always the same people. Again, Jubilee is about sight for the blind; it has something to say about the truth of our vision of the world around us, about integrity and transparency. Yet how can we speak about sight for the blind when we cannot even see what it is that we are eating because of the resistance to proper labeling?

Considering the impact of Biotechnology and local communities.

Jubilee invites us to see from a particular point of view, a point of view that acknowledges our place in a creation that is interdependent, and is an expression of the divine love, and, within which, each part has a place. Jubilee invites us to a perspective that privileges the hopes and fears of the most vulnerable; the hungry, the landless, the marginalized and excluded, and is sensitive to those who may become further excluded as a result of changes in the structure of agriculture associated with biotechnology. The Jubilee invites us neither to be dazzled by our own technological virtuosity, nor to demonize what is new and different, but to see it from the context of the new society that God is creating amongst us. The Jubilee calls on us to confront the challenges of biotechnology, not with some studied neutrality or detached objectivity—the so-called view from nowhere—but out of a passionate commitment to see and participate in the redemptive purpose of God and creation. The call to share in that vision and hope is something the poet Gerard Manley Hopkins so beautifully expresses when he reminds us that despite our exploitation of nature and each other, "The Holy Ghost over the bent world broods with warm breast and, with ah! bright wings."[3]

Thank you.

Notes

1. V. Shiva, *Biopiracy: The Plunder of Nature and Knowledge* (Boston: South End Press, 1997) p.2.

2. Ps. 24:1.

3. "God's Grandeur" from *Gerard Manley Hopkins: The Major Works*, Catherine Phillips, ed., Oxford: OUP, 2002, 128.

Renewable Energy and Creation— Experience in South Africa

—JOE MCGERVEY

God made the two great lights . . . God set them in the dome of the sky to give light upon the earth.

—Genesis 1:16–17

Slide 1

Good afternoon. Thank you for inviting me to speak here. The subject I'm going to talk about today is Renewable Energy and Creation. The talk describes the experiences that my wife, Katie, and I have had during our time serving as volunteers for mission to the Church of the Province of Southern Africa.

Slide 2

The low-cost electricity generated from coal dominates energy in South Africa. The story of South African energy is electricity. South Africa has the cheapest electricity in the world with wholesale prices of about 1 cent

---

Energy in South Africa

- South Africa: Low cost electricity from coal. Most petroleum imported. Wood and coal common in poorer households.
- Rapid Electrification through the grid. Renewable and off-grid installations are rare a small part of energy picture.
- South Africa has 40,000 MW of capacity, mostly coal plus one nuclear plant. Greater than all of the rest of Africa.

---

per kWh and retail rates of about 5 cents per kWh. This electricity is transmitted through an extensive grid connecting power plants, industry and homes. South Africa is probably the only country on the continent with enough electricity for all of its needs and which has connected more than half of its people to the electricity grid. Petroleum, mostly for transportation in cars and trucks, is not produced in significant quantities in SA and is imported. In poor households, wood and coal are used for cooking and heating. The government of SA has embarked on an aggressive electrification program since 1994.

This program is primarily connecting homes to the electricity grid using conventional connections. Smaller communities in remote areas will be receiving electricity through rooftop solar photovoltaic (PV) installations.

SA has 40,000mw of electricity-generating capacity. 90% of South African electricity comes from coal power plants. There is one large nuclear plant near Cape Town and a number of small hydro electricity stations.

To put this into perspective, 40,000mw is about 1/10 of the generating capacity of the US, but South Africa's capacity is greater than the rest of the generating capacity on the continent of Africa.

Slide 3

Understanding the status of energy in SA is important because SA is the political and economic leader of the continent. President Mbeki has taken a lead role with the African Renaissance and SA is active in all significant international activities within Africa. Economically, many businesses of SA have expansion plans that include establishing markets throughout the continent. For these reasons, seeing how energy is used in SA provides a template or model for how energy will play a role in the development of the rest of the continent.

> **Energy in South Africa (cont.)**
>
> • South Africa is the political and business leader in the continent. Expected to take a major role in the future of Africa and it is a template for how development may occur elsewhere.
> • Increasing demand for electricity will compel South Africa to build more power plants in 5-15 years.
> Will be coal, nuclear or renewable?
> Or will the growth in demand be curbed?

At this time, SA has sufficient generating capacity for all of its needs. In the next 5–15 years, demand for electricity will require the construction of new power plants. As we prepare for the World Summit on Sustainable Development, two questions about SA electricity are: what kind of power plants will be constructed and how much capacity is needed? SA gets most of its electricity from coal, but there are major environmental impacts from these coal power plants. Eskom, the national electricity supplier of South Africa, is spending millions developing a new nuclear powerplant design that could help meet growing demand in South Africa and bring grid-based electricity to new markets in Africa or be exported to North America or Europe. Another option is to curb electricity demand so that new powerplants are not needed while bringing service to millions of new customers.

Slide 4

During 2002, Katie and I had the opportunity to live at St. Andrews Mission in the Diocese of Umzimvubu. St. Andrews is located outside the small town of Lusikisiki in the Eastern Cape Province of South Africa. Lusikisiki is in the former Transkei, one of the "homelands" established by the South African governments under Apartheid. The people of

> **Energy Choices in the Transkei**
>
> • Transkei: Rural, high population density, environmental degradation
> • Sub-subsistence farming
> • Electricity is desired but affordability is a problem. Wood use is very common.
> • Other issues: Litter, sanitation, loss of nature, burning of wood, waste and fields.
> • Harvesting and carrying of water

the Transkei grow basic crops on small homestead plots. Regular rains make the poor soil of the region somewhat productive, but the population density has increased at least tenfold in recent decades and the land is suffering. Erosion, loss of forest cover and loss of endemic species is rampant, while the poverty of the Transkei pushes environmental protection down on the list of priorities.

Homesteads in Lusikisiki grow staple crops, such as corn, cabbage and potatoes, for their own use. Most families also raise livestock, especially cows that have social value and are allowed to graze freely. Private ownership of land is rare and most families have a "permission to occupy" their homesteads which are officially owned by the traditional leaders. Farming combines traditional practices and some modern techniques, including tractor plowing and purchased seeds and fertilizers. The homesteads do not produce sufficient food for most people and households are dependent on an outside source of income, often a government pension received by one of the older family members. We have heard these homesteads described as sub-subsistence since they depend on outside money to remain viable.

At night, we could see electricity service coming to homesteads south of the mission while we lived at St. Andrews. The dull, orange light of the evening's cooking fire was replaced by the bright white of a light bulb outside the entrance of a home. People want electricity service. It brings light, it extends the working day for many, and it can replace the smelly and dangerous use of wood and paraffin for lighting, cooking and heating. One obstacle is price. Although low by US standards, electricity service is expensive for a family that has a cash income of $1 or $2 per day. Despite the arrival of electricity, the rampant clearing of forests for wood collection continued at an alarming rate at St. Andrews Mission.

There are other environmental issues in Lusikisiki. Almost everyone discards or burns household trash, which has become a terrible problem as plastics and other artificial materials begin to dominate the waste stream. The tiny public water system in Lusikisiki delivers clean water to a small number of houses and there is no wastewater system. Homes have pit toilets but many people relieve themselves along roadsides and in the bush. It is not surprising that cholera outbreaks are a recurring problem in places like Lusikisiki. The loss of forest cover is the most obvious damage to the environment but invasive species and population pressures are squeezing out the remaining areas of unspoiled nature. Traditional practices and modern lifestyles produce a condition of nearly constant burning of the wood for cooking, trash and fields.

Water must be collected on a daily basis in most homes. Some homes harvest rainwater from tin roofs but most commonly the women and young girls of the home will walk to a stream or tap for cooking, drinking and bathing in the home. The collection of water combined with the collection of wood consumes much of the time available to get things done in the home.

Slide 5

South African industry thrives on its plentiful, low-cost electricity and this energy powers a mining industry that makes South Africa a world leader in the export of many precious metals and minerals. The great wealth from mining produced a sizable wealthy elite and a significant upper mid-

> ### Energy: Where are We Today?
>
> - Industry is dependent on plentiful, low cost electricity. World's largest producer of platinum, gold and chromium and a leading producer of diamonds, palladium and other precious metals
> - Formal homes are electrified. Hot water, cooking and heating from electricity.
> - Informal homes: Some are electrified, but most use wood, coal or paraffin.
> - Health problems: air pollution, poisoning, fires
> - Cost and access are the major factors in choosing energy sources.

dle class that lives in formal homes that are not unlike middle class homes in the US with electricity, modern kitchens and multiple televisions and other electronic equipment. Electricity heats the water, cooks the food and heats the rooms, although I would add that this energy is often used inefficiently.

Since the end of Apartheid, the government has built hundreds of thousands of new homes for the poor. Typically, these are single-family homes clustered on tiny plots of land on the edge of established towns. These government homes have electricity but are often uncomfortable because their cheap construction precludes insulation and proper orientation of the house to take advantage of natural patterns of sun and wind.

Most South Africans still live in traditional or informal homes often made of tin and cardboard. While some of these homes are electrified, most are not and people must use wood, coal and paraffin. The health implications of using these fuels for heating, cooking and light are important. Air pollution inside the home is terrible and we have visited communities where most children have asthma and the sound of the classroom is a steady stream of coughs. Outdoor air pollution is bad in areas where large numbers of homes use wood, coal and paraffin. To add paraffin to lamps and small stoves, people often store it in small bottles, but this leads to thousands of accidental poisonings. Finally, the high winds common to much of South Africa produce terrible fires in informal settlements where homes are built one against the next.

Bad health and limited economic opportunities are two effects of poor energy choices. People want better options, and in South Africa that means electricity. Access is one obstacle although the government's aggressive electrification effort is finding some success. The greater barrier may be cost. In a country with 60% unemployment, even the cheapest electricity in the world is too expensive for many.

Slide 6

Where does the electricity in South Africa come from? Eskom is the state-owned corporation that has a monopoly on the generation and transmission of electricity. That means that Eskom owns the powerplants and the high-tension lines that link the powerplants to the different regions of the country. Under

> ### Electricity in South Africa
> - Eskom (state-owned): Monopoly on generation and transmission. Plans to privatize in the next decade.
> - Retail through municipalities and Eskom.
> - Grid expansion: 67% of homes (51% rural)
> - Pre-pay meters most common for new connections.
> - Free 50 kWh/month program.
>   Current rural use 30 kWh/month.
>   Wealthy homes 1000 kWh/month.
> - Photovoltaic home: 5-10 kWh/month. No hot water, heating, kettle or cooking possible.
> - Free electricity program would use about 700 MW of 40,000 MW total capacity. (<2%)

pressure from international financial institutions (IMF and World Bank), South Africa plans to privatize Eskom within the next decade. Eskom sells electricity to municipalities that sell the electricity to homes. This is the retail side of the electricity business. The municipalities make large profits from the sale of electricity and these funds represent the largest revenue source for many small governments. In recent years, Eskom has become more active in selling electricity directly to customers.

The government's electrification program aims to bring service to all South Africans within ten years. Two-thirds of all homes, including more than half of all rural homes, are now connected to the grid. Most new connections use pre-pay meters that require customers to go to a store to buy a card with a number to be keyed into the meter in the home. The pre-pay meter shows how much electricity remains before another card must be purchased. Once the meter runs out, the electricity is off until a new card number is keyed. These meters are very popular with the municipalities and the customers. The municipalities are paid before the electricity is used, so there is no problem with collecting delinquent accounts. Customers like knowing that they will not generate a large debt to the municipality.

The government recently announced a new program to give every South African home 50 kWh of electricity every month. This amount is enough to run several lights and a small TV every evening and to cook on an electric stove for two hours a day. For comparison, a typical rural home uses about 30 kWh of electricity each month and a formal home in the city may use 1000 kWh per month-comparable to a middle class home in the U.S. Sales to homes that use more the 50 kWh per month will pay for the free 50 kWh that goes to everyone.

The government plans to install solar photovoltaic (PV) systems in 300,000 homes that are too remote to connect to the electricity grid. Customers in these homes will pay up to $10 per month for the service. These solar homes will use 50 or 60-watt solar panels that can provide 5–10 kWh per month of electricity, depending on the weather. The systems will not be able to provide hot water, heating or cooking, requiring people to rely on wood, coal or paraffin for these tasks. It is unclear how the solar home systems will be received because the free electricity program has raised expectations. People will question why they must pay for a level of service ($10 for 5–10 kWh of electricity) that is less than the government has said should be delivered at no cost (50 kWh).

The free electricity program will require about 700 MW of capacity to deliver 50 kWh of electricity for each home. This represents less than 2% of the country's total capacity. Put another way, 98% of the electricity will subsidize the 2% that the government wants to give people for free.

Slide 7

This chart shows the countries of the CPSA and several measures of technology, including electricity, telephones and television. The gap between South Africa and its neighbors is astounding. Perhaps not all countries in South Africa will achieve its level of wealth, but I'll say again that I believe South Africa represents the *direction* that we can expect for the rest of the continent in the twenty-first century.

Energy and Technology in the CPSA

	Angola	Lesotho	Mozambique	Namibia	South Africa	Swaziland
Electricity Produced (kWh/capita)	143	0	119	666	4,287	341
Electricity Consumed (kWh/capita)	133	25	16	1,082	3,954	180
Homes connected to grid (estimated)	15%	<25%	<10%	<25%	60%	<25%
Main Source of Electricity	Hydro	None	Hydro	Hydro	Coal	Coal/hydro
Persons per fixed-line telephone (1997)	166	110	297	18	9	33
Persons per mobile phone (1997)	1,461	1,743	1,049	no data	22	37
Persons per radio	16	21	27	8	3	7
Persons per television	69	41	287	30	8	52

Slide 8

Renewable energy has a mixed record in South Africa. I have discussed solar homes as part of the government's electrification effort and I think there may be some consumer resistance to these systems. Many of the solar homes that have been built in the past have succumbed to theft or disrepair or have been discarded once grid-based electricity became available.

Renewables in South Africa

- Solar home systems, solar schools and solar-powered telephones – mixed results
- Wind-farm in Darling in Western Cape
- Technology for the poor versus technology for the wealthy
- Biomass
- Summary: Renewables are swamped by cheap electricity from an extensive power grid

In the mid-1990s, the government installed solar panels at thousands of rural schools that did not have electricity. Because the program did not involve school administrators, the systems did not last. The solar schools program only installed lights, which were of little use since schools operate only during the day. Lacking anyone who cared that the system succeed, panels were quickly stolen or vandalized. Another program to bring rural telephone service through solar-powered radio telephones in homes has not succeeded because the technology was unreliable and was subject to theft. Cellular telephone technology delivers reliable service in rural areas at a cost within the reach of millions of poorer South Africans. Overall, the results of these renewable energy programs have been mixed.

In Darling, north of Cape Town, a private company has built a wind farm that will deliver electricity into the national grid. Eskom fought the project but the courts decided that Eskom must purchase the electricity from this renewables program. Eskom is researching some grid-based renewable technologies but none is operating. One obstacle for renewable technologies is that they are sometimes presented and received as "technologies for the poor." The wealthy of South Africa live in electrified homes that do not use renewable technologies. Solar panels and solar cookers gain the stigma of poverty and people do not aspire to use things that are only used by the poor.

One class of renewable technologies is biomass. Because trees, vegetation and animal wastes are somewhat renewable, some people view biomass as renewable. My experience in South Africa is that biomass is not gathered or used in a renewable manner. I would not consider wood to be renewable.

In summary, renewables can work in South Africa and renewable technologies have met with mixed results in various projects. Looking at the big picture, though, the availability of cheap electricity from the grid overwhelms the impact of renewables in South Africa. The electricity grid in South Africa functions very well—it is reliable and delivers electricity to almost every corner of the country at world's lowest prices.

Slide 9

There are important questions about South Africa's energy picture, which have important implications for the rest of Africa.

Is grid-based electricity the answer? Eskom is committed to the grid because it can deliver a high level of service while taking advantage of low-cost electricity sources.

Questions for South Africa's (and Africa's) Electricity
- Is grid-based electricity the answer?
- How do we deal with 40,000 MW of coal capacity?
- How serious are Eskom's nuclear ambitions?
  The Pebble Bed Modular Reactor
- Is electricity service a 'right'?
- How can these systems be sustainable?
  – Economic and environmental sustainability
  – Impacts on industry and affordability
  – Gov't blocks access to generation market
  – Non-payment for service – 95% in Soweto
  – Grass-roots initiatives affected by free electricity program

South Africa has about 40,000 MW of coal-powered electricity. What should be done with it? While these plants produce electricity at low prices, the environmental impact of these plants is air pollution and a carbon dioxide emission rate that rivals some European nations.

Eskom is developing the Pebble Bed Modular Reactor, which represents a new generation of nuclear powerplant. After committing millions of dollars to this program, will Eskom seek markets in Africa where it can be used?

Is electricity service a "right"? I have seen how electricity can improve the health and wealth of people who had been restricted to dirty fuels in the past. Should electricity be made available to all? Should people have to pay for it and how much?

How can these systems be made sustainable? I ask this as an environmental and economic question. High energy costs can inhibit economic growth, especially in areas where prices have been historically low. Stringing electricity lines to homes is pointless if people cannot afford to use it. In Soweto, the massive township near Johannesburg, 95% of customers are not paying for their electricity.

Finally, the government is implementing a number of major programs affecting energy use in the home, mostly around electricity. These programs change expectations and have shifted the economics of energy. One downside of these actions is that they may be diminishing the attractiveness and effectiveness of grass-roots energy projects. For instance, many projects in Africa help people pay for solar installations in their homes. Imagine the impact in an area where people have paid a lot of money to have photovoltaic systems installed in their homes and then Eskom brings in the grid with 50 kWh of free electricity every month.

Slide 10

Looking at the big picture or working in our own little worlds, we sometimes forget that the church must work on all four levels to bring energy choices to people that are healthy for them and help preserve creation.

> ### Working on Four Levels
>
> 1. Global: WSSD, National policies, lobbying transnational corporations
> 2. Nation or region: Government policies and large programs
> 3. Community: Programs for people
> 4. With Individuals: on the ground
>
> The Church needs to work on all levels.
> Planning times and complexity increase in larger systems.

Globally, we must work at venues such as the WSSD to share stories and exert our influence. As I have outlined in South Africa, national policies and the behavior of transnational corporations can have a big impact. Coming down a level, one nation's government or the conditions in a region can be important. Church members must understand what is happening and see how these policies and programs affect creation.

The community, which may be a single church, is where people are really part of the picture and the church can be a very powerful agent. Finally, as individuals, we must be informed and we must act responsibly because everything we do has an impact on others and affects God's creation.

The church must work on all levels to be effective.

Slide 11

We must work in our homes and churches to care for creation. We must grow our capacity for social development. This means that we must help our fellow churches and share our stories. We are called to press our governments and corporations to act responsibly.

Energy and the Church

- Work in our homes and churches to care for creation.
- Grow our capacity for social development
  Help our fellow churches
  Share our stories
- Press our governments and corporations to act responsibly

Contraction and Convergence

—THE RT. REV. JOHN OLIVER

The earth has warmed through many periods of climate change. Ice Ages have alternated with warmer periods over hundreds of thousands of years. But what has been happening in the last hundred years is without precedent. There has been a very rapid rise in temperature co-related precisely with human industrial activity and energy consumption on a very large and rapidly increasing scale.

It is possible to measure the presence of greenhouse gases in the atmosphere at different historical periods. Using air trapped in Antarctic ice, these measurements can take us back to prehistoric times. Pre-industrial levels of greenhouse gases were about 250 parts per million volume (ppmv). Present levels are 380 ppmv, and they are rising fast. They have a dramatic effect on the climate, causing a steady rise in temperature, wet years to become wetter and dry years to become drier, and extreme weather phenomena, such as hurricanes, to become more frequent. Sea levels rise as the sea temperature rises and polar ice melts.

These climatic effects have very serious implications for the human race and for biodiversity. There is general agreement among scientists that greenhouse gas levels must be stabilized at not more than 450 ppmv if catastrophic consequences are to be avoided.

The Kyoto Protocol, which derived from the World Conference on Environment and Development in Rio in 1992, is the first attempt to achieve international agreement to limit climate change. But it is a flawed process, unscientific, inequitable, and inadequate.

Another plan, called "Contraction and Convergence," offers a comprehensive post-Kyoto strategy which involves every nation in the world and which allows a fair and equal permission to pollute to every human being. It requires the highly polluting developed nations to achieve dramatic reductions in greenhouse gas emissions (Contraction), while there is Convergence towards equality, to be achieved by a set date, e.g., 2050. The system of worldwide emissions trading would allow the developing countries to sell their permission to pollute to richer nations during the period of Contraction and Convergence, and the income from such trading would enable developing countries to buy clean energy technology from the developed world.

Contraction and Convergence is scientific, equitable and comprehensive. It meets all the objections raised by the USA and Australia to the Kyoto Protocol. This Anglican Communion Global Congress in South Africa in 2002 has endorsed it, and believes it offers a solution to the greatest problem facing the human race today.

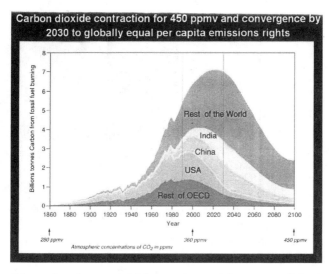

Illustrating the proposal "Contraction and Convergence", leading to stabilization of atmospheric carbon dioxide at 450 ppm (from GCI).

Global Warming and the Transition to Green Energy

—The Rev. Sally Bingham

I would like to speak with you about two programs we started through The Regeneration Project in California: Episcopal Power and Light and California Interfaith Power and Light. These are programs in response to climate change. Global climate change is a very serious issue. It affects all of the things we have talked about so far— land, water, food, and crop

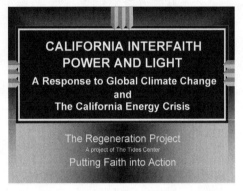

yield—and it will affect two things we have not yet discussed: air quality and disease. All of these things will be affected as our climate warms. All of the scientists have told us, and agreed, that it is the overabundance of carbon dioxide in the air that is causing the temperature to rise. Particularly in the developed world, our dependency on fossil fuels for energy is contributing to this problem. The US is 5% of the world's population, but creates 25% of the greenhouse gases, which are causing the warming trend.

Of all the nations, the United States is the largest producer of CO_2 emissions. Those of us who work in the faith community in the United States feel that if our Administration and our government is not going to cut its CO_2 emissions, not sign the Kyoto Protocol, then we will have to go around the federal government and organize the faith community to respond in a positive way.

We are the people in the pews who profess a love of God. We are the people that are called to protect creation. We are the ones who have to lead by example and show the rest of the communities how to get electricity that does not pollute our neighbors' air and eventually destroy creation. So, we are starting with the Episcopal churches. We have worked church by church in California, asking people to put solar power on their roofs. That was the first step that we wanted them to take, but if they could not afford to put solar on their roofs, then we asked them at least to find a green energy provider and purchase clean electricity. In America now, the electricity industry has deregulated, making it possible for some people to have a choice of where their electricity comes from. This makes the possibility of change much easier.

Our EP&L program became so popular in California that other denominations have joined us. We partnered with the California Council of Churches and have formed the California Interfaith Power and Light Program. It has also been taken up in Maine, Massachusetts, Texas, Tennessee and seven other states. The mission statement says: "California Interfaith Power and Light seeks to be faithful stewards of God's Creation by responding to global warming through the promotion of energy conversation, energy efficiency, and renewable energy. This ministry intends to protect this earth's ecosystems, safeguard public health, and ensure sufficient sustainable energy for all."

Traditionally, we have had no choice about where our electricity came from. Most people in the United States have taken electricity for granted for a long time. You turn on the light switch and you expect that you are going to have light. The only time you really think about it is if your lights don't come on. And you are particularly concerned if your neighbors' lights are on and yours are not. Now we had, in California, what we called "an energy crisis" where there was an actual shortage of electricity. So the natural question, after wondering whether or not you're going to have electricity, is "Where does this electricity come from?" What has happened now is that we have a choice: you can see the dirty burning coal plant, so we can choose to buy something that is clean and renewable. We are the generation in the United States that is having a choice. This is good. Nothing about the electricity system changes in terms of the wires, transmission or the distribution—only where it comes from.

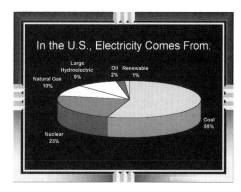

Largely our electricity in the United States comes from coal. I believe that is true here in South Africa and Africa too. These are the statistics for the USA: Coal—59%, Nuclear—23%, Natural Gas—10%, Large Hydroelectric—9%, Oil, 2%, and Renewable—1%. Coal is the dirtiest burning power generator that we have. Comparing CO_2 emissions internationally, one finds that the United States leads in those toxic emissions.

These are the human health and environmental damages from our traditional power-burning plants: acid rain and global warming (which we are focusing on in our work), as well as smog, toxic emissions, atomic radiation, the destruction of rivers, and the extinction of aquatic species.

Acid rain is chiefly caused by coal. It destroys forests, damages crops, destroys all life in many lakes and rivers, and damages buildings and cultural artifacts. Smog is a huge problem too.

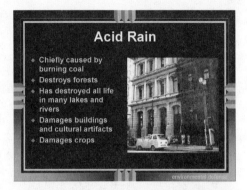

It obviously has a very detrimental effect on human respiratory systems. It can also cause premature deaths; it exacerbates asthma, reduces lung function generally, and produces chronic eye irritation.

The people that live near power plants are largely the poorer communities, and they suffer from the higher rates of asthma, lung disease, and cancer. We don't think that nuclear power plants are a viable way to generate energy. We are trying to move away from that. As you know, with nuclear energy there is no safe way of disposing of the waste, which remains highly radioactive for up to 300,000 years, and the cooling of the process of operating a nuclear reactor actually heats up nearby rivers and oceans, killing wildlife. Now that there are threats from terrorists, we think that it would be much safer for all of us if these power plants did not exist.

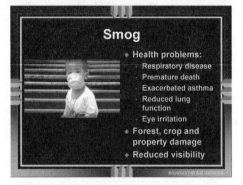

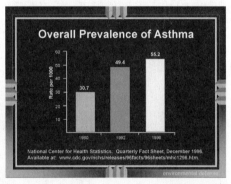

If terrorists are going to attack a power-generation plant, wouldn't we rather it be wind turbines or a solar-generating plant rather than a nuclear power plant? It is still very expensive and while it does not produce CO_2 emissions, there are all those very serious disadvantages with the production of nuclear energy.

We think that the days of the big hydroelectric dams are over, as we heard in a previous presentation. These big dams flood canyons, and they change the flow of water. They upset migratory fish patterns, and in some cases, entire cultures have to be moved. There are environmental immigrants now, refugees, in all parts of the world, who have had to be moved and displaced because their homes and habitats in river valleys have been flooded. Those dams also eliminate the natural flow of sediment, change water temperature, and block the migratory patterns of fish. I often say to people: Why do we, as humans, think we know better than God does as to how water ought to move? It is as though our rivers and streams were very intricately and beautifully created, and we in our arrogance have tried to change the flow of water, and we think we know better than God does where it ought to be.

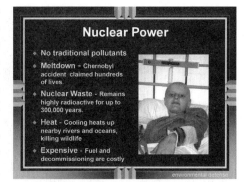

Next, let's think about the global warming issue. We are already seeing melting polar ice caps, more droughts, and more floods. I was in South Africa the week before coming here. I read in the newspaper that George Bush is being blamed for the floods in Europe, which, I thought, was interesting. It was a way of protesting that Bush was not signing the Kyoto Protocol, making a connection between that and the recent floods in Europe, Russia and Prague.

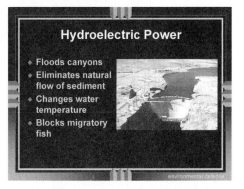

You know that there is an increase in the occurrence of epidemics. We are seeing a great deal more of unusual diseases, as the climate stays warmer. The magnificent Creator of ours set up a natural greenhouse effect which has made life, human life, possible, but we in our stubbornness about fossil fuels, have upset the balance by creating too much CO_2 and putting it into the atmosphere. Also, we have been cutting down our trees at an unprecedented rate, and trees as you probably know, are CO_2, carbon sinks. They absorb the carbon dioxide, so clearcutting and destroying forests only makes the climate change problem much worse. As a result, we are going to see a great deal more flooding, more severe storms, more droughts, and more serious weather problems all over the world.

So, why is the Church involved in this? The Church is called to do justice. The folks who are going to be the most adversely and most quickly affected by global warming are the people in poor and developing countries. And it's not as if this is going to happen in the future; it is happening now.

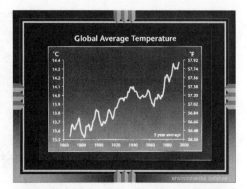

Take, for example, the small island in the South Pacific called Tuvalu. Tuvalu is going underwater. As the sea rises, the 11,000 people who live there are looking for a new home, and I understand they are trying to move to Australia. They are waiting to see if the Australian Government is going to take them. Entire cultures are being lost. In the developing world, when the sea levels rise and crops are destroyed, countries like Bangladesh don't have the disaster relief and emergency management programs that we have in the United States. They are on their own. That is another reason why it is an issue for the Church.

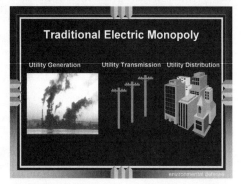

Globally, the average temperature has increased seven degrees Fahrenheit in the last thirty

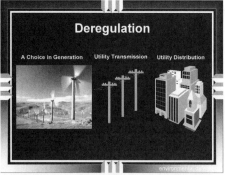

years, according to the *New York Times*. Sometimes people say that this figure and the science behind it are just not good enough. They say climate has changed many times through the millennia, over thousands and thousands of years. However, this has happened just during the industrial revolution, and there has been a continuous rise. We are creating this problem ourselves.

Now, let's consider briefly what we have been doing about this through "Episcopal Power and Light" and "California Power and Light," and other interfaith initiatives we have helped to create. In California, we have more renewable energy in the grid, compared with other parts of the United Sates. We are asking the state legislators, however, to require 20% renewable by the year 2020. Once people in the pews understand that turning on their light switch is polluting the air of the poor people around them, they think about doing it less and having clean energy. When people begin

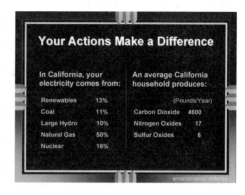

to understand that, then they do choose to have the cleaner electricity. The faith communities are playing a major role in this. We influenced the Governor in California to sign a bill cutting CO_2 emissions in cars in California. It was a landmark, and I was invited to stand behind the Governor when he signed the bill. I am not patting myself on the back, but the religious community's voice is being heard in governmental decision making now, and that is remarkable!

So, let me say again: We are the people in the pews who profess a love of God. We are the people that are called to protect creation. We are the ones who have to lead by example and must show the rest of the communities how to get electricity that does not pollute our neighbors' air and eventually destroy creation.

Solar Light for Africa, Ltd.—
An Example of How Churches Can Provide
Solar Light and Energy in African Communities

—THE RT. REV. WILLIAM RUKIRANDE, REPRESENTING SOLAR LIGHT FOR AFRICA (THE RT. REV. ALDEN M. HATHAWAY, FOUNDER)

Through Solar Light for Africa (SLA) churches, NGOs, and governments form partnerships to provide solar light and energy sources in rural African community facilities, particularly in Uganda and Rwanda. Founded in 1997 by Bishop Hathaway, SLA provides small solar packages capable of powering fluorescent lights and appliances in community facilities such as medical clinics, orphanages, schools, churches, and also in private homes.

To date, solar packages have been installed in more than 1,000 East African facilities, often with the assistance of the program's Annual Youth Mission, which operates during the summer months. This Mission involves American and Ugandan high school and college-age young people who live together for three weeks as they work in teams installing solar units.

The installation of solar units has numerous benefits: it decreases environmental and human degradation by providing a clean energy source, replacing the noxious fumes of kerosene lanterns that shorten people's life spans; it aids in economic development by providing light after the sun goes down for increased productivity and the enabling of students to study at night; it facilitates young people's access to the twenty-first century by providing solar power for computers and televisions, enabling global education and internet connection through satellites.

Currently, SLA has more than 12,000 requests from churches, clinics, schools, and orphanages in East African countries for the installation of solar units. To meet this need, Solar Light for Africa is seeking tax-deductible donations and grants for this important and lifesaving endeavor. SLA has been a participant in the UN Framework Convention on Climate Change and the U.S. Department of Energy's Initiative on Joint Implementation (USIJI). Solar Light for Africa, Ltd. can be contacted by e-mail at solarlight@starpower.net, or at the following address: 2300 Cathedral Avenue NW, Washington DC 20008; telephone (202) 232-7490; FAX (202) 232-7909. *Web* www.solarlightforafrica.org/contact.htm

Global Warming and a Fragile Environment—
A Christian Response

—THE RT. REV. GEORGE BROWNING

Let me say a little about the problem of climate change and energy consumption from the standpoint of Australia. It is said that Australians produce more CO_2 per person than any country in the world: 37 tons for each Australian. It is a huge amount; the accumulative impact on Australia is enormous. We are the oldest and most fragile continent in the world. Our ecosystems are very, very vulnerable. We are also the driest continent. The impact of climate change could mean that by the year 2050, we can expect to be 40–60% drier than we are now. This is almost impossible to believe. At the moment, the whole of eastern Australia is in the grip of the worst drought ever experienced. Droughts and floods are well-known cycles on our continent, but there is real evidence that this drought is made far worse as a result of global warming.

If we were an underdeveloped country, we would be in famine. At the moment we are importing food to keep our livestock alive. Yet our country, like America, refuses to participate in agreements or protocols which could begin to address these issues.

Because of the gap in the ozone layer, we Australians have the highest rate of skin cancer in the world. Almost every Australian will know someone who has had a cancer removed from their skin. My wife has had treatment to her face, which she says resulted from putting nappies on the line when the three boys were young! It is a very prevalent problem in our country. And yet, the world has so changed its behavior in relation to aerosol cans, etc, that there is a reasonable prospect that within a relatively short period of time the ozone hole could be repaired. If we can change our behavior in this regard, why can't we do it with global warming?

In the 200+ years since white people came to Australia we have totally changed the environment. Most of this has happened unintentionally. There has been large-scale land clearing to create space for agriculture and pasture for animals. European animals have been introduced. Sheep, cattle and horses have hard hooves; Australian native animals, like the kangaroos, have padded feet. Hoofed feet damage the topsoil. White settlers could have farmed native animals, but we chose to adopt the agricultural and grazing patterns of the Northern Hemisphere. We now experience serious downsides of these practices, the most notable of which are land degradation and salination. We are as slow to respond to these issues at home as we are to sign international protocols abroad. As a Christian in Australia, it is very difficult to cope with the inaction. We must share responsibility with the whole world to ensure that future generations have the opportunity of living in a world that is sustainable.

Notwithstanding the myriad of environmental issues we face, some of which I have fleetingly referred to, I am convinced that CO_2 and global warming must receive priority focus. We must face the fact that CO_2 stays in the atmosphere for approximately 100 years. Every year that goes by without a strategy to limit the expansion, let alone reduce the accumulative effect, means that we are several generations away from an improvement. I understand that if this UN Summit agrees to new protocols, the earliest we can expect an improvement will be about 2030–2050. If we do not make decisions now, then improvements may be 2060–2070 at the earliest. If we continue to put off the time when we bring the matter of climate change into some kind of balance it is a very, very serious matter.

What are we doing about it? What is the Church doing about it? I have become convinced that the Christian Community must take the initiative. It is after all our core business. We are stewards. I have recently established in our diocese the first Commission for the Environment in Australia. We are very fortunate that my Diocese is based in Canberra, the National Capital, and I can bring onto the Commission people who hold influential positions in public service. The head of the Department of the Environment, an Anglican, is on our Commission.

While there are many issues worthy of our attention, we have decided to make energy our main focus. The Diocese owns a large wool-growing property where we are planting tens of thousands of trees to make it more sustainable, but energy is the important thing for us.

We are beginning with an audit of Diocesan institutions—the Schools, Aged Care Facilities and Retirement Villages, Welfare Agencies, Central Office, Theological Center, Parishes. The aim of the audit is to find ways of reducing our energy consumption and to use green energy. Despite the fact that at the moment green energy is more expensive, we hope to have a cash positive result through energy savings.

Currently Australia has less than 10% green energy on our national grid. This is primarily sourced from wind and biomass. It is a reasonable aim to increase this to 25%. The only way of achieving this goal is through public demand.

My hope is that within a reasonable period of time we will have our major institutions buying green energy off the grid. In the process each institution will have examined its overall energy consumption and will have reduced it. There are wins all around. The institutions will have a lower energy bill (notwithstanding the higher price). The percentage of green energy on the grid will be increased. Individuals associated with each institution will have been encouraged to put the same ideals into practice at home. The environment will become more sustainable. It is not unreasonable to hope that progressively each Diocese in Australia can follow suit.

Anglicans are currently 22% of the total population of Australia. If every Diocese, every institution within each Diocese and every Anglican family were to come on board, this could make a huge impact. The company we are negotiating with is prepared to negotiate a credit to the Diocese for each Anglican family that signs up.

Nothing happens without it first being imagined. It is not too hard to imagine that through the Anglican Church alone we have the potential to touch almost one quarter of the Australian population. We now must find the will to do what our political leaders won't do.

In order to put this vision into reality we must convince the Anglican Community that this is core business. This is Gospel business. This is Kingdom business. At the moment our actions show we are not convinced, or at least not convinced enough. The reality is that the majority of Anglicans in the rapidly growing Churches do not believe that environmental matters are core in the same way that evangelism, or nurturing new believers, is core. I believe that evangelism is absolutely core, but so is Christian living of which environmental stewardship is a core component.

I have a mantra of five reasons:

1. I believe environmental stewardship is core business because of the biblical stories of creation in Genesis, the Psalms, Job, etc.

2. I believe environmental stewardship is core business because the call to stewardship is biblically one of the core vocations of every human being.

3. I believe environmental stewardship is core business because of what I believe about Jesus. (cf. the Prologue to the Gospel according to St. John, or the Hymn to the Universe, Colossians 1:15–20)

4. I believe environmental stewardship is core business because I am committed to social justice. The wealthy create most environmental degradation: environmental degradation creates poverty.

5. I believe environmental stewardship is core business because my faith teaches that we human beings must exercise inter-generational responsibility. We are children of previous generations and parents of those yet to come. To live at the expense of future generations is to steal from our children.

The letter we send from our Congress to the Anglican Communion is, for me, more important than the statement we issue to the World Summit. Every single Anglican, there are 70 million of us, should be able to influence ten people. That means we can influence 700 million people. If we can influence twelve, then we can influence a billion people. It is our core business. We should not ask others to do what we are not doing ourselves. Through the exercise of our faith and its implications for our living, we Anglicans can make a big difference to the world environmental crisis.

"Deep in the Flesh": The Body of Christ, HIV/AIDS and Sustainable Development

—Denise Ackermann

We know that the whole creation has been groaning in labor pains until now; and not only the creation, but we ourselves, who have the first fruits of the Spirit, groan inwardly while we wait for adoption, the redemption of our bodies.

—Romans 8:22–23

Questions and context

I have two questions, both of them burning in their immediacy, both related and both central to this paper and this Congress. First: *What does sustainable development mean in a context stricken by the scourge of HIV/AIDS?* Following on this is my second question: *How can the Body of Christ, itself infected with AIDS, find and bring hope into this context?*

I ask these questions as a woman, a theologian and a member of the Anglican Communion.[1] My context—the South African reality—is described as one of the areas worst affected by HIV/AIDS in the world. The statistics (those we are allowed to see) are a nightmare. We are in the midst of the first truly global pandemic in world history. Over 500 people dying daily, over 1,500 new infections in South Africa. I cannot begin to describe the misery and plight of hundreds of thousands of orphans, the faltering health services, the dire effects on our fragile economy, the growing shortage of teachers, and the enormous toll that the virus is taking on our labor force. I *can* state without fear of contradiction that the Body of Christ has AIDS. The church is not a community of people remote from the context in which it finds itself. We are the church with AIDS facing, in the words of the Secretary-General of the United Nations Kofi Annan, "a tragedy on a biblical scale". This tragedy is our challenge.

I turn to my first question: *What does sustainable development mean in a context stricken by the scourge of HIV/AIDS?* To begin with, what is meant by sustainable development? Sustainable development is described, somewhat blandly, as social and economic development within biophysical environmental constraints that meet the needs of the present without compromising the potential of future generations to meet their own needs. It calls for the improvement of the quality of life for all the world's people without increasing the depletion of our natural resources beyond the Earth's carrying capacity. So far so good. When probing further, however, it becomes clear that sustainable development is a complex process, often fraught with contradictions. As a woman who lives in Africa I wonder:

Who determines what constitutes sustainable development on my continent? Is it simply access to the market economy and capitalism? To what extent are those who make decisions prepared to address the fact that environmental factors are intricately linked to economic conditions and that this knowledge comes with a price? How can poverty and social injustice caused by weak national economics that force people to overconsume natural resources and women to be at the bottom of the economic scale be addressed?[2]

Let me come clean. The phrase 'sustainable development' makes my antennae quiver with caution, even skepticism. Can yet another large United Nations' conference such as the World Summit on Sustainable Development (WSSD) hold out hope for meaningful change for women and children on our continent? We are, on the one hand, a continent endowed with a wealth of biological diversity and, on the other, with dreadful poverty and ecological degradation. What we urgently need is the implementation of truly sustainable, gender sensitive, people-centered development. How can this come about in an environment that is ravaged by HIV/AIDS? I suggest that the place to begin is to recognize that this pandemic is in essence a gendered pandemic.

A gendered pandemic

African theologian Teresa Okure startled her hearers at a theological symposium on AIDS held in Pretoria in 1998, by saying that there are two viruses more dangerous than the HIV virus because they are carriers enabling this virus to spread so rapidly.[3] The first virus is the one that assigns women an inferior status to men in society. This virus fuels the sex industry in which young women, themselves the victims of abuse, become infected with HIV and then pass it on to others, even to their babies. This is the virus that causes men to abuse women. This is the virus that is responsible for the shocking fact that in many countries in Africa the condition that carries the highest risk of HIV infection is that of being a married women. I would like to add here that the first virus related to the HIV/AIDS pandemic is not only about women's questionable status in society, but it is more specifically about the disordered nature of relationships between women and men as expressed sexually and emotionally.

According to Okure, the second virus that enables the HIV virus to spread at a devastating rate is found mostly in the developed world. It is the virus of global economic injustice that causes dreadful poverty in many parts of the developing world. Capitalist market economies are thrust on societies that are not geared for them, as well as structural adjustment programs that are designed to meet the requirements of the developed world rather than those whose need is the greatest. Global economic systems disrupt traditional societies, displace economic and educational infrastructures, as the market demands of such systems, and make access to prevention and treatment of disease difficult and expensive, a reality that has a severe impact on the health of the most vulnerable members of society—women and children. It is ironic that international organisations like UNAids and the United Nations call on countries to restructure their spending in order to ensure that "national budgets are reallocated towards HIV prevention", when these very countries are most often hamstrung by crippling foreign debt. Peter Piot, executive director of UNAids, pointed out that in the year 2000, African countries were paying US$15 billion in debt repayments and that this was four times more than they spend on health or education.[4]

I want to add a third virus to Okure's list—the virus of denial. I have no trouble understanding people who, suspecting that they may be infected with HIV, refuse to be tested because the prospect of disease and death is simply too shattering. Neither do I blame people who are HIV positive for remaining silent about their status. Who wants to add the burden of stigma to an already fraught situation? Sadly, these kinds of denial do not assist in changing patterns of behavior or in protecting those who are uninfected, and consequently, the virus' progress becomes more rampant. More pernicious than individual denial has been the denial by the South African state that its citizens are trapped in a pandemic. As the world watches in dismay and people die daily, President Thabo Mbeki and his cabinet have spent more than two years debating "scientific questions" in regard to HIV/AIDS, opinions which were greatly informed by dissident views on the subject, while refusing virtually free treatment to pregnant women which would greatly reduce the number of infected babies born. Documents on HIV/AIDS are distributed to the ruling party which bear all the hallmarks of scientific twaddle and racist anti-Western sentiments that run contrary to the African National Congress' long tradition of non-racialism. One of South Africa's most eminent scientists, Professor Malegapuru Makgoba, recently and stingingly rebuked the South African government.

> When the government is provided with answers—the best scientific opinion in the world that is available—they simply refuse [to accept them] and this behavior is the *sine qua non* characteristic of a refusenik or denialist. Government has rather enjoyed dabbling with scientific unproven ideas, which it uses as the basis of debate. In order for any government to make a policy decision it is duty bound to seek the expertise of the professionals . . . so that they can make informed decisions in the best interests of the public. Whenever they have been given this kind of information they have simply refused it.

Now, after more than two years of prevarication and obfuscation, the South African government has hopefully begun to reverse its disastrous AIDS policies. Since the third week of April 2002, South Africans have dared to hope that this dreadful scourge will in fact be tackled with all the resources we can muster.

Picking up on Okure's observations, I argue that the HIV/AIDS pandemic is a gendered pandemic exacerbated by poverty that is having a devastating impact on our ability to sustain people-centered development. South Africa is a society in which cultural traditions of male dominance, bolstered by a particular understanding of the place of men in the Christian tradition,[5] has resulted in continued inequity for women. Poverty, both in the rural areas and in the informal settlements surrounding our cities, is a further grinding reality. Understanding this unholy alliance should be at the heart of all HIV/AIDS programs whether located in the churches or in state structures. Gender inequality and the snail-like pace at which poverty is being tackled are the main problems blocking effective HIV/AIDS prevention. By this I do not mean that HIV/AIDS does not have devastating consequences for *all* South Africans, regardless of age, race, class or economic status. Of course it does. But for South African women and children the AIDS pandemic is particularly perilous.[6] While it is cutting a deadly swathe across the educated classes in the 20–40 age group, its greatest impact is on the most vulnerable members of society: *the poor, the marginalized and the displaced.* This makes HIV/AIDS a crisis for women, particularly poor women in rural areas and those struggling to survive in shacks on the outskirts of cities.[7] It goes without saying that when women are affected, children suffer. Quoting from UNAids (1997), Vicci Tallis points out that "almost four-fifths of all infected women live in Africa; in sub-Saharan Africa, there is a ratio of six women to five men infected; in the 15–24 year age group the risk of HIV infection for young women is even more disproportionate, with young women outnumbering young men by a ratio of 2:1."[8]

Probing beyond the statistics, it appears that women's vulnerability to HIV/AIDS occurs on a variety of levels: biological, social, individual, maternal and care giving. For instance, an HIV positive pregnant woman runs the risk of transmitting the virus to her child, either during pregnancy, during birth or after birth through breast feeding.[9] Rural women who have little or no education and who live in traditional patriarchal relationships have scant access to information on HIV/AIDS, and generally lack the skills and the power needed "to negotiate safer sex". Tallis continues:

> According to UNAids (1997) studies in Africa and elsewhere [show that] married women have been infected by their husbands (as their only sexual partner). Simply being married is a major risk for women who have little control over abstinence or condom use in the home, or their husband's sexual activities outside the home.[10]

Strategies to deal with HIV/AIDS have failed these women because they insist on preventive behavior, which they, the women, have little power to implement. There is a growing body of well-documented research in the social sciences that shows that women in patriarchal societies are "unequipped for sexual negotiation".[11] Research on teenage girls found that many experienced their first sexual encounter as coercive.[12] In the province of KwaZulu/Natal, 72 percent of teenage girls attending clinics related that they had refused to have sexual relations with their partners but were usually unsuccessful at doing so and that attempts at refusal could result in physical abuse, termination of the relationship or financial hardship.[13]

What emerges from present research into HIV/AIDS in sub-Saharan Africa is the fact that the role of men needs to be addressed, particularly attitudes and behavior that are sexually irresponsible and that result in a certain death sentence not only for themselves, but also for millions of women and children. The theoretical and practical implications of the growing awareness of men's role in the HIV/AIDS pandemic are now being tackled by social scientists on our continent.[14] Heavily male institutions such as the military, sports clubs and trade unions are being focused on for HIV prevention.[15] Suffice it to say that the need to deal with inequities within relationships and society remains a central concern.[16] This does not imply that I am negating the importance of other strategies for dealing with HIV/AIDS such as advocating closed sexual relationships, the use of preventive measures, the need for appropriate treatment such as post-exposure prophylactics, AZT, or nevirapine for pregnant mothers.[17] I am simply saying that gender relations, exacerbated by poverty, are powerful contributing factors to the present pandemic in southern Africa.

In summary, African women, who produce over 70 percent of the continent's food, manage the continent's natural resources, nurture, care and provide skilled knowledge to eke a living from fragile ecosystems, are now being threatened by a deadly virus.[18] Yet the New Partnership for Africa's Development (NEPAD) championed by President Thabo Mbeki, is not only short on gender analysis, but it pays no heed to the effects of HIV/AIDS on its grand designs. Can sustainable development, in Esther Njiro's words, be no more than an oxymoron?[19]

As I have said, the Body of Christ has AIDS. As a Christian theologian I cannot let go of hope. To hope means being actively involved for change that can bring about that for which one hopes. My second question is: *How can the Body of Christ, itself infected with AIDS, find and bring hope into this context?* I now want to suggest several issues for our consideration as members of the worldwide Anglican Communion which may help us to both find hope and to bring it to the suffering who seek to live with dignity in the midst of poverty, disease and environmental degradation.

1. The body and relationship

First, I suggest that we begin by acknowledging that our social reality is an *embodied* reality. So is HIV/AIDS and poverty. So is the degrading of our environment. As the Body of Christ we are an embodied community of people. We cannot shy away from the reality of embodiment. In Elaine Graham's words, "The effects and dynamics of power, truth, reason, good and evil never exist as transcendent ideals; they remain to be embodied, enacted, performed in human communities as forms of bodily practice".[20] Our bodies are more than skin, bone and flesh. Our bodies encompass the totality of our human experience, our thoughts, our emotions, our needs and memories, our ability to imagine and to dream, our experiences of pain, pleasure, power and difference, as well as our beliefs and our hopes. Ethicist Christine Gudorf reminds us that the body is synonymous with the self. "The mind is not over and against the body but rather is part of it, as are the emotions".[21] Our bodies are, in fact, the intricate tracery of all that is our self. Again in Graham's words, ". . . embodiment is more than an 'issue' exciting our compassion; rather, it points us to the performative, incarnational nature of all theology. Bodily *praxis* is the agent and the vehicle of divine reality and the faith practices of the Body of Christ are 'sacraments' of suffering and redemption".[22]

Why is this important? It is the starting place for our sense of community— when one limb of the body suffers, we all suffer. The body carries our scars, our memories, our hopes and the clues to our identities. Bodies know that their well-being is "never secure, never predictable".[23] "Blessing in biblical traditions is matched by curse," Melanie May reminds us in her book *A Body Knows*.[24] Blessings and curses are woven into the very fiber of our bodies. The curses lie in the breakdown of our relationships with ourselves, with God, with others and with God's creation. The blessings are in the body's ability to come to terms with its afflictions. The body knows the presence of the One who promises us resurrection and new life. The body knows what it means to take up the challenge to find new ways of being in the world. These blessings enable May to say, "Knowing what my body knows, I am freed to be a believer". This I have seen countless times in the triumphs of people living with HIV/AIDS, who refuse to succumb to hopelessness and live fruitful even joyous lives. The recognition that sustainable development is about people's bodies is the place to start.

2. Stigma and the body

Women who are HIV positive are at the receiving end of prejudice, social ostracism and violence. Countless women in South Africa who are HIV positive have been the victims of sexual violence, perpetrated within a cultural order in which power is abused and women are used for male purposes. The results? Once their status has been verified, they are often ostracised.[25] In a patriarchal system women's cries of distress are insufficiently heard and they often disappear under a veil of silence. Breaking the silence about one's status can be life threatening. Gugu Dlamini became South Africa's first AIDS martyr when, in December 1998, she was stoned to death for speaking out about her HIV status. HIV/AIDS is nourished by silence in South Africa. The dark mystery that lies at the heart of the pandemic in this country is the stubborn multilayered silence or what is called 'the denial' by professionals.

When the HIV virus enters, lurks, then makes forays into the immune system of a person, life changes forever. The body is not only diseased but it also becomes the focus of stigmas. Stigmas are socially constructed ways of marking people. Stigmas brand or disgrace individuals or groups, tainting them and making them alien to the dominant culture. The question of stigma is particularly poignant when it is attached to persons suffering from HIV/AIDS. Ignorance, prejudice, stereotypes, issues of power and dominance all conspire to stigmatize sufferers and, in so doing, to label them and to distort their true identities. You simply become "an HIV positive", a statistic whose identity is now subsumed in your status. This denies the active, meaningful and contributing lives led by increasing numbers of HIV positive people. Stigmas have a way of rebounding on those who stigmatize. When I, who am not an HIV/AIDS sufferer, encounter a person who is, I am suddenly faced with the realization that this person, in the words of Iris Marion Young, "whom I may project as so different, so other, is nevertheless like me."[26]

Erving Goffman's influential theory of stigma points to the link between stigmas and assumed identities. He asserts that stigmas are specially constructed relationships.

> Historically, stigmas were imposed on individuals in the form of physical marking or branding to disgrace them. In modern societies, however, stigmas arise through social processes of interaction whereby individuals are marked or segregated because of an attribute they possess or because of something discrediting known about them. Hence stigmatized identities emerge through interpersonal interactions rather than as a psychological reaction to events. . . . The mere existence of stigma ensures that social interactions between stigmatized and non-stigmatized persons are usually uncomfortable, tense, and frustrating.[27]

Goffman's work on "stigmatized identities" refers to the disabled. As he points out, stigmas are located in the bodies of persons with disabilities. Goffman's paradigm strikes profound chords in our context. Women who are known to be HIV positive are stigmatized by a large section of South African society.

Fortunately, within the body of people living with HIV/AIDS there is an increasing band of people who are slowly gaining power by defining their experiences and claiming their reality, speaking out and breaking the silence around the disease. There is also a new brand of social activism emerging in South Africa, as bodies march in the streets demanding affordable treatment for HIV/AIDS.[28] We cannot sustain any form of just development in communities which are a breeding ground for stigmas. As members of the Body of Christ, we ourselves have to demonstrate the truth that all members are equal in value and dignity.

3. The power of narrative

Human beings cannot survive without a narrative identity.[29] Telling stories is intrinsic to claiming one's identity and in this process finding impulses for hope. For those living with HIV/AIDS there is a need to claim and to name their identities in order to move away from the victim status so often thrust upon them. Narrative has a further function.[30] Apart from claiming identity and naming the evil, narrative has a sense-making function. The very act of telling the story is an act of making sense of an often incomprehensible situation, of a suffering and chaotic world in which people wrestle with understanding and, in so doing, seek to experience relief. I trust that the WSSD will make sufficient space to hear the stories of marginalized people and treat them with respect.

I hope too that in our Communion there is space for communal narrative. Then we will see that the stories of people living with HIV/AIDS are not only stories of suffering. They are also stories of triumph, of resistance and of hope which can change communities of faith. Churches should offer a supportive and empathetic environment for storytelling in the search for meaning. Stories, writes Joan Laird, are "to be thought of as narratives within the narrative".[31] The stories of people living with HIV/AIDS are individual tales within the metanarrative of the pandemic. Hearing and engaging with these stories in communities of faith has the potential to draw members into relationship. We all have stories to tell. As our stories intersect, they change. We become part of one another's stories. In this process, we are all changed. Hearing and telling stories begins a process of openness, vulnerability and mutual engagement that challenges stigmas, ostracization and the loneliness of suffering, and hopefully leads to acts of engagement, affirmation and care. Most importantly, narrative has the power to break the silences surrounding this crisis and to give it a human face.

Grace Jantzen comments: "And if the incarnation is about the solidarity of God with humankind, then practical identification with people with AIDS can send us back to reading the New Testament with joyous insight that we didn't have before."[32] The real metanarrative is *the* story of our faith: the story of the God of Israel acting to create and redeem, culminating in the ministry, the suffering, death and resurrection of Jesus Christ. Thus storytelling becomes a two-way conversation—hearing stories of suffering and triumph, and retelling *the* story of suffering and triumph in our communities of faith. The intersecting of our life stories with the Jesus story is our ultimate hope.

4. The Body of Christ as moral community

In South Africa today there is much talk, and very necessary talk, about abstinence, prevention and medication in the face of the HIV/AIDS crisis. The Roman Catholics say abstinence is the only answer. The Anglicans say yes, but if you must, use condoms. There is very little being said, however, about the moral and ethical issues raised by the HIV/AIDS pandemic. So far the church has not grasped this nettle. The recognition that the Body of Christ is a community of sexual human beings[33] is slow in coming and centuries of ignoring any matter related to human sexuality is merely feeding the silences around HIV/AIDS. It is simply not good enough merely to preach fidelity and abstinence in sexual relations. This message cannot be heard, understood or followed as long as it is communicated without a properly constructed debate on what constitutes a moral community. This is a debate in which both men and women must take part. The church's failure to develop an adequate theology of sexuality is indeed deeply ironic ". . . in a religion that is named after one who was incarnate love . . .", Jantzen comments.[34] Moral choices, moral accountability and a community in which women are respected as equal partners in the church itself, as well as in their sexual relations, are essential to this debate.

What makes a moral community? Christian ethics are communal ethics. How people live with one another and our faithfulness to God are two sides of the same coin. The people of Israel received the law, according to Rowan Williams, "when God had already established relations with them, when they were already beginning to be a community bound by faithfulness to God and to each other".[35] Williams continues:

> When the Old Testament prophets announce God's judgement on the people, they don't primarily complain about the breaking of specific rules (though they can do this in some contexts) or about failure to live up to a moral ideal; they denounce those actions that signify a breaking of the covenant with God and so the breaking of the bonds of faithfulness that preserve Israel as a people to whom God has given a vocation.[36]

In the New Testament, Paul deals with ethical dilemmas (for example, Rom. 14 and 15, 1 Cor. 10) by arguing that any decisions taken should be guided by the priority of the other person's advantage, by avoidance of judgmentalism and by acceptance of one another and thus by the ultimate imperative of building the Body of Christ more securely. For Christians, ethical actions flow from involvement in community with God and with one another. Actions that promote the good of another are actions that are designed to be for the good of the Body of Christ.

How can the shaping of a moral community begin? Bernard Brady in his book *The Moral Bond of Community* has a chapter entitled "You don't have anything if you don't have stories". He writes: "Narratives form and inform our values, our dispositions and how we 'see the world'."[37] It is indeed possible to argue that narrative is *the* medium of moral communication. What is certain is that narrative is at the heart of our faith, a narrative which "sets up the conditions for the possibility of the moral life".[38] Instead of a negative ethic of human sexuality which consists only of injunctions on what not to do, people's stories can be countered with other stories—stories from our source book. Once the stories of the Bible and from our traditions interact with our own stories, then moral consciousness, the ability to distinguish the "is" from the "ought" and the choices this involves, can be nurtured. Acquiring moral agency does not separate "being" from "doing" or character from decision making and action. To be a member of the Body of Christ means "the formation and transformation of personal moral identity in keeping with the faith identity of the community".[39]

To put it differently, a moral community is one whose goal is the common good of all. Common good makes sense if it is translated into sustained people-centered development. A moral community upholds the integrity of life, values the dignity of the human person, and includes those who are on the margins or excluded, while not avoiding the reality of structural sin. The moral claim is to "respect and enhance the integrity of life *before God*".[40] The main task of a moral community is to nurture the moral capacities of its members, by storytelling, by involvement in the work of justice and charity, by upholding the integrity of all created life, affirmed by our liturgical practices. In this way the community becomes one of moral deliberation and praxis. "In both Jewish and Christian traditions, faith's truth is finally a 'performative' one".[41] It becomes real when it is embodied. Moral truth and a way of life go hand in hand.

Bruce Birch and Larry Rasmussen in their book *Bible and Ethics in the Christian Life* tell the story of Dom Helder Camara meditating in the middle hours of the night about the attitudes of the rich towards the poor and then writing a poem. This poem speaks to those of us in the church who are not HIV positive and who may be tempted to feel virtuous about our status, perhaps even indifferent to those who are infected.

> I pray incessantly
> for the conversion
> of the prodigal son's brother.
> Ever in my ear
> rings the dread warning
> "this one [the prodigal] has awoken
> from his life of sin.
> When will the other [the brother]
> awaken
> from his virtue?"[42]

5. The language of lament

I suggest that the ancient language of lament offers a vehicle for expressing the raw emotions arising from situations such as the one I have tried to sketch.[43] The language of lament also offers the Body of Christ the opportunity to say: "We are suffering; we stand in solidarity with all who suffer; we lament while we believe that there is hope for all in the saving grace of Jesus Christ".

What is lament? Lament is a form of mourning. It is also more. It is somehow more purposeful and more instinctive than mourning. Lamenting is both an individual and a communal act that signals that relationships have gone awry. While lamenting is about past events, it also has present and future dimensions. It acknowledges the brokenness of the present because of injustice and our role in contributing to the troubles of the world. It instinctively creates a link between healing and mourning that makes new just relationships possible in the future. Lament is not utilitarian. It is as primal as the child's need to cry. Lament is more than railing against suffering, breast-beating or a confession of guilt. It is a coil of suffering and hope, awareness and memory, anger and relief, desires for vengeance, forgiveness and healing.[44] It is our way of bearing the unbearable, both individually and communally. It is a wailing of the human soul, a barrage of tears, reproaches, petitions, praise and hopes that beat against the heart of God. It is, in essence, supremely human.

Once the wail is articulated, the lament usually takes on a structured form. This does not mean that lament should be tamed or domesticated, but rather, that it happens in spaces that are contained by liturgical boundaries and rhythms. Nevertheless, lamenting remains risky speech. Walter Brueggemann acknowledges this, saying that it is "dangerous, restless speech".[45] It is risky because it calls into question structures of power, it calls for justice, it pushes the boundaries of our relationships with one another and with God beyond the limits of acceptability. It is a refusal to settle for the way things are. It is reminding God that the human situation is not as it should be and that God as the partner in the covenant must act. Lament is never an end in itself. It is undergirded by the hope that God not only can, but that God *will* hear the cries of the suffering and the penitent and *will* act with mercy and compassion.

As HIV/AIDS decimates families and communities, as we are inundated with reports on how the earth is doomed, the Body of Christ can find hope and comfort in the psalms whose undimmed quality comes to us through the ages, expressing the rawness of suffering as well as trust and hope in God. In Brueggemann's words: "Israel unflinchingly saw and affirmed that life as it comes, along with joy, is beset by hurt, betrayal, loneliness, disease, threat, anxiety, bewilderment, anger, hatred and anguish".[46] Israel also saw that lament and praise go hand in hand. On the one hand, the psalmists almost assault God with facts about the human condition. On the other hand, they reveal trust and confidence that God will deliver them.

When the language of lament becomes the language of the Body of Christ in circumstances of suffering, it has a number of grave implications. First, it has important implications for the political and social witness of the churches and the impact of their message. The credibility in society of the churches as institutions that claim to be inclusive, caring communities is in doubt if they are not seen to lament the injustice of the patent lack of support from our government for those suffering from HIV/AIDS. Lamenting can be politically subversive and therefore dangerous, as it is never about the preservation of the status quo.

Second, the language of lament can enrich our liturgies and our pastoral care. I have seen lament at work in St George's Cathedral in Cape Town where people faced one another across the racial divide, told their stories, wept and joined in prayers of petition and prayers. Then I understood why so many prayers of praise are impoverished. Too often praise is not praise that emerges from grappling with radical doubt about God's presence in the world and our disquiet about suffering. I also saw how painful memories, experiences of exclusion and stigmatization must be brought into the open. They need to be told and, when words fail, the psalms offer a valuable resource for lament as they honor people's pain and offer hope. Hope is nurtured in community. When the community of faith joins in lamenting, the suffering person feels that her or his pain is validated. The locus of pain is shifted from the inner world of private suffering to the outer reality of the community of faith in a movement that is potentially cathartic.

Third, why are we not lamenting the rape of our planet? Why are we not lifting our voices to God in lament and penitence for our sins of disrespect, waste, pillage and despoiling of the generous and life-giving creation we are integrally part of?

Finally, the practice of lament can contribute to a more intimate and authentic relationship with God. People living with HIV/AIDS grapple with guilt, fear and anger. Death as judgment for sin weighs heavily on some. The ability to cry out to God, to lament sin and seek forgiveness, as David (Ps. 51) did, offers another way. Fear of the suffering associated with death from AIDS-related diseases is only human; anger at being a victim of infection raises legitimate questions about God, about justice and about God's presence and power in a suffering world. Is God's justice and care for us reliable and, if so, where is it? There is much cause for lament, yet its loss stifles our questions about evil in the world. Instead we settle for a God who is covered with a sugarcoated veneer of religious optimism whose omnipotence will 'make everything right in the end'.

Religious optimism is deeply different to a life of faith, which is unafraid to examine suffering but is nonetheless grounded on hope. Religious optimism prefers to sanitize God by removing God from the ugliness of evil and suffering. This is a God whom we dare not approach with our genuine grief and with whom we are in a relationship of eternal infantilism. Prayers of lament that are direct, truthful about suffering, that name the unnamable to God, are powerful in their potential to heal our doubts and address our lack of trust and restore our faith in God's power to act on our cries. The church with AIDS must raise its voice in lament, the only language that can adequately express our response to our situation with integrity.

6. Life and death

How to live productively and hopefully with the knowledge of premature death raises questions about the relationship between life and death that demand attention in the Body of Christ. What has the Good News to say to someone who is infected with HIV or who is dying of AIDS? What has it to say in a world with depleted forests, increasing ozone gaps, threatened species and devastating climatic changes?

I suggest that the place to begin is to affirm that God is a lover of all life, so much so that life continues into eternity. Certainty about this comes from the promise of the resurrection of the body and in the hope for the restoration of the world. Hope is the key to questions about life and death. Not "pie in the sky when you die" kind of hope which is nothing more than the thin skin of religious optimism, but creative, imaginative, expectant and risky hope, maintained only with struggle. Hope is demanding, because we have to live our lives in such a way that that which we hope for can come about. This kind of hope takes our confessed belief in "the life everlasting" as not only something for one day when I die, but as a confession of how I will live my life this day, in this moment. It has profound implications for my conduct as a human being dependent on my ecological environment for sustenance.

Life, death and resurrection all belong together—they make up the whole of life. Resurrection cannot be reduced to 'life after death' alone. When John (1 John 3:14) writes "We know that we have passed from death into life, because we love one another", he stresses that love is passionate about life, that we must say a hearty "Yes" to life, life which leads to death. What the resurrection of the body means is the subject of theological speculation; resurrection talk, however, remains body talk according to our creeds. Resurrection does not mean a deferred life—something we put off until after we die. In Moltmann's words: "I shall live *wholly* here, and die *wholly*, and rise *wholly* there".[47] Eternal life is all of me, all of everyone, all of creation, all healed, reconciled and completed. Nothing will be lost. Christian faith is shaped by the experience of the dying and the death of Christ and by his resurrection. The process of the resurrection of the dead begins in Christ and continues in the Spirit, 'the giver of life', and will be completed in the raising of all the dead.[48] So, I would say to the person dying of AIDS, "Death is not your end. *Every life remains before God forever*". To be raised to eternal life means that nothing has been lost for God: ". . . not the pains of this life, and not in moments of happiness".[49] Thus death both separates and unites. "Eternal life is the final healing of this life into the completed wholeness for which it is destined."[50]

Unfortunately, there are Christians who believe that AIDS is God's punishment for sin. Susan Sontag in her interesting book *AIDS and its Metaphors,* says that "Plagues are invariably regarded as judgments on society . . ."[51] We are very quick to link any sexually transmitted disease with sin as if there are no innocent victims. Insensitive zealousness has resulted in persons dying of AIDS being told: "Your sin has caused your death". I am cautious, even suspicious, of this language of fear. Despite those terrifying mediaeval pictures of judgment tempting women and men to seek comfort and salvation in the arms of the church, people have not stopped sinning. The mere mention of HIV/AIDS raises fear. It seeps into places where we did not know it before: fear of sexuality, fear of bodily fluids, fear of the communion cup, and as Sontag comments "fear of contaminated blood, whether Christ's or your neighbour's."[52] (Not surprisingly, Nietzsche commented acerbically on what he called the "holy lie"—the invention of a God who punishes and rewards by holding out the afterlife as some sort of "great punishment machine".[53]) Death can be caused directly by sin. We kill one another. We are destroying our environment. But death is not God's ultimate judgment on us. Admittedly, Christian thinkers like Paul, the old church fathers and Augustine saw death as punishment for 'the wages of sin'. James (1:15) writes that ". . . then, when that desire has conceived, it gives birth to sin, and that sin, when fully grown, gives birth to death". Undeniably, death can be caused by sinful acts.

There are other traditions in Christianity that do not see death as a judgment on sin. Schleiermacher and liberal Protestant theology of the nineteenth century disputed the causal connection between sin and physical death.[54] Moltmann argues that death may called the 'wages of sin' but that this can only be said of human beings. Angels are dubbed immortal but according to Peter (II Pet. 2:4), they sinned! Animals, birds, fish and the trees don't sin, yet they die. Through human beings, death has been brought into non-human creation. Death has been with us from the beginning. God's first commandment to human beings was "be fruitful and multiply". We were mortal right from the beginning. From a pastoral point of view, theological speculation about the relationship between sin and death is not particularly helpful for the person dying of AIDS.

The body is implicated in the process of sin. The very context in which we live is affected by sin. Innocence suffers. Everything that is 'born' must die. It is part of our condition. Our responsibility is to live and to die in loving solidarity with that sighing and groaning community of creatures described by Paul (Rom. 8:23), all waiting for "the redemption of our bodies" (Rom. 8:23).[55] We all need redemption. "The death of all the living is neither due to sin nor is it natural. It is a fact that evokes grief and longing for the future world and eternal life."[56] We all await what Letty Russell calls "the mending of creation".[57]

At the center of our efforts to understand the link between life and death is Christ. For Paul, community with Christ, who is the subject of our hope, extends to the living and the dead. "For to this end Christ died and lived again, that he might be Lord both of the dead and of the living" (Rom. 14:9). Moltmann reads this verse as follows:

> I understand this in the following sense: In dying, Christ became the brother of the dying. In death, he became the brother of the dead. In his resurrection—as the One risen—he embraces the dead and the living, and takes them with him on his way to the consummation of God's kingdom.[58]

As we struggle to understand what it means to live hopefully, we are reminded that life remains unfinished. We have tried to live according to the plan for our lives, but we have failed. We are wounded, incomplete, not yet the persons that God intends us to be. We mourn the death of those we love. We grieve precisely because we have loved. Yet in grief we try to hold on to hope. There is no quick fix for those who suffer. Life in the midst of suffering and death is a constant struggle; it risks moments of despair and loss of trust and it seeks hope even in the darkest places.

7. The body of Christ in the Eucharist

By grace, failure does not have the last word in the Christian life. Our hope is in Jesus Christ, the embodiment of our faith, whose life, death and resurrection we celebrate in the Eucharist.[59] Michael Welker reminds us that the Eucharist was instituted "in the night that Jesus Christ was betrayed and handed over to the powers of this world"[60]. Its origins do not lie in success or triumph but in the human betrayal of the Son, and it is precisely here that we dare to hope. I want to conclude my reflections with a few thoughts on embodied hope in the Eucharist. In the Eucharist I find a coming together of the different themes I have raised that takes me into the heart of the Gospel.

At the outset of this paper I said that the church as the Body of Christ has AIDS. I see a link between the violated, hungry and diseased bodies of countless people and the crucified and resurrected body of Jesus Christ whom we remember and celebrate in the bread and the wine at the Eucharist. Deep inside the Body of Christ, the AIDS virus lurks. As we remember Christ's sacrifice, we see in his very wounds the woundedness of his sisters and brothers who are infected and dying. But in Robert Jenson's incomparable phrase, "God deep in the flesh" draws us all into the Body of Christ, the One who takes the church as his bride, makes it his Body and through this nuptial act sets before us the possibility of relationships in love which are the antitheses of the disordered and morbid relationships that lead to disease and the spoiling of our wondrous earth.

The Eucharist is the bodily practice of grace. Nancy Eiesland writes: "Receiving the Eucharist is a body practice of the church. The Eucharist as a central and constitutive practice of the church is a ritual of membership. The Eucharist is a matter of bodily mediation of justice and an incorporation of hope".[61] Because God chose to live with us in the flesh, sacramentality takes physical reality very seriously.[62] We are bodily partakers of the physical elements of bread and wine, Christ's presence in our lives and in our world. The very bodiliness of the celebration of the Eucharist affirms the centrality of the body in the practice of the faith. "The Supper", writes Welker, "centers on a complex, sensuous process in which the risen and exalted Christ becomes present. The Supper gives Christians a form in which they can perceive the risen and exalted Christ with all their senses."[63]

The celebration of the Eucharist makes the Reign of God present 'to us' in the form of Christ's body broken 'for us' and Christ's blood shed 'for us'. Christ invites us to the feast, and he is "both the giver of the feast and the gift itself".[64] In other words, the gift of the Reign of God is quite simply present in the person of Christ himself—Christ crucified and risen. Thus the communion meal mediates communion and true life-giving relationship with the crucified one in the presence of the risen one. It becomes a foretaste of the messianic banquet of all humankind. It is the meal at which the bodies of all are welcome. In Christ's Body, the Eucharist is *the* sacrament of equality. Only self-exclusion can keep one away. At the communion table we are offered the consummate step in forging an ethic of right relationship, across all our differences. "We who are many are one body for we all partake of the one bread". This visible, unifying, bodily practice of relationship with all its potential for healing is ours. For the Eucharist to have meaning in our lives, we need to feel its powerful pull to the radical activity of loving relationships with those who are different. "The Eucharist involves a commitment (*sacramentum*) to sharing with the needy neighbor, for Jesus said, 'The Bread that I shall give is my own flesh; given for the life of the world' (John 6:51)".[65]

A covenanted Eucharistic community is a community in relationship with one another and with God. Paul describes us as the Body of Christ, a body which, though it has many members, is one body. "If one member suffers, all suffer together with it; if one member is honored, all rejoice together with it" (1 Cor. 12:26). It is a body in which the weakest are to be treated with respect, for ". . . God has so arranged the body, giving the greater honor to the inferior member, that there may be no dissension within the body, but the members may have the same care for one another" (1 Cor. 12:25). The picture here is one of solidarity in suffering, of mutual support and of a moral community in relationship with one another and with God, practicing an embodied ethic of resistance and affirmation. Just imagine what that could mean in the midst of an HIV/AIDS pandemic and a world struggling to survive human acts of destruction!

Finally, much has been made of the text in 1 Cor. 11:27–29, 31–32 about eating the bread and drinking the wine in an unworthy manner, about examining ourselves and about the threat of judgment. Welker comments: ". . . [then] the Supper is no longer a feast of reconciliation but rather an anxiety-producing means of moral gate keeping. In a sad irony, the feast of unconditional acceptance of human beings by God and among each other was misused for intrahuman moral control!"[66] There is a tension here. Welker points out that in the celebration of the Eucharist, God accepts us unconditionally, while at the same time Paul's concern is that Christians celebrate the meal in accordance with the meal's identity. Rightly so. How we partake of the Meal is deeply significant for how we live as a moral community. "The Eucharist may be understood as nourishment for moral growth and formation",[67] writes Duncan Forrester. A community with a moral code and a moral identity partaking in a meal of grace, memory and new life, brings resistance to evil and hope for now and tomorrow for the church with HIV/AIDS.

Conclusion

As long as WSSD or NEPAD or any other grand design does not address the HIV/AIDS pandemic in Africa, there will be no sustainable development for African people. This places a heavy burden on the Body of Christ to be a voice of truth in the midst of denial and prevarication. We can speak into the moment by acknowledging the central role of gender in this pandemic and holding fast to the truths of our faith, which we must put into practice day by day. It will not be easy. Deep in the flesh lives the paradox of blessing and curse. We know the curse of disease, abuse and diminishment. We also know the blessing of resistance, affirmation and hope. In the midst of this bewildering paradox, there is the human capacity for indignation and moral outrage. We are enabled to say "yes" when all else shouts "no".

Notes

1. See the Statement of Anglican Primates on HIV/AIDS, Canterbury, 16 April 2002, for the official stance of the Anglican Communion on HIV/AIDS which touches on a number of points raised in this paper.
2. Esther Njiro, "Sustainable development: An oxymoron?", *Agenda*, 52, 2002, 6–7. Esther Njiro outlines four areas of concern for women in Africa as we approach the World Summit on Sustainable Development. First, the

adverse effects of economic globalization which have had a negative impact on local industries, job opportunities, and national capacity production; second, access to and control over resources such as land, education and skills training; third, environmental security and health in which African women are at the receiving end of degraded environments, lack of clean water, sanitation; fourth, exclusion from governance for sustainable development as women's participation in governance at national and local levels remains deficient, in terms of unequal property and inheritance rights.

3. See Kevin Kelly, 'Conclusion: a Moral theologian faces the new millennium in a time of AIDS' in James F. Keenan (ed.) *Catholic Ethicists on HIV/AIDS Prevention* (New York, Continuum, 2000), p. 325.

4. Trengove Jones, *Who Cares?*, p. 15. Harvard economist Richard Parker commented in 1996 that "we have begun to understand the perverse consequences caused by specific models of economic development (most often imposed from above) that have in fact functioned to produce and reproduce structures of economic dependence and processes of social disintegration". See Richard G. Parker, 'Empowerment, community mobilization, and social change in the face of HIV/AIDS', paper presented at the XI International Conference on AIDS, Vancouver, July 1996, 4, 11.

5. This is illustrated by the fact that there are churches in South Africa which are part of mainline denominations, in which communion is served in the following order: first the men, then male adolescents, then women and lastly female adolescents—as a confirmation of the headship of men, e.g., refer 1 Cor. 11:3.

6. For statistics, see Quarraisha A. Karim, 'Women and Aids: the imperative for a gendered prognosis and prevention policy', *Agenda* 39, 1998, 15–25. See also Whiteside and Sunter, *AIDS*, p. 12 for a discussion on mother-to-child transmission. HIV/AIDS is our *kairos* because as long as we are unable (even unwilling) to deal adequately with this scourge, development that is truly sustainable, gender sensitive and people-centered will not come about. It is a time when the ordinary rhythm of life is suspended. Will it be a time of doom or will we find a new unveiling of God's presence and love for us here and now?

7. See Hilda Adams and Anita Marshall, 'Off target messages—poverty, risk and sexual rights', *Agenda* 39, 1998, 87–93.

8. Vicci Tallis, 'AIDS is a crisis for women', *Agenda* 39, 1998, 9.

9. See Gill Seidel, 'Making an informed choice: Discourses and practices surrounding breast-feeding and AIDS', *Agenda* 39, 1998, 65–81.

10. Tallis, 'AIDS', 9–10.

11. See *inter alia*, A. Kline, E. Kline and E. Oken, 'Minority women and sexual choice in the age of Aids', *Social Science and Medicine* 34, 4, 1992, 447–457: D. Lear, 'Sexual communication in the age of Aids: the construction of risk and trust among young adults', *Social Science and Medicine* 41, 9, 1995, 1311–1323; L. Miles, 'Women, Aids, power and heterosexual negotiation', *Agenda* 15, 1992, 14–48; I. Orubuloye, J. Caldwell and P. Cardwell, 'African women's control over their sexuality in an era of Aids', *Social Science and Medicine* 37, 7, 1993, 859–872.

12. See Human Rights Watch Report, *Scared at School*, p. 27 for a report on a recent Gauteng study in which nearly 50 percent of male youth said they believed a girl who said "no" to sex meant "yes" and 24 percent thought a girl who had been raped had "asked for it". Nearly a third of both men and women surveyed said that forcing sex on someone you know is not sexual violence.

13. See Rachel Jewkes, C. Vundule *et al.*, 'Relationships dynamics and teenage pregnancy in South Africa, *Social Science and Medicine* 52, 2001, 733–744. See also Christine Varga and Lindiwe Makubalo, 'Sexual non-negotiation', *Agenda* 28, 1996, 33.

14. See C. Baylies and J. Bujra, *Aids, Sexuality and Gender in Africa: The Struggle Continues* (London, Routledge, 2000); J. Bujra, 'Risk and Trust: Unsafe Sex, gender and AIDS in Tanzania', in P. Caplan (ed.) *Risk Revisited* (London, Pluto Press, 2000); K. Carovano, 'HIV and the challenges facing men', Issues Paper 15, New York, UNDP HIV Development Programme; K. Nkosi, 'Men, the military and HIV/AIDS in Malawi' in M. Foreman (ed.) *AIDS and Men* (London, Panos Publications/Zed Press, 1999).

15. See also Janet Bujra, 'Targeting men for a change: AIDS discourse and activism in Africa', *Agenda* 44, 2000, 6–23.

16. Karim, 'Women and AIDS', 23.

17. See Whiteside and Sunter, *AIDS*, pp. 147, 148.

18. Njiro, 'Sustainable development', 5.

19. Ibid., 3.

20. Elaine Graham, 'Words made flesh: Embodiment and practical theology", paper read at the International Academy for Practical Theology's Biennial Conference, Seoul, Korea, 1997.

21. In Anne B. Gilson, 'Embodiment' in L. M. Russell, and J. S. Clarkson (eds.), *Dictionary of Feminist Theologies* (Louisville, Westminster/John Knox Press, 1996), p. 82.

22. Graham, 'Words made flesh'.

23. Melanie A. May, *A Body Knows: A Theopoetics of Death and Resurrection* (New York, Continuum, 1995), p. 107.

24. Ibid., p. 108.

25. Sick without resources these women often die. The story of Nosipho Xhape, who died in a strange shack where she tried to find shelter, is not uncommon. This woman left her two children in the Eastern Cape to find work in the city. She could only survive by linking up with a man who would look after her. When it became apparent that she had full-blown AIDS, he turned her out one night. She found shelter in a toilet until a neighbor gave her a blanket and water and she moved to a broken-down shack. Fifteen hours later she was dead. See *Cape Times*, 12 February 2000.

26. Iris Marion Young, *Justice and the Politics of Difference* (Princeton, Princeton University Press, 1990), p. 147.

27. Quoted from Eiesland, *The Disabled God*, pp. 59–60.

28. Here I have in mind the Treatment Action Campaign headed by the intrepid Zackie Achmat who is HIV positive and who refuses to take antiretroviral drugs until they are available to all who need them in South Africa.

29. Robert Schreiter, *Reconciliation: Mission and Ministry in a Changing Social Order* (Maryknoll, Orbis Books, 1999), p. 34.

30. I am grateful to Bernard Lategan for pointing out that the narrative has the further hermeneutical function of sense making, an understanding he attributes to the work of Jörn Rüsen's concept of *Sinnbildung*.

31. Joan Laird, 'Women and stories: Re-storying women's self-constructions' in M. McGoldrick, C. M. Anderson and F. Walsh (eds.), *Women and Families: A Framework for Family Therapy* (New York/London, W. W. Norton, 1991), p. 133.

32. Jantzen, 'AIDS', p. 306.

33. Peter Brown has documented the variety of ways in which Christians in late antiquity found sexuality a problem. See his *The Body and Society: Men, Women and Sexual Renunciation in Early Christianity* (New York, Columbia University Press, 1988).

34. Jantzen, 'AIDS, shame', p. 308.

35. Rowan Williams, 'On making moral decisions'. Unpublished address to Lambeth Plenary Session, Canterbury, July 22, 1998.

36. Ibid.

37. Bernard V. Brady, *The Moral Bond of Community: Justice and Discourse in Christian Morality* (Washington, Georgetown University Press, 1998), p. 1.

38. Ibid., p. 22.

39. Bruce B. Birch and Larry L. Rasmussen, *Bible and Ethics in the Christian Life* (Minneapolis, Augsburg, 1989), p. 45.

40. William Schweiker, *Power Value and Conviction: Theological Ethics in the Postmodern Age* (Cleveland, Pilgrim Press, 1998), p. 153. See also Cahill, *Catholic Ethicists*, p. 286.

41. Birch and Rasmussen, *Bible and Ethics*, p. 137.

42. Ibid., p. 47.

43. See also the following articles by me: 'Lamenting tragedy from the other side' in James R. Cochrane and Bastienne Klein (eds), in *Sameness and Difference: Problems and Potentials in South African Civil Society*, (Washington D.C., The Council for Research in Values and Philosophy, 2000); 'Tales of terror and torment: Thoughts on boundaries and truth-telling', *Scriptura*, 63, 1997, 425–433; 'On hearing and lamenting: Faith and truth-telling' in H. R. Botman and R. M. Petersen (eds.), *To Remember and to Heal: Theological and Psychological Reflections on Truth and Reconciliation* (Cape Town, Human and Rousseau, 1996); '"Take up a taunt song": Women, lament and healing in South Africa' in Leny Lagerwerf (ed.) *Reconstruction: The WCC Assembly Harare 1998 and the Churches in Southern Africa* (Zoetermeer, Meinema, 1998).

44. Walter Brueggemann, 'The shape for Old Testament Theology, II: Embrace of pain'. *Catholic Biblical Quarterly* 47, 400, describes lament as "a dramatic, rhetorical, liturgical act of speech which is irreversible". It articulates the inarticulate. Tears become ideas.

45. Brueggemann, 'The shape', 401.

46. Walter Brueggemann, 'From hurt to joy, from death to life', *Interpretation* 28, 1974, 4.

47. Ibid., p. 67.

48. Ibid., p. 69.

49. Ibid., p. 71.

50. Ibid.

51. Susan Sontag, *AIDS and its Metaphors* (New York, Farrar, Straus and Giroux, 1989), p. 54.

52. Ibid., p. 73.

53. Friedrich W. Nietzsche, *The Will to Power*, tr, W. Kaufmann and R. J. Hollingdale (New York, Random House, 1967), p. 90.

54. For an explanation of these views, see Moltmann, *The Coming*, pp. 87 and 89ff., who discusses Karl Barth's adaptation of Schleiermacher's views. From pp. 87, 88: "Schleiermacher, and with him modern Protestant theology, distinguished strictly between person and nature; and he restricted himself to the religious and moral experiences of the human person. . . . With these presuppositions it is quite logical that Schleiermacher would have declared death *per se* to be neither evil nor a divine punishment but the natural end and temporal limit of the finite existence of men and women. It is only a God-consciousness deranged by sin that will experience this natural death subjectively as an evil, and fear it as a punishment. Death is not caused by sin, but is through sin that it acquires spiritual power over human beings. . . . Liberal Protestant tradition developed Schleiermacher's position further. The underlying exegetical assumption was that the biblical traditions are talking about death both literally and in a transferred sense. In the transferred sense, 'death of the soul' means a breach of fellowship with God, while 'eternal death' is its loss. These experiences in the God-consciousness must be uncoupled from physical death. The consequences of sin are spiritual disintegration, lack of inner peace, moral corruption, and fear of eternal damnation. To derive physical death from this source is nonsensical. Physical death cannot be put down to religious and moral causes. . . . Liberal Protestant teaching concludes that the death of the soul and eternal death follow upon sin; but it removes the death of the body from this cohesion, because it distinguishes strictly between person and nature".

55. Moltmann, *The Coming*, p. 92, writes "The modern separation between person and nature (as in Schleiermacher) or between covenant and creation (as in Barth) does neither justice to human nature nor to the community of creation. It is an expression of the anthropocentrism of the modern world, an anthropocentrism destructive of nature. . . . The patristic church's doctrine of physical redemption was more comprehensive in its cosmic dimensions".

56. Ibid., p. 92.

57. This term is used by Letty Russell in many of her works to denote the eschatological implications of the Reign of God.

58. Moltmann, *The Coming*, p. 105.

59. See Jürgen Moltmann, *The Church in the Power of the Spirit: A Contribution to Messianic Ecclesiology*, (Minneapolis, Fortress Press, 1993), p. 244, who discusses the different ways of naming the celebration and who chooses to call it the "Lord's supper", the term used by the ecumenical movement. See also Michael Welker, *What Happens in Holy Communion?* tr. J. F. Hoffmeyer (Grand Rapids, Eerdmans, 2000), pp. 56–59 who argues that the supper is more than a 'thanksgiving'. I shall use the term *Eucharist* for no other reason than that it is in keeping with my tradition.

60. Welker, *What Happens*, p. 43.

61. Eiesland, *The Disabled God*, p. 112.

62. Susan A. Ross, 'God's embodiment and women', in C. M. La Cugna (ed.), *Freeing Theology: The Essentials of Theology in Feminist Perspective* (San Francisco, Harper and Row, 1993), p. 186.

63. Welker, *What Happens*, p. 18.

64. Moltmann, *The Church*, p. 250.

65. Duncan B. Forrester, *Truthful Action: Explorations in Practical Theology* (Edinburgh, T&T Clark, 2000), p. 96.

66. Welker, *What Happens*, p. 70.

67. Forrester, *Truthful Action*, p. 95.

The Meaning of "Biodiversity" and the Situation in Madagascar

—Dr. Chantal Andrianarivo

Where were you when I laid the foundations of the earth?

—Job 38:4

Just to remind everyone: What is the definition of biodiversity? Biodiversity is the variability of life in all its forms, levels and combinations. This includes variability within ecosystems—terrestrial, aquatic, or marine ecosystems, all species, and genetic materials. Biodiversity is not only species diversity, it also includes whole ecosystems, habitat diversity, and genetic diversity from the biggest to the smallest living organisms. We cannot see genes, but genes make me different from you and us different from dogs and from plants, for example. What is the importance of this biodiversity? Diversity, as we know it today, has been produced over three billion years of evolution. Yet it's not something only of yesterday. It is alive; it is the living earth. It has taken a very long time for this biodiversity to evolve, to create species, to have new ecosystems, new genes on the earth.

It is also the basis for the evolution of all species including humankind. Without biodiversity, life would not be possible on earth, because it is the condition of life. Take, for example, the Amazonian forest. It gives us 60% of our earth's oxygen. If we lose that forest, we cannot live on earth because we will not have enough oxygen. Biodiversity gives us elements, medicine, and water in the ecosystem. It is the source of life on the earth.

What are the threats to biodiversity? The threats are, first, the economic situation. In many developed and developing countries people say that biodiversity is "free resources"—it's for them. It's not for the state; it's not for animals; it's for human living, they believe. Within this particular economic system, poverty is one reason for the threat to biodiversity. Why? Because if you live in a developing, poor country, you will see a forest as a source of energy. Forest products can be used for building materials and also for medicines. People will naturally ask why we can't use these "free resources." It's really the situation of life for the rural populations. The second kind of threat to biodiversity is human action. Human action means harvesting forests and collecting species for illegal trade. Cultural values are part of the problem here. It's also due to unsustainable agriculture, but my point is that it's really a vicious circle of many different threats to biodiversity on the earth as a whole.

Due to the economic system of human action, we also have climate change as a threat to biodiversity. We talked about climate change yesterday, and most of the reasons for climate change are human action. Part of this threat is related to poverty, but it's also due to the differences between North and South. We have very, very rich regions in the North and very poor regions in the South. This situation creates a huge problem because the South wants to be like the North in terms of the economic system, but with it we have climate change.

Climate change is due to direct human action, in part, while another part is a natural consequence of this action. We have lost many, many regions of forest. We have an increase in atmospheric temperature. We are losing adequate freshwater. All this is really the cause of these very large hurricanes and cyclones we are witnessing recently. The effects of El Niño are one result of climate change. Natural disasters happen very often due to human action, but this is not always obvious.

At the WSSD Conference, the Convention on Biological Diversity will have a spokesperson in the Secretariat from Canada. What is the history of the Biological Diversity Convention? In 1989, the governing council of the UN recognized the need to increase efforts to protect biodiversity. In February 1991, a formal negotiating process began, and in May of 1992, in Nairobi, the nations of the world worked on the adoption of a global convention on biological diversity. In June 1992, at the United Nations Conference on the Environment and Development in Rio, 150 states signed it. One big state that has not signed it is the USA. In December 1993, the Convention went into effect officially when 90 countries ratified it.

What is the Convention on Biological Diversity? The Convention is a framework; it is an agreement between parties, between countries who have signed it. This convention has three main objectives. The first is conservation as it relates to protected areas. The second is conservation in terms of the sustainable use of biological diversity. If we can practice sustainable use, then we can have sustainable development, but at the moment, there really is no sustainable development or use. The third objective is benefit sharing, which is important because traditional knowledge of local ecosystems is sometimes stolen by scientists and others working on behalf of corporations and universities for the purpose of economic development. There is no benefit in this for traditional practitioners among the local people. Currently, benefit sharing is a very important part of the Convention.

I'm thinking also about Madagascar in relation to benefit sharing and the Biological Diversity Convention. Madagascar is the twelfth ranked country for mega-diversity. It comes after South Africa, Brazil, Zambia, Malaysia, Canada and other countries. What is mega-diversity? It is when you have, for example, one kind of ecosystem, one kind of species, only in that country. You cannot find that species in another country. Madagascar has a high rate of mega-diversity. We have about 12,000 plants. The nomenclature of some of these plants is still unclear, but we know that it's between 10,000 and 12,000 plants. Ninety-nine percent of our amphibians are under threat; 30 percent of the land is covered by natural ecosystems, while only 2.7 percent of those areas are protected.

By "natural ecosystem," I mean that we have wetlands, rivers, lakes, forests, mangroves, coastal areas, and so on. As a whole, Madagascar includes 5,000 or more square kilometers, but only 30 percent is covered by natural ecosystems. That means that we have very few natural ecosystems remaining in Madagascar. In a workshop held in 1995, we had to prioritize the most important ecosystems to be protected, to be classified as "protected areas." During that five-day workshop, scientists decided that 30 percent of our land must be classified as protected areas.

But what about the people that live there? That is a very real issue, so we later decreased the number of terrestrial protected areas, but we increased our coastal and marine protected areas in Madagascar. We cannot do more for protected areas because the local population needs natural resources in order to live, but we must learn to use those resources in a sustainable way. This is true everywhere, not only in Madagascar.

What are the main threats to ecosystems and biodiversity in Madagascar? These threats include, first, the exporting of biological resources. Resources are exported not only by the local human population, but also by industry. The second threat is agriculture linked with rice cultivation. This is a very difficult and important issue because of soil depletion. The third threat involves the trade in species, illegally. As I said, we have a great many rare and endangered species which the larger, developed countries want. Most of our species are listed in the international convention of endangered species. It is forbidden to export and trade many species from Madagascar, and most of the actual trade is illegal.

What are the reasons for these threats? I think, primarily, it is the poverty in Madagascar, which is also the case in underdeveloped countries more generally. There is a severe lack of alternative strategies for exploiting forest resources, that is in a sustainable way. We have no policy for the sustainable use of ecosystems in Madagascar, and everyone does as he or she likes. We are now beginning to develop contracts with the people. For example, if they are planting or reforesting an area, then after 20 years, this area is owned by the population who has worked there.

And what are the effects of responses to these threats? The effects are, first and foremost, the loss of biodiversity. The impoverishment caused by slash-and-burn agriculture simply adds to the poverty. We have had this same situation since the beginning of the last century. So, we adopted, in 1990, a Charter for the Environment, which is an environmental policy for the country. In this charter, we have created national executive agencies which are funded by the World Bank. These agencies include the National Association for Environmental Action, which was created to grant some activities for sustainable development in Madagascar. This association has established, within the last ten years, 3,000 small-scale sustainable development projects in rural areas. Another national agency is the Ministry of Water and Forests, which manages all the forested areas in Madagascar, except for the protected areas. Protected areas come under my association, the National Association for Protected Areas. Also, we have the National Center of Geographic and Environmental Training. And then later, we created the Indian Ocean University.

Following this Charter for the Environment, our national environmental action plan was made to include three phases of five years each. We are now at the end of the second phase of the national action plan. The first phase was for implementing all the agencies and their activities in Madagascar. The second phase, which we are in now, is to develop sustainable projects; and the third phase, beginning next year, will be to have a sustainable financing strategy for all these activities. So, you see, we have been doing quite a lot.

The diversity of life in a very small space.

Biodiversity and Ecojustice

—The Rt. Revd. Geoff Davies

There are two areas that have been largely neglected by the Church, but which are at the centre of what the Bible is saying to us and which have to be central to the church's witness in the future. They can be encapsulated in one word, "ecojustice", which embraces economic justice and ecological justice. The word "ecology" (*oikos* "house") is the study of relationships among organisms and the environments in which they live, including all living and non-living components.

We have too often neglected economic justice in the church because most of us think we don't know anything about economics and we should leave it to the "specialists", and we have also singularly failed to recognise our responsibility to uphold ecological justice.

Ecological justice

God told us to care for the world. In the very first chapter of the Bible, God mandated us to "rule" or "have dominion over" God's creation. We are doing a shocking job of it!

"Rule" or "have dominion over" can only be understood in Christian terms as caring for, looking after, nurturing for future generations. I appreciate what Bishop George Browning from Canberra has said about this being "gospel business". We know full well in South Africa that when people "rule" for their own benefit, without caring for others, the consequences are disastrous and justice is forsaken. The Blacks suffered gross injustices under apartheid. And in fact, the totality suffered, including the environment. If you travel to the so-called "homelands", you see the effect on the natural environment, where too many people were forced to eke out an existence on too little land. Everybody and everything suffered the injustices of apartheid.

This situation applies to the world today. Because of world economic injustices, everybody and everything is suffering the consequences.

Our mandate to rule is not just to care for fellow human beings, but all of creation: *have dominion over . . . every living thing that moves upon the earth* (Genesis 1:28).

And in Genesis 9:15–17 we hear that God established *an everlasting covenant between God and every living creature of all flesh that is upon the earth.*

Last night, someone referred to the attitude of some of my fellow bishops. Some bishops have challenged me and said: "Human beings are the pinnacle of God's creation and God really doesn't care about vermin, such as the monkeys you see here; it is only human beings God cares about." That is why a great many people criticize us for not caring about other species.

So this mandate—and it is a mandate—is obligatory on us all. Seeking environmental justice and environmental care is not just another justice issue that we are trying to foist on the churches. Just as we had to concentrate on the abolition of apartheid in South Africa, we now have to recognise and acknowledge that environmental responsibility is central to the Gospel—it is integral to our Faith. After all, are not we Christians the ones who worship a creator God?

We are going to be roundly condemned by future generations for destroying so many natural habitats and allowing the extinction of so many species—and not only that—for upsetting the balance of nature so much that the existence of life as we now know it is threatened.

We know that the tropical jungles are the lungs of the earth. Yet we continue to destroy them. And we know that the buildup of carbon dioxide and greenhouse gases is likely to bring about dramatic climate change. If global warming increases, and if the polar ice caps—which contain 90 percent of the world's fresh water—melt, the consequences and the human suffering is going to be catastrophic. Dramatic climate change will threaten food production, disease and pests will increase, and the majority of the world's cities, Bangladesh, and island nations will be flooded.

You have in your folder a handout that talks about the "sixth extinction". It explains how we've had five extinctions in the history of the earth. We now face the sixth extinction, but this one is exceptional because we are causing it; we are bringing it about. A recent UN report warns that 12 percent of bird species and nearly a quarter of all mammal species are regarded as globally threatened, with perhaps 50 percent of all species becoming extinct in the next 100 years. We are also now using 20 percent more of the planet's natural resources than can be regenerated by natural means.

And so, I want to suggest a resolution to the Anglican Communion to try to take Churches on board:

> That this Anglican Congress on the Stewardship of Creation,
>> meeting in South Africa for the World Summit on Sustainable Development in August 2002,
>> and recognising the responsibility God mandated us with in the first chapter of the Bible to care for the world; and recognising further that caring for God's creation is central to the Christian Faith;

and acknowledging in penitence that we have failed in our
God-given responsibility;
and realising that the future of life on earth hangs in the balance;

Resolves

1. to ask all Churches to place environmental care on their
agenda;

2. to ask all Christians to make their own personal commitment to care for God's world, respecting all life, for "The
Earth is the Lord's and all that is in it". (Psalm 24:1)

I now want to make a radical proposal—is that not what the Church
should be about, making prophetic proposals that lead the way?

I do this because I have a desperate concern over the loss of biodiversity.
We need to understand that biodiversity is like a brick wall. You can
remove a few bricks, and it will remain standing. But if you remove too
many, the wall will collapse and that is what is going to happen to life—
in other words, extinction. We, humans, are bringing about the rapid
and uncontrolled extinction of hundreds, no, thousands, of species.

The world community has accepted, in principle, that in cases of genocide
and ethnic cleansing—and now extended to include terrorism—there
should be international intervention. We cannot allow such behaviour
against fellow human beings. The United Nations Charter of 1945, in
effect, made national sovereignty absolute, as we wanted to stop one
country invading another to acquire its territory. But in 1948 the same
nations also ratified the Universal Declaration of Human Rights and the
Convention against Genocide. This states bluntly that there are some
crimes so heinous that even sovereignty cannot protect their perpetrators.
And so, with the conviction that "Human rights rank above the rights of
states; human liberties constitute a higher value than state sovereignty",
the international community intervened in the Balkans over Kosovo
(though they failed, earlier, to intervene in Rwanda) and, as we now know,
they have intervened in Afghanistan over the issue of terrorism.

But why do we stop here? Is God concerned only about humans? Did
God not mandate us to look after all His creation? When somebody is
hungry, they are going to kill that protected animal in order to survive.

My proposal is for a resolution to the United Nations that calls on the
international community to provide for the international protection of
threatened habitats and species.

It would cost a fraction of what President Bush spends on his armaments
and war programmes, to subsidise countries to look after endangered
species, and to provide personnel to ensure the protection of these species.

So I want to suggest this resolution for your consideration:

> That this Anglican Congress on the Stewardship of Creation,
> Aware of the responsibility we have before God to care for creation,
> And recognising the responsibility the international community
>   has to intervene to prevent acts of genocide, ethnic cleansing
>   and terrorism;
> And recognising that our responsibility is not limited to the care
>   and protection of fellow human beings only;
>
> Resolves
> to ask the World Summit on Sustainable Development and the
> United Nations to undertake to ensure the protection of endan-
> gered habitats and species so that the tide of extinction is stemmed
> and survival guaranteed for future generations, realising that this
> could require subsidising the countries involved as well as provid-
> ing international protection.

There are two reasons why this is so important:

1. We have to respect life if we ourselves are going to live in peace and with justice.

2. Our children are going to shake their heads in amazement and disbelief that we could be so irresponsible, so selfish and self-centred that we allowed the extinction of so much of God's creation and so many magnificent creatures.

Maybe Pythagoras, 2,600 years ago, told us why we should be so concerned:

> For as long as Man continues to be the
> ruthless destroyer of lower living beings,
> he will never know health or peace.
> For as long as men massacre animals,
> they will kill each other.
> Indeed, he who sows the seeds of murder
> and pain cannot reap joy and love.

Edward O. Wilson has written:

> The worst thing that can happen—will happen—is not energy
> depletion, economic collapse, limited nuclear war, or conquest
> by a totalitarian government. As terrible as these catastrophes
> would be for us, they can be repaired within a few generations.
> The one process . . . that will take millions of years to correct is
> the loss of genetic and species diversity by the destruction of nat-
> ural habitats. This is the folly our descendents are least likely to
> forgive us.

The Great Apes

I make this proposal particularly for the protection of the great apes whose genetic makeup is 98 percent the same as ours. In protecting their habitat, we are, of course, assisting our own survival by protecting the tropical rainforests, our planet's lungs. But we also have to put a stop to the horrific traffic in "bush meat", which verges on cannibalism and also seems to be a source of the Ebola virus.

Consider some of the newspaper reports in Rwanda:

> Africa's great ape massacre—A growing fad for "bush meat" on the tables of the elite in Central Africa spells death for the endangered gorillas and chimpanzees of the region. The hunters are also destroying what could be a key to curing AIDS.
>
> Time is running out for the great apes—Conservationists have launched a desperate attempt to stop humanity killing its closest relatives.

It is clear that human beings are not going to stop killing each other in a hurry. While we continue with our strife, we are bringing about the extinction of other creatures. We are also not going to stop greed in a hurry. As the loggers cut roads into the jungle, so the hunters follow to take their pound of flesh—and so increasing numbers of animals face extinction.

I hand out to you a document, a proposal, which I hope we can endorse at this Congress:

A Call By Representatives of the South African Council of Churches to the World for Environmental Justice

We call on the people and nations of the world to live in harmony with nature and each other, treating all as "our neighbor". Only as we live in harmony with nature, establishing justice and caring for its natural life supporting systems of air, water, and soil, shall we humans live in harmony with ourselves.

Just as we in South Africa had to abolish the unjust structures of apartheid in order to establish justice, so too we need to establish just economic structures in the world to overcome the impoverishment and enslavement of the majority of humanity.

We therefore call for the establishment of just economic structures, fair trade in investment and the cancellation of odious debts. We call on the United Nations World Summit on Sustainable Development to overcome not only the poverty of the world, but establishing fair economic structures. We also call for protection and prevention of the economic exploitation of people and the destruction of the natural environment.

We make this call because:

1. It is immoral that the resources of the world are controlled for the benefit of the wealthy minority.

2. It is immoral that both individuals and nations should have more wealth than they need while others starve.

3. It is immoral that "developing" countries are subjected to the regulations of "free trade" while the countries of North America and Europe protect and heavily subsidize their agricultural industry.

4. It is immoral that the direction of human activity is led by economic self-interest. Economic decisions must be subservient to moral and ethical considerations. Like other resources, money is a tool to be used for good or bad. It is God's direction that we must follow and turn from allowing money to be a God.

5. It is immoral that with the demands of Globalization, environmental standards are lowered.

6. It is immoral spending over US $600 billion on weapons of war annually. This money would solve the development problems of the world and create far more employment than the armaments industry.

7. It is immoral using violence to bring about peace solutions. In all areas of confrontation, negotiations should replace armed conflict.

8. It is immoral and evil to bring about the extinction of other species brought into being by God.

9. It is immoral to destroy the habitats of other species. Since the nations of the world have agreed that it is right to intervene and in cases of genocide, ethnic cleansing and terrorism, the nations of the world now need to intervene and when necessary provide financial subsidy to ensure the survival of threatened habitats of other species.

Call for Intervention to Ensure the Survival of Species

The forthcoming World Summit on Sustainable Development (WSSD) will rightly emphasize sustainable development for people and, hopefully, procure some correction to the gross economic disparities and injustices prevailing in our world.

Justice has to be established between us, the people of the world, and so Valli Moosa, South Africa's Environmental Affairs and Tourism minister, is right to say that issues of debt relief, investment and trade access should be key themes at the summit. But equally, we must not neglect the critical need to seek justice for the rest of creation.

There is a danger, particularly in South Africa where we are struggling to overcome the injustices of Apartheid, that in seeking environmental justice for people, we neglect the need to establish equity for the environment. The danger is that we cannot meet our human needs without also taking care of the natural environment. It is obvious that if we want clean air and water and soil in which to grow crops, we have to take greater care of the environment. It is also obvious that expanding human populations cannot continue making limitless material demands on a finite, limited planet.

One of the greatest dangers facing us now is that of biodiversity loss and species extinction. This is critical for the future survival of life on earth, including our own. If too many species become extinct, the fabric of life will collapse. It is also urgent, as we hold in our hands, within the next ten to twenty years, the fate of thousands of species. But at present, we continue the destruction of forest and other ecosystems as we pursue our own human conflicts, strife and self-interests.

This generation must realize as a matter of urgency:

• Extinction is forever. We cannot bring extinct species back to life.

• Our responsibility is to look after and preserve the world, making it a better place for the next generation. This is what sustainability is all about. Our children will shake their heads in disbelief that we have been so irresponsible as to allow the extinction of so many forms of life, caused considerably by our own greed. A world without cheetah, great apes, and cranes, whales—and their accompanying habitats—is a vastly impoverished world denied the variety and beauty God intended.

• We need in particular to protect primates because our genetic makeup is 98 percent the same as primates. Eating this "bush meat" is virtually cannibalism.

• The human gene pool is hardly in danger of extinction, with six billion of us while some gorilla species are down to less than ninety. Their extinction in the wild is a real probability unless there is serious intervention.

In order to bring about meaningful action, we must call on the United Nations and the forthcoming WSSD to implement steps to stem the tide of extinction. In recent years, the world has established the principle of intervention in the face of genocide and ethnic cleansing and now terrorism. This principle cannot, however, be limited to humans. We cannot sit back and witness the destruction of natural habitats and the extinction of species. To ensure their survival is not only the responsibility of the countries concerned but of all humanity.

The West, especially the United States, has a particular responsibility. It has the financial resources and capacity. All that is required is the moral conviction that the survival of our fellow creatures and their habitats is our responsibility.

There seems to be no end to the internecine strife between humans, fuelled by the armaments industry "which provides jobs in the 'developed' countries". Because we humans continue with the killing fields is no excuse for bringing about mass extinction in the process. Billions are being spent in combating terrorism in Afghanistan. At a tiny fraction of the cost, peacekeeping forces could be established for areas of critically endangered species, including the reserves and homes of primates. We humans have now become terrorists to the rest of creation, showing blatant disrespect for life.

We must take adequate steps to protect other species from extinction and their habitats from destruction. Since our present world assesses everything in financial terms, the way ahead would be to "commercialize" the protection of habitats and species, paying the local communities to protect their forests or other threatened areas.

The Anglican Church of the Province of Southern Africa, at its Standing Committee meeting in October last year, passed the following resolution:

Whereas we recognize the responsibility of the international community now has to intervene to prevent acts of genocide, ethnic cleansing and terrorism;

And whereas our responsibility is not limited to the care and protection of fellow human beings only;

Therefore this Standing Committee:

1. Petitions the South African department of Environmental Affairs and Tourism as well as the United Nations to undertake to ensure the protection of endangered habitats and species so that the tide of extinction is stemmed and survival guaranteed for future generations;

2. Recognizes that this could require subsidizing the countries involved as well as providing international protection.

The South African Council of Churches at its National Conference in August 2001 asked its national Executive Committee to "take appropriate action so as to ensure that endangered habitats and species are protected".

People are poor! Instead of catching and selling exotic birds and animals, or killing primates for "bushmeat", pay indigenous communities to protect their animals and birds. Eco-tourism would soon pay the way. In the meantime, wealthier countries must pay local communities, rangers and foresters to patrol and protect the threatened areas, ensuring that further destruction does not take place. It would only be the price of a few luxury cars or yachts, or a jet fighter and a missile or two. The West's military spending is in excess of US $645 billion a year. Establish justice for people and secure threatened habits and endangered species instead of expending all that money on weapons of destruction.

The protection of tropical forests, the lungs of the earth, is necessary for the well-being of the planet and our own survival, rich and poor alike. All we need to do is convince the political leaders of the world of its importance and urgency.

The JITUME Foundation's Tree Planting Program:

An Example of the Interdependence among Community Empowerment, Climate Change, and Biodiversity

—THE DIOCESE OF MPWAPWA (THE ANGLICAN CHURCH OF TANZANIA)

The JITUME Foundation was established as a corporate body under the Trustees Incorporated Ordinance of Tanzania in order to manage the process of enabling people to organize themselves into small solidarity groups in order to combat the problems of poverty and environmental degradation. The JITUME Foundation has taken over the management of the diocesan initiatives which were previously known as the Tanzania International Small Group and Tree Planting Program (TIST), developed by the Institute for Environmental Innovation. JITUME is an acronym for the Swahili words which stand for the Tanzania Initiatives for Sustainable Development.

The specific objectives of the JITUME Foundation are:

a) To promote sustainable development with the use of Small Loans for Agriculture and Microenterprise Development (MED) among the people in Mpwapwa Diocese, especially women, young people, and other disadvantaged groups;

b) To promote programs and projects related to the Clean Development Mechanism (CDM) of the Kyoto Protocol of the United Nations Framework Convention on Climate Change;

c) To document best practices that can be appropriately replicated in other locations in Africa and elsewhere in the world.

The Setting

Mpwapwa, Tanzania, is located seventy miles east of Tanzania's capital, Dodoma. Tanzania is the fourth poorest country in the world, with a per capita yearly income of $260, and Mpwapwa is one of the poorest areas of Tanzania.

Here are some telling statistics:

- Infant mortality: 98 deaths/1,000 live births
- Life expectancy: 52 years
- Adult literacy: Male, 80%; Female 57%
- Population below poverty line: 51%
- Percentage of households with a car: Negligible

Background of Program Activities

In July of 1999, the Anglican Diocese of Mpwapwa, headed by Bishop Simon Chiwanga, sponsored a "visioning" exercise with a group of lay leaders and clergy. In small groups of 10–12 people, members of the diocese identified a holistic vision of church growth with the goal of eradicating famine and seeing their land reforested. The resultant objectives were as follows:

- Reforestation
- Food security
- Economic stability
- Church growth
- Small group development

The strategy chosen for achieving the first four objectives was using small groups, hence the need to put small group development as one of the key objectives of the whole program.

Beginning in December 1999, local and expatriate consultants have worked with small groups in the Diocese of Mpwapwa to develop a program that would respond to goals set during the visioning process. Since that time the program has grown to a large, pilot phase, sustainable development project. It is now pioneering methods by which people in developing countries can take charge of their own development and leverage previously untapped resources. These include the ability to create inexpensive carbon credits that can supply the demand of carbon-intensive multinational corporations around the world.

Key Strategies

The major Program Elements are implemented through "small groups" of 10–12 people. Members of each small group commit to the following covenant:

- Group members agree to live in community with each other, to tithe, to develop the gifts of each member, and to encourage each member;

- Groups agree to set aside ten percent of their agricultural produce and business profits as an emergency fund for group members;

- Groups agree to repay all loans made to the group on the agreed upon basis. Each member is responsible to assure that the group pays the loan. Loans can be repaid in cash, in crops that are stored by the groups, or through seedling growth and tree planting;

- Groups agree to follow and help develop "best practices" by developing small groups and by creating a sustainable environment, sustainable agriculture, and sustainable economic development;

- Groups agree by the use of "best practices" to plant, care for, and establish a minimum of one thousand trees per year. Each group is responsible for the protection of all other groups of trees that have been or will be planted, wherever they are planted;

- Groups agree to enter into such agreements as necessary to transfer their greenhouse gas credits created from the trees;

- Groups agree to meet at least one time per week and to use all small group "best practices" including rotating leadership;

- Groups agree to report group activities to the Program Head Office on a regular basis and to cooperate with verification efforts necessary to establish greenhouse gas credit creation.

Effective Social Systems

The churches and their associated administrative structures are among the strongest social units in Tanzania. The program builds on this infrastructure by training Tanzanians who already have the demonstrated potential to manage small group training, small group recruitment, systems implementation, and program management.

The Tree Planting Program

Certain small groups are being encouraged to run tree nurseries. Local species are grown from seeds collected at the end of the rainy season. These trees have proven their ability to survive in the harsh drought conditions of recent years. Tree planting is encouraged in specific areas to provide shade for dwellings, windbreaks, or where crops are planted to help cut down on soil erosion. Trees that produce nuts or fruit of value to the farmers will also be used in order to maximize the benefits to the participants.

Tree Planting for the Clean Development Mechanism (CDM)

While small group members intensify their efforts in tree planting for their sustainable development objectives, they put in place carbon sequestration systems. The JITUME Foundation is doing so in order to enable small group members to enter into greenhouse gas business as an added value to their trees and as an assured long-term source of income. The JITUME Foundation seeks to seize new opportunities offered under the Clean Development Mechanism of the UN Kyoto Protocol on Climate Change.

Carbon Sequestration

By the end of Phase III, the program will have planted nearly six million trees of assorted local species. The program is encouraging mixed groves of trees planted near villages, around houses and along farm borders, including fruit and nut species that may be successful in certain micro-climates in Tanzania.

Quantification

In order for the program to quantify amounts of carbon sequestration, the planting and growth of trees must be rigorously recorded and verified. Present models show that the trees planted through the pilot program, Phase III, alone should achieve between 500,000 tons and 3,000,000 tons of CO_2 sequestration. The soil sequestration results from restoring soil fertility are speculative at present, but are expected to be substantial. Workers from the local area have been trained in the use of GPS technology, measurement, and 3-Com's Palm-Pilot technology in order to collect information that is being used to quantify the tonnage based on the growth and age of the trees. They are referred to as "quantifiers."

Accomplishments to Date

Pilot Phase I: Program Feasibility and System Development

- Concept Development by forty Diocese of Mpwapwa small groups

- Initial small group Local Species Tree Planting Efforts

- Initial small group Sustainable Agriculture Training

- Initial Organizational and Quantification System Development

- Establish communication among small groups to develop "best practices" in tree planting and agriculture

- Initial germination and growth of 445,000 trees

Status: 100% complete
Completion Date: September 30, 2000

Pilot Phase II: Pilot Implementation and Program Modification

- Concept Implementation through approximately 400 diocesan small groups

- Initial Dry Season Local Species Nursery Development

- Sustainable Agriculture Training and Implementation

- Pilot Implementation of Organizational, and Quantification Systems

- Initial Training and Feasibility Evaluation in a second location

- Program Review and Modification; Initial Quantification Review

- Initial germination and growth of 1,500,000 additional trees

Status: 40% complete
Completion Date: September 30, 2002

Pilot Phase III: Near Commercial Operations 2003–2005

- Modified Program Implementation through approximately 1,000 small groups

- Replication in one or more African locations

- Dry Season Tree Nursery scale-up

- Capacity building underway to support commercial operations

- Advanced Sustainable Agriculture Training and Implementation

- Organizational, Administration and Quantification scale-up

- Program Review and Modification; Quantification Projection

- Initial germination and growth of 4,000,000 additional trees

Status: in progress
Completion Date: September 30, 2005

For more information, please contact: The Managing Director, JITUME, P.O.Box 2, MPWAPWA,Tanzania. Tel. 255 26 2324123. *E-Mail:* DMP@maf.or.tz <mailto:DMP@maf.or.tz>

Two members of the Congress Planning Team, David Shreeve and Claire Foster, with Archdeacon Tai (on the right).

Waterfall at Marakele National Park.

Eco-Justice and the Church

—The Rt. Revd. Geoff Davies

Hear this, O elders, give ear, all inhabitants of the land! Has such a thing happened in your days, or in the days of your ancestors?

—Joel 1:2

Two important areas the Church has to be involved in are: (1) Economic Justice and (2) Environmental Justice.

We have Biblical injunctions to witness and be involved in both areas, yet they have been seriously neglected by the Church in the past. We don't have to be economists to know there is something seriously amiss in today's world.

Let me state at the outset that I am not an economist, and I am not asking that we become economists. Our responsibility and challenge is to see that economic justice is established. How this is achieved is for the economists and politicians—but justice there must be!

You will find much helpful material in the two books by Professor Klaus Nurnberger: *Prosperity, Poverty and Pollution* and *Beyond Marx and Market* and another by Ulrich Duchrow: *Alternatives to Global Capitalism*. These are inspired by and based on scripture.

The Old Testament prophets are quite clear. I give just one example: *Let justice roll down like waters, and righteousness like an ever-flowing stream.* (Amos 5:24).

The prophets and Jesus are clear in their teaching about sharing and overcoming greed—that is establishing economic justice. We are also recognising the need to be involved in economic justice because of the gross inequalities prevailing in our world—people are being enslaved by our present world economic structure. The World Bank claims that it is helping poorer nations, while exacting its full share of interest, so that more money flows out of Africa annually in interest than is ever given in aid. There has never been such a yawning chasm between rich and poor, with the rich getting richer and the poor, poorer.

It is an affront to God, who provides for our needs, but not our greed. When the Lord fed the Israelites with manna in the desert, he commanded: *Gather as much of it as each of you needs. . . . The Israelites did so, some gathering more, some less. But when they measured it with an omer, those who gathered much had nothing over, and those who gathered little had no shortage; they gathered as much as each of them needed.* (Exodus 16:16–18)

Fifty years ago, the majority of people in Africa could feed themselves. Today a fifth of the world's population, over a thousand million people, don't have enough to eat.

Global Distribution of Income

UNDP 1992

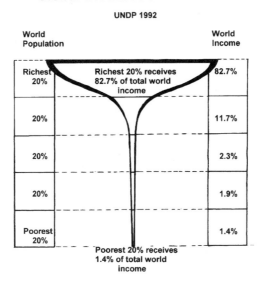

So I seriously question the morality of our present economic system, when we have a greater abundance of wealth and resources than ever. Unrestricted capitalism panders to our base instincts of selfish acquisitiveness and greed—and that is why it is an issue that involves us as people of faith.

Our purpose in life is NOT the acquisition of wealth and possessions: *Take heed, and beware of all covetousness: for a person's life does not consist in the abundance of his possessions.* (Luke 12:15)

Our utilisation of money should not be guided solely by the profit it generates. We have to make moral decisions as to how we utilise money. Do we spend money on armaments or on health and education? Do we spend our own money on a luxury car or helping others?

We received warnings as far back as Aristotle who analysed the difference between (1) the *oikonomia*, the household economy of needs, and (2) the money-accumulation economy.

Marxism arose in the first place in response to the extreme inequalities of the Dark Satanic Mills of William Blake's England. Because communism has failed, this does not mean that capitalism is right or has got all the answers. With globalisation, these mills have been exported, so that not only is the exploitation of people worse than ever, but also the rich nations are even dumping their toxic waste on the poorer countries of the world.

The CPSA Bishops have stated in their recent Millennium Message that *the prevailing economic orthodoxy of global capitalism is heretical, unjust and inhuman*. Apart from our worship of money, it is heretical because we treat it as a god, as if it has a life of its own! But money or capital is a commodity. We decide how to use it, whether we spend it on education or armaments.

The heresy is compounded because we have removed any basis of morality in our present global system. The one criterion of judgment used is whether something is profitable—the fact that it might cause thousands to starve, or tropical jungles to be destroyed, is not considered.

For I know how many are your transgressions, and how great are your sins—you who afflict the righteous, who take a bribe, and push aside the needy in the gate. . . . Hate evil and love good, and establish justice in the gate; it may be that the Lord, the God of hosts, will be gracious to the remnant of Joseph. (Amos 5:12, 15)

I have spent a few minutes on economic justice because the present financial system is a direct cause of environmental destruction and poverty. International odious debts are a direct cause of the over-exploitation of natural resources. This, combined with human greed, is bringing about the destruction of indigenous habitats causing the large-scale extinction of species and poverty. A country like the Philippines does not want to destroy its magnificent tropical jungles. It has a huge debt burden and the sale of timber brings in much-needed foreign currency. So we cut down tropical rain forests and we drill for oil in inappropriate and sacred areas, like the Arctic and the Andes. This is all to pay debt, which creates more wealth—for the privileged few.

The Global 2000 Report

Environmentalists have long been warning of the dangerous path we are following with the relentless exploitation and destruction of the world's natural resources. In 1980, The Global 2000 Report to the President of the USA stated: "If present trends continue, the world in 2000 will be more crowded, more polluted, less stable ecologically and more vulnerable to disruption. Serious stresses involving population, resources and environment are clearly visible ahead. Despite greater material output, the world's people will be poorer in many ways than they are today. For hundreds of millions of the desperately poor, the outlook for food and other necessities will be no better. For many it will be worse. Barring revolutionary advances in technology, life for most people on earth will be more precarious in 2000 than it is now—unless the nations of the world act decisively to alter current trends."

It is reputed that the new President of the USA in 1981, Ronald Reagan, shelved the report, yet all that it warned has come about. The in-depth World Commission on Environment and Development, *Our Common Future*, known as the Bruntland Commission after its Chairman, reported in 1987 on our threatened future. It served notice that "the time has come for a marriage of economy and ecology, so that governments and their people can take responsibility not just for environmental damage, but for the policies that cause the damage. Some of these policies threaten the survival of the human race."

The world responded by holding the Rio Conference in 1992. Many good decisions were made, but the world has not acted on them, led by President George Bush (Senior) who refused to ratify many agreements. The tragedy is that the predictions have come about.

Ecological Bankruptcy Report

A report by "Redefining Progress" in California has warned that a failure to rein in humanity's overuse of natural resources could send the planet into ecological bankruptcy. The consumption of forests, energy and land by humans is exceeding the rate at which earth can replenish itself

Scientists said humanity's demand for resources has soared during the past 40 years to a level where it takes the planet 1.2 years to regenerate what people remove each year. The impact by humans on the environment has inched higher since 1961 when we used 70 percent of the planet's regenerative capacity. "If we don't live within the budget of nature, sustainability becomes futile".

The Global Environment Outlook

The Global Environment Outlook, compiled for the UN, charts the environmental degradation of the last 30 years since the first world environment conference in Stockholm in 1972 and looks forward to how the world might look by 2032:

• Half the world will be short of water
• Urbanisation of 70 percent of land surface
• Another 2 billion mouths to feed

The destruction of 70 percent of the natural world in 30 years, mass extinction of species, and the collapse of human society in many countries, was forecast in this bleak report by 1,100 scientists on 23 May 2002.

The report paints four possible futures for the world:

1) The *current pattern of free trade and short-term profit* at the expense of the environment, which leads to disaster.

2) In a second, equally dangerous scenario, *security considerations dominate* with fear of terror and mass immigration into rich areas. It involves a world split into rich and poor, with freedom of movement and democracy restricted and rich enclaves like Europe and North America with barriers keeping out the poor and desperate. Apartheid is alive and kicking in the world!

3) A third offers a *strong policy-based option* where governments try to protect the environment with international treaties with varying degrees of success.

4) The fourth, where *all decisions are based on sustainable development* rather than short-term gain and greed, is the blueprint favoured by the report.

Klaus Toepfer, the UN Environment Programme Executive Director, called for concrete actions and an iron political will to change the existing pattern. "Without the environment there can never be the kind of development needed to secure a fair deal for this or future generations. It would be disastrous to ignore the picture painted."

So we must ask: Are we going to follow the way of justice and sustainability, or power and oppression? Do we bring morality into the world economic order? We can see from Zimbabwe what damage one leader can cause. I am not intending to be political, but President George Bush stands hugely accountable, as President of the richest, most powerful nation, which produces 70 percent of the world's pollution, uses 25 percent of the world's energy, and wastes the energies, natural resources, and finances of the world on armaments and defensive space shields. Kyoto—The USA's refusal to sign is wicked. The USA has to cut down on greenhouse gas emissions. An average American is responsible for 300 times the carbon dioxide emissions of a Mozambican. The West spends $600 billion annually on armaments. (The Space Shield: It is reported that an extra $2.8bn has been allocated for the USA ballistic missile defense programme in a budget that will total $328bn). If President Bush took that money, and all the people involved in armaments research and production, and used the money and the people to build schools, health facilities, water sanitation schemes, he could solve the problems of world poverty.

We were told long ago: *A king is not saved by his great army; a warrior is not delivered by his great strength.* (Psalm 33:16)

To find security we should: *Administer true justice, show kindness and compassion to each other.* (Zechariah 7:9-11)

Don't rely on your guns—seek Justice. That is the clear message of the Bible. The USA is now doing exactly the same thing on a world scale that we did under apartheid and which they rightly condemned us for—

keeping the poor of the world from sharing its resources. The US cannot just consider its own interests. If it wants to be involved in world trade, if Americans want to sell their Coke and KFCs to us, they must recognise they are part of the global community and accept their responsibilities. World leaders can no longer consider their own citizens only. They must recognize that we are inextricably one world community and we must establish justice for that world community.

Though I call for the establishment of economic justice, the challenge essentially comes back to us. We, Christians, need to be bringing about an attitudinal change, a conversion. Is that not our job?

We have to recognize that the care of the world is supremely the responsibility of Christians and Christian Churches because:

1. We are the ones who worship a creator God;

2. The present direction of the world is motivated by self-centred greed leading to serious spiritual misdirection and this is clearly a responsibility of the churches.

Christ tells us to love our neighbor—the present economic system leads us in the opposite direction. We have to start being responsible in two areas:

1. In the North, controlling our consumption;

2. In developing countries, limiting the number of children we bring into the world.

We need to challenge the accepted wisdom of the need for constant growth: it is not possible on a finite planet. But that does mean there needs to be limitation in population growth, fair trade and redistribution

of wealth. There has to be a radical change of direction and mind shift by the rich and powerful, and they are the least likely to want to change. Yet, South Africa is an example that it can be done.

Christianity can provide the answer, if we follow the teachings of Christ and not the heresies of prosperity cults! In Mark 8:34–37, Jesus challenges us to *deny oneself and take up the cross.* Are we prepared to do this, to make sacrifices and take up the cross, in our own lives, in our communities, in our countries?

In the little booklet, *Save Our Future,* we are encouraged to:

1. **Take responsibility** for our lives and the world around us, including the number of children we bring into the world.

2. **Re-examine our values,** recognizing the sanctity of life.

3. **Walk in the way of the cross, denying self, affirming life,** overcoming aggression and exploitation for co-operation and sharing.

4. **Respect diversity and promote unity,** recognising that God's purpose is that this creation of infinite diversity should live together in peace and harmony.

We know there is a struggle or even conflict between "brown" and "green" environmental issues—both are necessary.

Eco-Justice embraces economic and ecological justice.

We have to:

• Demand economic justice. Churches must be involved.

• Establish fair trade and just structures.

• Work to ensure that the world's resources are used for development and not the armaments industry.

We need a resolution that calls for:

• The establishment of *economic justice.*

• The *cancellation of odious debts.*

• The establishment of *fair trade,* so that if there is to be free trade, "developing" nations must be allowed free access to the markets of the "North".

• A *dramatic reduction in armaments expenditures,* recognising the immorality of spending so many resources on armaments. If those resources were directed to sustainable development, they would provide far more jobs, overcome the poverty of the world and help establish justice, thereby overcoming suspicion and tension.

How Good Intentions Go Wrong: An African Case Study

—Professor Richard Fuggle

I fear that what I might be saying to you now could be construed as opposition, or to be subtracting from what has been said over the past few days. This is not my intent, and I would not like it construed that way.

I would like to thank everybody very much for the invitation to be with you, to address you. I feel privileged to have participated in this Congress. I have found it particularly stimulating, especially the high level of intellectual interaction that has taken place. I now want to share with you some insights I have gained through over thirty years of professional practice as an environmental scientist.

During the last five years, I have been serving as a consultant to the Inspection Panel of the World Bank. I give advice on matters of ecological justice and economic justice for World Bank projects that are seen to be going wrong by the people they are intended to help. It is not commonly known that World Bank projects can be challenged; this is done through the formal structure of the Inspection Panel. This is a mechanism whereby investments that are being made to alleviate poverty may be challenged if they are in fact causing harm. The Panel's web site is: www.inspectionpanel.org. On this Web site, you will find the entire range of policies to safeguard people and environments from being harmed by projects financed by the World Bank.

In a strict sense, the World Bank does not actually exist. Most people don't know that. The "World Bank" consists of different bodies: the best known are the International Bank of Reconstruction and Development (IBRD), which charges a nominal rate of interest, and the International Development Agency (IDA), which provides money at very low interest over 40 years. The others are the International Finance Corporation, the Multilateral Investment Guarantee Agency, and the International Centre for the Settlement of Investor Disputes. So when one talks about the "World Bank", you have to be very careful which organization you are actually talking about.

Both the IBRD and IDA have developed a series of safeguard policies to ensure that their investments minimize harm. There are safeguard policies to protect the environment, biodiversity, indigenous peoples, people being resettled, natural habitats, forests, water resources, and others. Many of the documents we see popping up in debates relating to the

WSSD, for example, are based on the thinking already encapsulated in these safeguard policies. I am not here to defend the World Bank. What I am trying to show and share with you today is my experience. I will do so using a case study of Lake Victoria, Central Africa.

The World Bank was asked to come in and provide the money for a structure to allow for sound environmental management and to relieve poverty in this area. Yet once underway this project was challenged because some affected people thought the project was doing more harm than good. This is when the Inspection Panel was brought in. The Panel had to investigate the facts of the matter.

But before I continue, let me state what I hope you will get out of this case study. Firstly, I'd like you to end with the impression that many of our searches for solutions to problems of eco-justice are too simplistic. The world wants a villain, whether from television or modern Western approaches to movies; I'm not sure where it comes from, but we want a villain. We want the villain to be someone else; we don't want the villain to be our societal or personal values, or our comfort with what we are personally doing. The second point I would like you to understand is that the villain is not science or economics, but rather the arrogance that we display in assuming that we will find answers from these modes of analysis. The villain is not science or economics, but arrogance. We seek a scapegoat because we are too arrogant to examine the values we use to make our economic and technical choices.

The third point is the blind faith we have in quick-fix solutions. We want to change one specific thing, we want to change the World Bank's policy, we want to change world trade, and we want to do one thing or another. I am reminded of the acronym every ecology student is taught "YCCJOT"—"You cannot change just one thing." To look for simplistic solutions in the intricacies of our social and economic systems is silly. When we try, we often make problems worse.

The fourth thing that I hope you will gain from the case study is that we refuse to acknowledge the limitation of human knowledge. Caution is advised when tackling problems without complete understanding. That is what I spoke about when I dealt with the "precautionary principle" two nights ago: our refusal to recognize our limitations as well as our refusal to recognize the limitation of human knowledge.

The final point about which I think we have to be very watchful is the cult of shifting the blame. That is, "We are not at fault, someone else is", the polarization between "we" and "they". The poor countries blame the rich; the rich countries blame the poor. This is the failure to accept that the best agents for change that we have are the hands at the ends of our own arms, and our own minds and hearts. We want someone else to do it. This is the message I hope you will get out of this case study.

Now let's consider the plight of thirty million people living around Lake Victoria. For those of you who do not know the area, let me sketch this very briefly. Lake Victoria sits astride the equator, 400 kilometers from north to south, 350 kilometers east to west. It's the second largest freshwater body on earth, the world's largest tropical lake. The volume of water that discharges out of Lake Victoria over Owen Falls is 1,200 cubic meters per second, which is awe-inspiring. However, living around this volume of water are people in immense distress. The area has the highest incidence of malaria in the world; the highest incidence until very recently of HIV/AIDS (the locus of the highest incidence of this scourge has now shifted south to Botswana, Zimbabwe and South Africa). The levels of poverty are extremely high. When John Speke first stumbled across the shores of the lake in 1858, he found very few people there despite the abundant pure freshwater and fertile soil. Mosquitoes and tsetse flies were the problem. He named it Lake Victoria for the British monarch and essentially moved on.

When did things start changing around Lake Victoria? British colonization took place in the 1890's; one of the first problems that the British and Germans encountered was the ongoing Arab slave trade. The slave trade had been banned in Europe and North America, but it was continuing here. The decision was made to bring in troops to stop the slave trade. They had to get the troops in, internally, behind the Arab settlements on the coast. The decision was made to build a railway line to transport troops to the interior to stop the slave trade. It was thought that troops would come in and that soldiers were the answer to the problem, and that was that.

But what happened when that railway line was constructed was something else. The first thing was that so many people had been taken away in slavery, particularly the males, that the British could not impinge on the local population for additional labor, so they imported labor from another colony. Indentured labor was bought in from India to build the railway line. Some indigenous people were used, and this was not good for local agriculture. So the people that worked on the railway line as well as the soldiers who opted to stay in East Africa became the first foreign settlers. They imposed upon the Colonial Government to allow them to acquire land, which they were given on 99-year leases; they started clearing the tropical forest and to teach the local people commercial rather than subsistence agriculture. Bush was cleared and agriculture was promoted. Soon production systems were being used to meet both local needs as well as for export to support a cash economy. However, that was not the intention of the railway line, and not the intention of the early farmers.

The net effect of this agricultural development was the creation of new human settlements. The population increased and the population needed to be fed. The protein that was received was mainly from the lake. Lake

Victoria is the richest natural lake in the world in terms of biodiversity, with over 500 species of fish native to it. The local people were using rather crude methods of trapping small finger-sized fish, but sustained themselves quite adequately. As the population grew, it could no longer sustain itself. The first thing that was used to increase fishing yields, as suggested by scientists, was nets. So gill nets and twine nets were brought in from Europe, and immediately, many more small fish were caught, which fed the growing population. However, the gill nets significantly decreased the number of fish from the lake because they were more efficient at harvesting the fish than the older methods.

When the fishing pressure started getting too high, people were no longer getting the fish and protein they required. More scientific research went into the problem, and it was realized that an excellent eating species lived down the Nile. So Tilapia were brought into Lake Victoria to feed people, with the best of intentions. People who were hungry for protein were satisfied. But Tilapia are not sport fish and were not meeting this need. So the thinking was: "Let's develop a tourism industry and also increase the productivity of this vast volume of water whose fishery potential is simply not being tapped. Let's bring in some really decent fish. It can be sport fishing, but it can also feed a lot more people". So the Nile Perch was bought in.

The Nile Perch, the world record, hold your breath, is 282 kilograms—it took four people to hold that fish. The average Nile Perch is about 7–8 kilograms, but as indicated, this fish can grow into an absolute monster. This is very different from the finger-sized little fish that used to live in the lake, eating algae and decaying parts of natural plants. When agriculture started in the lake basin, fertilizer was needed to improve production. The water running off from tea and coffee estates carried excess fertilizer into the lake, as well as sediment eroded from areas no longer protected by natural vegetation. The little fish that were living in the lake used to gobble the algae that flourished because of the added nutrients, and kept it pretty much under control. This all changed with the introduction of the Nile Perch.

In one sense, the introduction of the Nile Perch has been a great success as it has created an industry that employs, in total, close to one million people. The Nile Perch is now exported to the tables of Europe and the Far East, and is a significant contributor to the import/export earnings of a number of East African countries. The governments see this as very important, and a lot of money has flowed in and a lot of people are employed. However, the large perch are carnivores and eat the smaller fish. The Nile Perch has virtually wiped out many of the small indigenous species that were there. What this, in turn, has done is to change the whole energy balance and nutrient balance of the lake. The reduced numbers of small fish mean that they no longer consume the algae which removed the phosphates and nitrates that wash into the lake from the surrounding areas. The entire nutrient cycle of the lake has been inadvertently changed. The once-clear nutrient-poor lake waters became muddy, cloudy nutrient-rich waters.

Another thing that happened inadvertently was that on the western side of the lake, settlers in Rwanda had tried to beautify their homesteads by adding a rather attractive plant from South America into ornamental ponds. This was the Water Hyacinth. The Water Hyacinth is really a quite remarkable plant. It mops up nutrients from water at a great rate, and it is the "proverbial plant" that doubles in size every week. It can float around on the surface; it can root in shallow water. It can propagate vegetatively or sexually. As a scientist, one really has to admire this plant. But when it escaped from where it was intended and ultimately got into Lake Victoria, it found all the nutrients that were there because of farming, high water runoff, and the changed fish populations in the lake. This enabled it to grow and grow. The Water Hyacinth, which found its way into Lake Victoria, simply said, "What a lovely place to be", and within a very short time it was significantly covering the lake. Now Water Hyacinth forms dense mats that are virtually impenetrable by boats. These mats block the harbors, so the trawlers that were going out to fish for the Nile Perch could not get out. Other trade between Kenya and Uganda, and Kenya and Tanzania, could not take place. The economy of the areas close to the lakes started collapsing, because trade could not take place— not only the national economy, but also the local and domestic economy of peoples living on the land.

For example, women, who used to be able to catch a lake ferry for seven shillings to take their produce to sell in the town market, and catch the ferry back in the afternoon, now found that they could not use the ferry. They had to take one of the mini-bus taxis which went around the lake, where road infrastructure is not kind, and it cost them seventy shillings, ten times as much as before, and also took two days to make the round-trip, so they simply gave up going to towns to trade. Further, the traditional economy of the area required that women catch small fish in nets, close to the edge, and dry them in the sun, and trade them throughout East Africa. Sun-dried fish were a staple. But when the large Nile Perch that weighed many kilograms became the staple of the commercial fishing industry, women could not handle them. The economy changed, the fishing economy changed, it became male dominated. The fish that were being caught by the males go through a fish-processing factory and over 2,000 tons of fish fillets are flown out to the rest of the world each year. The women are no longer even able to catch sufficient small fish to feed their families. So there is protein malnutrition, especially among the children, around a lake that is actually exporting 2,000 tons of good fillet a year and earning lots of money. The domestic economy has been totally changed by the good intentions that have been brought into this entire system.

You must remember that neither the Water Hyacinth nor the Nile Perch was introduced with evil intent. They were introduced to meet human needs, to feed hungry people. The farming that was started was not with evil intent, but to feed hungry people. In each case people assumed that they had the answer and that they knew what was going to happen. Experts looked for simple straightforward solutions to specific problems. Little thought was given to the ramifications of the actions; little precaution was taken.

But once Water Hyacinth was seen to be wrecking their economies the governments of Kenya, Uganda and Tanzania asked the World Bank for money to solve the problem, and were granted 20 million dollars. With this funding the Lake Victoria Environmental Management Programme was initiated. But in the nature of scientific inquiry the Water Hyacinth problem got worse while it was being investigated. So the Government of Kenya commissioned a "quick-fix" solution and hired a company to use barges to mechanically chop up the floating mats of hyacinth. This led to significant protests from local people who thought that this intervention was going to result in even more harm than they had already experienced. People were getting poorer; the Inspection Panel was triggered to investigate this problem.

So the Panel went in, wanting to know what had happened. It is a complex story which is fully documented in the Panel's report. This report shows that neither people nor the environment had suffered significant losses as a consequence of the project. However, it did find: ". . . there has been a serious lack of attention to the scientific underpinnings of the water hyacinth shredding pilot . . ." And further, "The Panel witnessed first-hand the dilapidated state of the building housing the laboratory. The laboratory had inadequate equipment, glassware, reagents, water supply, electricity supply and cleaning service. Any results emanating from it would be highly suspect". Yet records showed that the laboratory and equipment had been paid for. The Panel also found: ". . . that procurement and disbursement practices which result in the relatively easy purchase of vehicles and office equipment, while laboratories, field and scientific staff essential to meeting the objectives of the pilot are starved of funds, need urgently to be corrected. . . ."

Where does all this lead? We get into an area in which we find that the actual situation on the ground is primarily a result of internal values: what politicians and officials are putting pressure on or not putting pressure on; what they are prepared to act on, and what they are not prepared to act on. In a situation where one has denial, the policies of the international community (such as the World Bank's safeguard policies) are meant to correct practices that subvert eco-justice (economic and ecological) in the local country. Why is that needed? It is needed because the money that is asked for, and is going there, has not been used for the purposes for which it is required. The answer that we are geared to look for is based on money and science.

I hope I might have demonstrated to you that, although we give money with good intent, as was done with the railway to stop slavery, the introduction of agriculture to feed people, the introduction of fish to meet the protein needs of a large number of people—in each case, we have not foreseen the consequences that have come. The precautionary principle has not been followed. Each action has been trying to achieve economic or ecological justice, not in quite the same sense that we have were talking about here, but with good intent. You should remember neither the Water Hyacinth nor the Nile Perch was introduced with evil intent. They were introduced to meet human needs, to feed hungry people. The farming that was started was not with evil intent, but to feed hungry people. In each case people assumed that they had the answer and that they knew what was going to happen.

Yet all of the solutions adopted proved to be too simplistic. They have not realized the complexity of the system, and have not tried to get at the underlying values by asking: "Is there not something in the human psyche, in the human spirit, that is important here? Are we doing things the right way? Are there structures in which resources are flowing incorrectly?"

I suggest that each of us in our own way, using our own hands at the end of our arms, need to examine what we can do, and possibly should do in our presentations at the WSSD, so that we are not overly simplistic. We must stop blaming others, be it the World Bank or the world economic order; we must stop looking for external villains. We must recognize that within the complicated issues that humankind faces, we do not have all the wisdom that we should have to solve ecological problems. If we try to solve the problems of economic justice, ecological justice, by only trying to change one thing, we should know that it is going to fail. We have to appreciate the complexity of natural systems and that our interventions are based on the values we bring to them. Good intentions are not enough. We must first address our own actions.

It is incumbent upon the faith communities, and gatherings such as this, to ensure that the religious and moral values underpinning ecological and economic justice are not forgotten in the scientific and economic debates that do dominate and will no doubt surface at the forthcoming World Summit on Sustainable Development.

Economic and Ecological Justice

—THE RT. REV. DAVID BEETGE

Good morning. It is lovely to be here with you this morning. I want to say a few things, but first, I think you need to know the point of view from which I am speaking. In a former incarnation, I studied economics, yet I am not here to talk from an economic point of view. I became Bishop of a new diocese, which was part of the diocese of Johannesburg in 1990. This happened between the years of 1990 and 1994 when we were moving towards a new constitution in South Africa. Within my area, 8,500 people died of political violence. I spent those four years ducking bullets, mediating, and helping to resolve the political violence in the area. For most of my adult life, I've been a pacifist. I never did military service, although this was not because of my pacifist stance. But in my diocese, I was a pacifist in one of the most violent areas of the country for those four years. The violence of seeing children abused and a woman raped and the destruction of the area through that violence had an incredible effect on me, and today it is part of my own testimony.

Some time ago I took my own personal vow of trying to live a life of non-violence in all its forms. For violence is not just something like me hitting you. Violence is much more complex than that. Obviously, there is direct and immediate violence. There is nothing romantic, as the media might portray it, about seeing children with their legs blown off. There is nothing romantic about the landmines that are created in the form of toys that are still found in Angola where the children will pick them up and have their arms and limbs blown off. And then there is structural violence. Structural violence includes cultural violence, economic violence, and ecological violence. What I want to say to you today is mainly about economic violence. I came to the position that Gandhi found himself in, when Gandhi said, "Poverty is one of the worst forms of violence." I think that is my starting point for anything that I want to say to you this morning.

We are a society, a world, and a global village that is committed to violence in all its forms. There is direct violence. We resolve our disputes through direct violence. The treaty against Iraq is a case in point. It is interesting that Simone Weil, in 1966, said that the culture of the West and the spirituality of the East will one day be in conflict. I think this is exactly what we are seeing now. But we should not forget that violence can never be contained in one area. It spreads like a cancer. We found in the political violence of the early 1990's, at a community and at a national level, that the incidents of abuse against children and against women grew and increased during that time. If you allow violence to operate at one level of your life, ultimately you are going to use it at other levels as well. It is a cancer. It is a social cancer. As John Dear has said, "To break our addiction to violence, we need to look coldly at our violence." It is not something that is out there. It is something internal and we need to admit that we are addicted to violence, to break our denial of violence, and begin the process of transformation into non-violence.

Now having given you that little brief introduction, there are really two areas that I want to look at this morning, quite briefly. One is military expenditure; the cost of military expenditure is of considerable concern. Bishop Davies mentioned it, and I want to go into it in a little more detail. Let me just read to you again some of what is happening in terms of the military. This is a quote from John Dear:

> As I write this, millions of people are starving in Africa, while the United States continues to spend its resources on war and world domination. The violence that plagues our culture is reaching astronomical proportions and our inner cities stand on the brink of explosion. During the 1980's and the 1990's the US Government spent each fiscal year hundreds of billions of dollars for war and nuclear weapons. Yet, funding for education, health-care, the homeless and AIDS research was cut. Over forty wars are being fought around the world and over 60,000 children die from starvation every day. Sexism, racism, greed, consumerism, torture, poverty, and militarism tear our world apart. Even after the cold war our addiction to violence threatens to destroy us all.

I don't want to single out the US, because they are not the only culprit. I could name other countries as well. Don't forget that most of the third world debt, particularly in Africa, is a result of governments providing Africa with obsolete weapons that they now have to repay. That is a fact. But let me just quote from Dear again, because he is a Jesuit and he is from the United States:

> The US has legally spent over $11,000,000,000,000 (trillion) dollars on making war and killing people since 1946. The US budget for fiscal year 1993 included over $232,000,000,000 (billion) for war making purposes. The world spends over $900,000,000,000 (billion) dollars each year on war and killing people. A fraction of those funds could end world hunger in two weeks, house the world's home-less, prevent disease, and improve life for millions of people. If one tenth of this money were diverted to world needs, it would be more than the total amount the World Bank estimates would wipe out world hunger. The Reagan administration spent $1,140,000,000,000.00 (1.14 trillion) dollars for war between 1984 and 1987.

That is only four years. One trillion dollars is a lot of money. How could that money have been spent differently? Here is the answer from John Dear:

> For one trillion dollars you could build a $75,000 house, place it on $5,000 worth of land, furnish it with $10,000 worth of furniture, put a $10,000 car in the garage, and give all this to each and every family in Kansas, Missouri, Nebraska, Oklahoma, Colorado, and Iowa. Having done this, you would still have enough left to build a $10,000,000 hospital and a $10,000,000 library in each of 250 cities and towns. After having done all that, you would still have enough left from the original trillion to put aside, at 10% annual interest, a sum of money that would pay a salary of $25,000 per year for an army of 10,000 nurses, the same salary for an army of 10,000 teachers, and an annual cash allowance of $5,000 for each and every family throughout that six state region, and not just for one year, but for generations to come.

That is the sort of alternative we should be looking at. Within Southern Africa and Africa the cost of the military has been exorbitant. Let me quote to you from what Dwight Eisenhower, a general and President of the United States, once said:

> Every gun that is made, every warship that is launched, every rocket that is fired, signifies in the final sense a theft from those who hunger and are not fed, those who are cold and not clothed.

If we look, for example, at the cost of the military, in Southern Africa, we see the following: military expenditures in the forty-four sub-Saharan African countries fell in real terms by 30.5% between 1990 and 1999. Now you would say that is very good, but listen more closely to the figures. As a proportion of GDP this amounted to an average of 3% in 1990 and 2.6% in 1998. As a proportion of central government expenditure the mean went to 11.8% in 1990 and 8.5% in the late 1990's. Full time members of the armed forces in sub-Saharan Africa totaled 958,500 in 1985 and 1,455,000 in 1999. In 1999 there were also some 300,000 reservists, and 238,100 paramilitarists.

The expenditure trends noted above might be interpreted as demilitarization within sub-Saharan Africa during the 1990's. However, for the lower income countries in particular, military expenditure reductions were in response to a very difficult economic condition and not part of any long-term plan. In addition, South Africa's reduced military expenditure over the period almost equals the entire reduction for all sub-Saharan Africa in the 1990's. South Africa, it might be noted, has subsequently begun a major military expense expansion. There is little evidence of any purposeful or sustained demilitarization in sub-Saharan Africa even though the trends seem to be in the right direction.

So often conflict can seem isolated, but let me quote you some figures from the book *Searching for Peace in Africa.* It shows that armed conflicts in the 1990's have affected many parts of the African continent. Mention has already been made that in 1998 there were no fewer than seventy-two violent armed conflicts on the continent, but these are some figures about deaths resulting from armed conflicts in Africa during the 1990's:

Algeria: 800,000

Western Sahara: 13,000

Ethiopia and Eritrea: tens of thousands (conservative estimates)

Somalia: 250,000

Sudan: 400,000—1.5 million (first civil war) to 1.9 million (second civil war)

We know there are reasons for this, and the reasons are the colonial legacy, ethnicity and religion, different levels of development, poverty, poor leadership, militarism, state and political conflicts, and foreign interests including oil in some parts. The Sudanese conflict, for example, has been fueled by oil, and there are other conflicts that are fueled by such things.

There are human costs, which also have financial implications, including those killed in armed conflict and those maimed in armed conflict. You know that there are landmines called "smart landmines." I have been in Angola twice recently in the last year. Smart landmines have been created so that they don't kill the person. It is far more demoralizing for a nation to have hospitals full of people with arms, legs, and limbs blown off than just to bury them. This is part of the violent culture that we are living with. Children used in war and child soldiers throughout the world know only a culture of violence. These circumstances will have a long-term effect on the economy of our world, because a general culture of violence affects every level of society.

Walter Wink, author of *The Powers That Be,* a very good book and worth reading, has written a trilogy on non-violence. I quote him here:

Again the means used in a war must be proportionate to the end sought, but how can we know in advance what level of destruction will follow the armed conflict? Even beyond casualties, ruined cities, refugees, a gutted economy, women raped or reduced to prostitution, children dying from malnutrition and intestinal diseases, how does one project into the future the continuing hazard of exploding landmines and bombs, drug addiction, alcoholism, mental illness, physical crippling and suicide?

How can this be weighed before or even during a war? It is true that both Mozambique's and Angola's economic sustainability are under threat for generations to come because of the land-mines that have been planted in those countries.

In the recent floods in Mozambique, many of those landmines were washed down to different places, which has affected new areas of growth. This is a personal matter, and from my perspective, a matter of deep vio-lence affecting the lives of everyone else.

I want briefly now to move just to the question of poverty. I will be shorter on this, but not because I am less interested. I will refer now particularly to South Africa. The "Human Development Report" of the United Nations published in 1999 ranks South Africa 101st in the Human Development Index. South Africa falls within the median human devel-opment category. In terms of human poverty in developing countries, South Africa is ranked 31st. It goes on to show that 23.4% of the popula-tion are not expected to reach the age of 40; 13% of the population are without water and sanitation; 9% of children under five are underweight; 23.7% of the population live below the income poverty line of one dollar a day. The population in South Africa is estimated to be around 43 mil-lion. This means that over 10 million people live below the income poverty line.

Someone once said to me that South Africa is a land of contrast in so many different ways: culturally, geographically and socially. The figures quoted above show this to be economically true as well. The figures related to GDP show a great difference between the poorest 20% and the richest 20%. The area of my diocese falls into the area of the greatest poverty. The number of people living in informal settlements has increased significantly over the last five years. People living in these areas come not only from different parts of South Africa, but from other parts of Africa. Such areas are Mozambique, Malawi, Sudan and Zimbabwe, to name a few. My wife is a community health nurse who works a lot of the time in informal settlements. She tells me that we're having people from far afield, right up north from Sudan even, coming down and looking for a place to live in this area.

From the standpoint of the city, it is clear that the concentration of eco-nomic power in a small number of areas has meant that the economic wealth of the country has not been properly distributed. The number of people suffering from poverty has increased. We are still living with the legacy of apartheid economically. Don't believe otherwise. The whole economy under the apartheid system was skewed to have pockets of eco-nomic wealth in the cities away from the so-called "homeland." They did not have the opportunity of being economically sustainable. There has to be some way of redressing that situation in the future.

In Johannesburg, you can see the wealth of the northern suburbs. My office is twenty-five miles away from them. In the area of my office, the area of unemployment is 37%. When you go to the poor rural areas of my poorest parish, the unemployment rate is up to 90%. Now that shows you, in a relatively short space, the economic violence that the system caused. The Human Development Report analyzes the changing face of poverty, and concludes that, compared with 1970, the lowest income levels for a person today are likely to be among Africans or Latin Americans, children or women or the elderly, low-wage or unskilled workers, laborers, urban refugees, or the internally displaced. This would seem to confirm the point regarding the informal settlements that have grown up around the towns and cities in the more developed economic areas of South Africa.

Driving though these areas, I am moved by the number of people who have nothing or very little to do each day. Women and children exist in small homes waiting for the chance of finding work and food, and being able to make appropriate choices for themselves. As the Human Development Report says, poverty means that opportunities and choices, the most basic human development, are denied. My brothers and sisters, it is for that reason that I believe there is economic violence in our society. Poverty affects every aspect of the human condition—children, gender issues, and internal personal securities, just to name a few. A single mother from Guyana once said, "Poverty is hunger, loneliness, nowhere to go when the day is over, deprivation, discrimination, abuse and illiteracy." A person from Botswana once said: "Wealth is the blanket we wear, poverty is having that blanket taken away."

I must end, and you have been patient. I want to remind you that real security does not come from abuse; real security does not come from force; real security does not come from violence; real security for us must come from governments taking serious responsibility for the needs of their people, which include poverty, unemployment, inequality, HIV and AIDS.

If governments care for their people, if governments really invest in their people, then we won't need the armaments that other countries don't want any longer. All of this comes back to my first issue—that we are in a world, a global village, totally committed to violence. You have the opportunity at your meeting here to begin a new world, a world of non-violence. Fernando Cordozo said: "The biggest challenge for multi-lateral organizations is to reinvent a sense of community and to make room for national solidarity." We need a real democratization of international relations. It will not be easy given the individualism of our time. It is the only way to insure that history's greatest transformation will be ethical. It is the only way development will again have human faces. Perhaps development will only be taken seriously when we have the courage to look past the numbers and see the pain and suffering on human faces, the pain and suffering that I have lived through as a Bishop and through all my episcopacy.

That pain and suffering in all its forms—direct violence, structural violence, economic violence, ecological violence, and cultural violence—has brought pain to many, many people. While I was in Angola recently, the depth of pain in that country was so great that I could not speak for two days afterward. It seemed a luxury. We must never forget those 60,000 children that will die of poverty each day in our world. Sixty thousand is a number. To their parents, their children are not a number; they are a precious face.

I was once giving an address on the armaments issue, and a lady came to me and said, "You must stop talking about the arms, because they create jobs." And I told her that I know personally a mother whose son was shot in the conflict of the South African political struggle. Her son was shot in the conflict. I wanted to say to her, "Don't worry about your son, because the bullet that killed your son created a job for someone in another country." You can't say that, not to her. All our decisions have moral consequences. The reason you have gathered here today is to remind us, as a church, that there is a morality to our actions and a consequence of our actions. When we lose sight of the faces, and just focus on numbers, as I have partly done here today, it reminds me of the enormity of the problem. We can so easily go down that slippery slope which justifies violence. We have the chance to say "no" to that violence, and to create a new order of non-violence. That is the decision, the moral choice, that we must make.

The Supermarket at Deipsloot "Informal Settlement".

Gender and Human Development

—Rosina Wiltshire

. . . in the image of God he created them, male and female he created them . . .

—Genesis 1:27

I was saying to the Minister of Barbados that I was coming here, and she said: "Oh, I am so heartened that the Anglican Community is coming together, to look at the issues of stewardship." I wrote a letter to all the churches in Barbados, about what role they see for themselves, and about how they could assist in the issues of environmental management and community awareness, and I never heard from the churches. So, it is, in fact, wonderful that we are all gathered here.

What I propose this morning is to speak for approximately twenty to twenty-five minutes. Hopefully, it will be less than that. I will leave seven to ten minutes for feedback; then, we'll have a period of group work, approximately forty minutes, with fifteen minutes report back time at the end. On the substance, I want to structure my presentation by clarifying what I see to be meant by "gender", the role of "women" in articulating the shifting of debate in United Nations conferences, leading to the World Summit on Sustainable Development, and in the Alliance of Women in Churches and The World Council of Churches. Gender, as you know, is an area of controversy, led by the Catholics and Muslims. And then, I will end with some questions on how the Anglican Community can enhance its positive role in promoting a perspective of gender equality and women's empowerment.

What is "gender"? Gender relates to the values, norms and roles assigned to women and men by society. A gender perspective refers to the different perspectives women and men bring to decision making because of their different experiences and knowledge arising from their gender-based norms and roles. A gender analysis refers to accessing and making a provision for the different impacts of a policy or plan of action on women and men.

Now, practically, you have been working with a number of issues, like food security. In Africa, 80 percent of domestic food production is conducted by women. So if one is trying to address food security in Africa, one has to deal with that reality. In Asia, the ratio is slightly different. I have seen water pumps, designed by engineers, where it was assumed that it was the men pumping water. The pumps were "up there", and the women, who were the ones in the villages who were responsible for pumping the water, were "down there". This means you had unused water pumps, or pumps in which people had to stand on one another to get the water. In North America, I have been in theaters where the architects have assumed that women and men needed the same amount of bathrooms. And we all know that because of physiology and clothing, women need more time. Each woman needs more time. If you are building bathrooms and designing a building, you need to construct twice as many bathrooms for women as men. This kind of information comes from gender analysis applied to different fields. Some of these are architecture, engineering, policy, food planning, budgeting, and wherever you sit, a gender analysis is necessary to come up with solutions that speak to the differential needs of men and women.

Now what was the role of women in bringing a gender perspective and shaping the debate and general direction of the present WSSD and general development of the environmental issue? I speak from my own experience, and that began in 1981 when I attended the UN Conference on Renewable Sources of Energy. It was the first conference in which there was fairly significant participation of women. I was part of the official conference, and within the Nairobi Center the delegates were mainly men, in jackets and ties. One day outside the conference center, I was standing on the stairway, and I saw dozens of women, many barefooted, coming to the conference center, dressed in traditional African clothing. And, as they came to the stairs, they were led by Wangari Maathai; many of them had walked for miles, from rural areas, and they came to talk to the delegates at the conference.

They did not get entry to the conference, and most people were not interested in what they had to say. But these rural women were telling us that based on their experience in collecting firewood for energy, they were experiencing a major degradation of the environment. They were having to walk farther and farther for firewood. The forest was being depleted; there was not as much water. They were talking about a whole different perspective on the environment. What I was hearing inside the conference room was talk about nuclear energy, a lot of science and technology, and some people talking about solar energy, but their voices were in the minority. It was like experiencing two different worlds; and, it really struck me—how the different positions and experience of these women, these "grassroots women", as we call them, and their understanding of what was happening to the environment seemed to link the issues like desertification, deforestation, water, energy, biomass, and all kinds of things. The men in that conference had no deeper understanding of it. They were not interested in it. The women's voices, as I said, remained on the stairway of the Nairobi Conference Center. The debate coming out of the conference had little reflection on the reality of environmental degradation as we understand it today.

The perspectives developed through the Nairobi Conference on Women in 1985, where the Southern Women's Network and the Development Alternative With Women For A New Era (DAWN) linked women across Africa, Latin America, the Caribbean, and the Pacific, presented a perspective, a linkage among women concerning environmental degradation, growing inequality, North and South, the debt crisis, the gap between rich and poor, increasing impoverishment and the call for the new definition of development. These were and are crucial matters: women's equality and the sustainable use of the environment. The DAWN voice was seen as a Southern voice; it was a voice of the Southern Woman. At Rio, the 1992 Earth Summit, the Southern perspective represented by DAWN and the Northern Woman represented by the Woman's Environmental and Development Organization (WEDO), led by Bella Abzug, came together.

We formed an alliance, and there was an Alliance Action Committee on which I served. We decided to hold a meeting of women across the world, which we called "The World's Women's Congress for a Healthy Planet", and we met in Miami. Out of that conference, the Woman's Agenda 21 emerged. The voices expressed and heard there addressed the role of values and spirituality in redefining the relationship of humanity to the earth, the relationship of people to one another, men to woman, rich to poor. There was a call for the re-examination of the value we give to forests, air, water, and women's work, which we talked about as the "care economy". We called for a shift in what was measured, in creating wealth in the GDP, and an acknowledgement of wealth depletion, as well as wealth creation, the visible and invisible economies. Maurice Strong was very receptive to the Women's Agenda 21, but not all were. I would say about five to ten thousand women were in Miami for The World's Women's Congress for a Healthy Planet.

We decided we would take the Alliance to the official Rio Summit and the preparatory process. We met and caucused for each Prepcom, lobbying delegates to get the vision of the human and the environmental considered as a whole and to get these issues into the debate. Initially at Rio, the scientists controlled the agenda and they were talking about forests and water, but they were talking in very technical terms, and the human and the environmental dimensions had not been fully integrated—not been integrated at all. There was also an alliance forming among the churches and other religious groups, through the efforts of The World Council of Churches, which brought together representatives from every religion: Jews, Muslims, Hindus, and many who met in Geneva just before the second Prepcom. I represented DAWN in that group; and we sought to merge our interests into what we called an "Earth Charter". I don't know how many of you know about the Earth Charter. The Earth Charter talked about many of the things we are discussing here, such as God's creation, the sacred nature of the Earth, the stewardship of the Earth. If I say so myself, it was an excellent document, but it was not accepted. In fact, we found that the official delegates were even more unwilling then than they were in 1948 to accept some of the basic proposals about peace, human responsibility to one and other, and the Earth.

As the gender perspective sharpened, as we moved towards the Gender and Population Conference in Cairo where we looked at the impact on women's education, on population, health, and the whole family, the importance of the linkages entered into the official level of discussion. So, the Church, especially the Roman Catholics and the conservative Muslim states, formed an alliance to oppose the whole proposal relating to gender and women's empowerment and women's equality. In Beijing, in 1995, that came to a head with the Roman Catholics and Muslims trying to get the issue of gender off the official agenda, and, at that meeting I was in charge of the UN Development Program delegation to Beijing. I was also involved in the development of the Beijing agenda—the Platform for Action. The Anglican Observer to the UN asked me to speak to a group of churches and religions (and all of them came except the Roman Catholics and Muslims) about what was meant by gender and what was meant by the issues. And I did that. In fact, that gathering of religious people bought an alternative perspective to the debates. They actually countered what was seemingly a monolithic church position.

In Beijing, we took forward the UNDP's Human Development Report that year, which focused on gender, with revealing gender statistics, gender issues generally, gender budgeting, and the issue of environmental economics which had come to the floor in Rio. And at the present WSSD, well, I should say before WSSD, the issues relating to children, which, I should say, men also brought to the floor in their gender perspective, culminated in the Children's Human Rights Agenda. Yet, we seem to be stuck and sitting in that meeting, hearing some powerful presentations, but so much of it reminds me of what we were trying to do in Rio.

One of the issues that we were grappling with in Rio, that we grappled with in Beijing, that we talked about with men and women across the world, was that it was not really a question of not knowing; it was not a question of lack of information. Instead, it was a question of fundamental values. Ethics and spirituality—that was and is the core of the challenge for human community. It is not as easy as putting money at the problem; it is not as easy as many of the solutions we have come up with so far. But, it is fundamental to the solutions that we seek.

The questions that I want to pose to you are these:

• How can we, the Anglican Community, the Church, begin to raise our understanding at a community level?

• How can we create a new understanding of wealth?

• What role is there for sharing love, joy, and compassion?

• What role is there for filling need rather than greed?

• What role is there in defining the role of the person, the family and society?

• How can we shift the value of manhood from making money, gaining power, expressing sexuality, and fathering children, to one that fully encompasses God's abundance, love, sharing and compassion?

Those questions are for each one of us, but they are also questions for the Church and the Church community. How can we integrate this into our teachings, living, and our being? If the Church cannot do it, no one else can. It seems to me that we, as an Anglican community, in the recognition of the need for a different stewardship toward the Earth, are well positioned to address these issues.

Water distribution at Deipsloot "Informal Settlement".

The Beauty and Spirit of Empowerment

—Wangari Maathai, founder of the Green Belt Movement
Presented by Juliana Mugure Muchai

> *. . . and where the Spirit of the Lord is, there is freedom.*

—II Corinthians 3:17

Your Grace, Clergy and Honored Guests,

Allow me to thank you most sincerely for the warm invitation to attend this Anglican Congress on the stewardship of creation in preparation for the United Nations World Conference on Sustainable Development (WSSD) here in Johannesburg. I am honored and privileged to share with you some hopes and dreams with members of your fellowship in the hope that it will encourage you to look deeper into yourselves and strengthen your commitment to God's creation.

As people of faith, the story of Genesis should inspire awe of the beauty and perfection with which God created the earth and the community of the living in it. If only we could see the earth with the eyes of God, when after every action of creation He proclaimed, "It is good!" How satisfied the Creator and the Great Source must have been!

Then, when we look around and witness the destruction of that Creation, the story in the Book of Genesis should inspire the spirit of repentance because of the destruction caused by the human species. What can we do to stop the deforestation and subsequent soil loss, desertification and loss of biodiversity? Stop the pollution of especially air, soil and water? Stop the excessive consumerism, pandemics like HIV/AIDS, landlessness and home-lessness, poverty with all

its manifestations? What sins of omission and commission do we stand accused of?

What will it take to convince governments that there are too many children in the streets, too many poor people who cannot meet their basic needs? What will it take to harness our appetite for consumer goods, which may not give us the happiness we yearn for but which have become prioritized by globalization, especially since the industrial revolution in Europe?

The troubling deterioration of the environment and the conditions of life on earth are in sharp contrast to the beauty and harmony which the author of the Book of Genesis envisaged as he narrated the story of Creation. The waters of the Euphrates and Tigris must have been clear of silt and agro-chemicals. Just like I did when I was a child, Adam and Eve must have fetched and drunk the waters straight from the rivers. How strange it must look to them that a few of us would only drink treated water from an equally treated bottle! When God looks at the deforested hillsides in Haiti and Kenya or the silt-laden Mississippi River, when the Source watches the species of plants and animals die from pollution, observes the poverty and hopelessness on the planet earth, when he looks into our hearts and minds, I can hear the words, "It is not good"!

During my service with the Green Belt Movement, I have learnt to recognize that Voice from the Source. It comes through the community of the living with whom I share these moments on this planet. I hear their cries and I have learnt to say to myself that I cannot stand their agony. I tell them that as long as I can I will do something for them even as I do something for myself because we are all under threat!

Therefore, I am restless! I am worried about the poverty I see, the hopelessness, the homelessness, the street children, the drugged and the alcoholics. I recognize these as symptoms of what has gone wrong with the Creation. I search for the causes. I look for solutions to these problems, and look forward to the day I shall be restful. I went to Copenhagen to look for solutions, then to Rio de Janeiro in 1992 and I was hoping that the fellowship in Johannesburg in 2002 might be better. I search without losing hope, sometimes afraid that the Source might be indifferent if the human species opts to remain ignorant and arrogant; that the Source might allow the human species to perish because of its ignorance (refer to the Book of Hosea, Chapter 10).

When I was a child, streams and rivers were clean and provided safe drinking water. Lush vegetation grew along riverbanks and bathed in the sweet waters in the streams. Rivers roared downstream and trout danced in the cold, clean and fresh streams.

Now I have my own children. In contrast, every time the rains fall, the rivers are red with the fertile topsoil. That is an indicator that something is wrong in the Ministry of Environment and Natural Resources as well as the agricultural sector: forests are being clear-cut indiscriminately upstream. Streams dry up and women walk long distances to fetch water. Rainfall patterns change and rainfall often fails. That leads to crop failure, hunger and malnutrition. Repeated cycles of this abuse to the environment produce poverty, insecurity and desperation. Can we honestly ask God to intervene, or do we write letters to the relevant ministers of government? Do we demonstrate in the streets to register our disappointment with poor governance of natural resources or do we ask the angels in Heaven to do something about it? Do we make the connection between environmental degradation and the problems which communities face every day?

When we make that connection, the God in us will move and energize us. It will guide us from apathy to action, from being observers to doers in the hope that those actions can make a difference.

That is the vision that inspired the Green Belt Movement. The Movement, in turn, gives us a forum in which to take action. In addressing the many issues and concerns tackled by the Movement at the grassroots, national and international levels, the questions which confront us both from within and without are: Why bother? What is the motivation? What inspires and sustains?

If there were easy answers to these questions, I would have packaged them and offered them for sale! There is no do-it-yourself formula! But the reasons we react in a certain way to various experiences come from the depth of our psyche, faith and personality.

In my case, the answer partly lies in my lifetime experiences not only within the Green Belt Movement but also from various education institutions of higher learning that I attended. I draw from my childhood experiences as I grew up in the rural areas, with peace and security and under the loving guardianship of my parents, one of whom was illiterate while the other could barely read and write in our mother tongue, *Gikuyu.*

A conducive environment in different schools enriched this background and I grew physically, socially, spiritually and intellectually. It was in this background and environment that the inspiration to initiate the Green Belt Movement found me. I believe that inspirations come to all of us, but if they find us unprepared, they fall on infertile ground and yield nothing. I was mostly lucky and owe it to other members of the community of living, who created the environment for my ideas to flourish. It is impossible to recall all the thoughts and feelings which are responsible for the irresistible urge to get involved in the issues, which impacted so negatively on so many people and which became the issues to be handled by the Green Belt Movement.

Sometimes I believe I plunged myself into these issues without appreciating the frustrations and the dangers these efforts expose a person to. This is probably because when the Spirit moves it is not always possible to explain why we react in a certain way. Perhaps the reactions respond to the God in all of us. This God speaks and guides us into action and in specific directions.

Besides my early experiences, my life has been influenced by the formal education I received during the early part of my life both at home and from abroad. My teachers, who were mostly foreign missionaries, were positive, self-giving and value-driven. They shared values, which shaped my psyche and personality and which later became some of the values introduced to the Green Belt members. These values include the spirit of volunteerism or service to others without expecting rewards, a deepening of self-awareness and self-worth and an appreciation for the interconnectedness of all members of the community of the living.

The privilege of a higher education, especially outside Africa, broadened my original horizon and was responsible for my deeper understanding of the linkages between the environment, governance, human and women's rights, justice and equity. It was that education which also helped me understand the value of working for the greater common good of communities so that a greater number of people benefit. Therefore, I learned to appreciate freedoms which dictators deny other citizens. I was moved to speak for those who do not have a voice, like the poor, women, children and the non-human members of the community of living, such as trees and animals. Was that not what Jesus Christ did when he confronted the mighty Roman Empire? To be His disciples in earnest is to emulate His actions, without hope of rewards. I was myself a beneficiary of common concern for others, often strangers, and, once successful, I too wanted to improve the quality of life of those I had left behind in my country in particular and in the African region in general. I was moved to do so through service to the environment. If the environment would improve in Africa, it would contribute towards an improved world environment. Many of these dreams have been realized, albeit to a lesser degree than expected due to many constraints, about which we shall not dwell.

The foreign experience deepened my spirituality, rather than my religion, and encouraged me to seek God in me and in others, rather than in buildings and in the heavens. I experienced the value of prayer, voluntary service, sharing and caring. I set out to share and serve in voluntary organizations. It took me time to appreciate the linkages between politics, governance and the issues I was dealing with. I eventually realized that unless the government, which managed the resources of the country, is transparent, accountable and responsible, there would be no change and conditions would only get worse. I realized that simply giving service and cleaning the mess behind governments, without demanding transparent and accountable governance, is not enough.

Giving alms is good, but not enough. Why can't the government promote equity and economic justice instead, so that those needing alms can become self-reliant? I also realized the need to mobilize thousands of people so that change could come faster and to more members of the community.

Most of us do not take action because we are afraid of repercussions: fear of neighbours, public opinion, authority and even friends. Therefore, we developed an empowering education programme to overcome fear. Even Jesus told his apostles, "Fear not, for I will be with you". We are not the only ones who fear!

Therefore, as His disciples, we set the example and are courageous for those who need protection, fairness, justice and peace. And lest we forget the log in our eyes, we start with ourselves: serving, standing up, empowering others and ourselves and practicing love, compassion, justice and equity . . . to be examples of what we claim the Master Himself would do.

How can one know all these things and not develop a feeling of restlessness? How can one not be bothered? How can the spirit not be moved from a state of apathy to action? And when the Spirit moved me in the early 1970's, I dreamt of an Africa that would re-discover herself, know herself and empower herself. An Africa that would appreciate herself better and seek solutions to her problems first from within herself.

The process of self-rediscovery should be enhanced by a new consciousness about the earth and the uniqueness of life on it as expressed in the Earth Charter. This growing awareness that the world is interdependent, inter-linked and a common neighbourhood should be a source of our inspiration. This awareness makes our man-made barriers and divisions irreverent and a hindrance towards appreciating other species in the chain of life.

In this we are experiencing a new global re-awakening. We should not be persuaded to believe that we are anybody's burden. We should appreciate our tenacity and the ability to have overcome the many obstacles put in our way in the course of history. We should relish the fact that a species less endowed would have become annihilated. Our life experiences from the primordial times to the present, both recorded and unwritten, should be a source of greater inspiration and empowerment. Ours has been a long journey along the millions of years we have been sharing life on this planet. Time has come to humble ourselves before the Source, The Great Creator, the God of many names. We must appreciate that all members of the community of living are important to the Source.

That is where the inspiration comes from. It is a long journey back to the Garden of Eden and, until we get back, there we must remain motivated and persevering.

When I feel alone and desperate, I ask myself, "What would Christ have done?" And the God in me answers, "Christ would never give up hope."

Therefore, my brothers and sisters, let us persevere to the end!

And the people of God said, AMEN!

SECTION II

Homilies

"We Are God's Handiwork"
The Rt. Rev. Dr. Simon E. Chiwanga

"Walk with Love and Care on God's Earth"
Archdeacon Taimalelagi Fagamalama Tuatagaloa-Matalavea

"Closing Homily and Blessing of the Participants' Commitments"
The Most Revd. Njongonkulu W. H. Ndungane

We Are God's Handiwork

—The Rt. Rev. Dr. Simon E. Chiwanga

In the Name of the Father, Son, and Holy Spirit, Amen.

I thank the Anglican Communion UN Observer, Archdeacon Faga, and her Team for inviting me to this historic Congress.

I thank Archbishop Ndungane, Bishop Geoffrey Davis and all their colleagues for their hard work to ensure the success of the Congress. My last visit to this country was in 1993, for our 11th ACC Meeting. It gives me particular pleasure to come to the new South Africa where the theme of reconciliation can be read everywhere, in the land and communities of this great country.

I bring greetings from my Diocese, my Archbishop Donald Mtetemela, and the Anglican Church of Tanzania.

I accepted this awesome honor of preaching at this Opening Eucharist service of the Congress with the understanding that I will not be expected to deliver a full-blown sermon like that I gave at the Opening Service of the 1998 Lambeth Conference or at the 73rd General Convention of the Episcopal Church of the United States in 2000.

I came here mainly to do two things. First, on behalf of the Anglican Consultative Council, and indeed on behalf of our President, the Archbishop of Canterbury, and our Secretary General, Canon John L. Peterson, to support and congratulate Archdeacon Faga and all those who got this vision and who have labored in various ways to bring this Congress into fruition. The holding of such a gathering is a clear indication of how those who initiated the idea, and you who have responded to the invitation, have taken seriously Lambeth Conference calls that it was a matter of urgency that the faithful be informed about "what is happening to our environment and to encourage them to see the stewardship of God's earth and for the care of our neighbours as a necessary part of Christian discipleship" (1988 LC).

Second, I came here to appeal to this Congress to do two things for both the participants here present and the Churches they represent. For the participants: if this Congress is intended to reach out to the WSSD Summit taking place in Johannesburg this month, it would be most helpful if participants were helped to understand what the Summit is all about. If the Congress is to be prophetic it needs to understand the context of the prophecy. I am aware that not all of us have access to modern information technology, which would easily give us the information we want. I had to struggle very hard to get even the minimum information on the Summit.

For the Churches represented, or Member Churches of the Anglican Communion: the Congress should encourage and show the way for Member Churches to take seriously environmental issues. Section 2 of Lambeth 98 observed as follows, "We therefore claim for environmental issues pre-eminence in time, energy and prayer. The matter is even more serious because of the relative lack of priority given to it at this Conference. There is little time. World governments will not prioritize these issues because of perceived political cost." Was that a reflection of the situation in dioceses back home? Is work on the environment an optional extra in the mission of the Church, and for the retired Bishops?

All of today's readings speak about the Source and Sustainer of all creation—God! "Where were you when I laid the foundations of the earth? Tell me if you have understanding." (Job 38:4). In Revelation we read, "I am Alpha and Omega." Psalm 65 acknowledges that all flesh is from God. In the Gospel, the farmers do not know how their seeds germinate and grow. Do some leaders of the world need to be reminded that "The fear of the Lord is the beginning of wisdom"?

Some of us in the Church have not fully recovered from the influence of seeing the world as secular and apart from sacred things the Church deals with. The holy monk Thomas Merton had something to say which may remind us to keep on plunging ourselves deep into the world as God's stewards. Writing on prayer and contemplation he says, "This age, which by its very nature is a time of crisis, of revolution, of struggle, calls for a special searching and questioning, which is the work of the Christian in his silence, his meditation, his prayer; for he who prays searches not only his own heart but plunges deep into the heart of the world in order to listen more intently to the deepest and most neglected voices that proceed from its most inner depths." (T. Merton, *Contemplation*. New York, Doubleday Image, 1999, p. 23).

There is a tendency at the WSSD to deal with issues of the environment and of poverty eradication or social and economic development separate from each other and from God. St Paul, in Ephesians, reminds us of the awesome task of the Church:

> Now, through the Church, the manifold wisdom of God should
> be made known to the rulers and authorities in the heavenly
> realms, according to his eternal purpose which he accomplished
> in Christ Jesus our Lord. (Eph. 3:10).

The Church needs to keep on highlighting the wisdom of God contained in the Bible:

> The earth is the Lord's, and everything in it, the world and all who live in it, for he founded it upon the seas and established it upon the waters. (Ps. 24:1).

It cannot be repeated sufficiently enough that ecological challenges are unlikely to be met satisfactorily without the moral and spiritual motivation nurtured by the churches. However, as Archbishop George Carey observed during the 1998 Lambeth Conference, "Our contribution to public debate about environmental responsibility has often been patchy and undistinguished."" In his message to this Congress, the Archbishop of Canterbury says, "By meeting immediately before the UN World Summit on Sustainable Development, your presence is an important reminder that all must take seriously the spiritual dimension to the ecological and humanitarian crises facing the planet." Therefore, this Congress has a unique opportunity to witness to the WSSD the holistic mission of God to God's world as we wrestle with interrelated and burning issues such as of the environment, poverty, HIV/AIDS, international debt, and globalization.

Another message that this Congress will convey to the world leaders is that of hope and confession that leads to ACTION. Within our readings for today we meet God's promise to "make all things new." This suggests to me that our environmental and sustainable development challenges will best be dealt with after personal transformation and return to God, and be "Doers of the Word" (James 1:22). There is need for genuine commitment to an agreed course of action, agreement reached indeed after careful and even painful debate in search for truth. The frustration comes when agreements are not honored.

Take, for example, the issues facing the WSSD. Some developed countries are reluctant to adhere to the key principle agreed upon in Rio in 1992, of Common but Differentiated Responsibilities, which is crucial for the implementation of the WSSD goals. Some developed countries want a level playing field for all, in order to strike a 'Global Deal' for sustainable development regardless of different capacities and capabilities of nations and the historical responsibility of developed countries for the current destruction of the environment and threats to sustainable development. The establishment of regional, sub-regional and national institutions for disaster management and to assist African countries to address the impacts of climate change, consistent with the provisions of the UN Framework Climate Change Convention, is another area of disagreement. Then, of course, not all parties have ratified the Kyoto Protocol so that it enters into force and leads to actions towards reducing the heat-trapping greenhouse gases, particularly by developed countries.

The means of implementation is also an area of deep divisions. This relates to issues of Finance, Trade, Technology Transfer including indigenous knowledge and intellectual property rights, Capacity Building and Education, Training and Awareness creation.

Key issues that are rejected by some developed countries, particularly the US, for inclusion in the final document of the Summit include: additional and new resources, time frames, provision of financial and technical assistance in the implementation of the outcomes of WSSD, increased Overseas Development Assistance, acceleration of HIPIC initiatives and debt cancellation. Privatization, like exclusive emphasis on domestic governance, democracy and rule of law, and domestic mobilization of resources need also to be tested against the dangers of micro-managing the internal affairs of developing countries and also avoiding the historical responsibilities of developed countries as the major cause of the current environmental degradation and the unsustainable production and consumption patterns which are threatening sustainable development.

These challenges also face churches around our Communion. The Gospel lesson compares the Kingdom of God to human agriculture. Yes, the process of sprouting, growing, and developing are mysterious; yes, "the earth produces of itself." But the parable speaks of a cooperation between the farmer and the earth. It is the farmer who scatters the seed and the farmer who goes in with his sickle in obedience.

In Tanzania, and in many other parts of Africa and the world, we need to confess our "deeds of iniquity" our selfish, short-term, unsustainable spoiling of the human-designed landscapes that sustain us. The earth does have powerful regenerative capacities, and we know God's promises to forgive our transgressions, lest these sins continue to be visited on our children, our children's children, and on our neighbor's children's children. We are co-creators with God, especially of our human-designed environment. We can be co-redemptors with God by improving these spaces, increasing the care of our stewardship—turning five talents into ten.

In my own Diocese of Mpwapwa, for example, it is drier than it used to be, just within my lifetime. I remember the plains and mountains both covered with trees, streams running well into the dry season, and no dust storms such as are common dry-season plagues these days. These things are due to local deforestation and soil erosion, or global climate changes, or some combination—who can tell?

In our cities and towns and villages, the trash is burying us. In the past, every kind of waste product was biodegradable, and so people would simply toss things away from their dwellings or burn them in trash pits. Now we have cheap plastic bags, bottles, and packaging, which degrades very, very slowly and is poisonous to burn, and glass and metal bottles, cans, caps and lids which cannot be disposed of at all.

If we succeed, all things will indeed be new. I want my youngest son, who is now fifteen, when he gets to be my age, to be able to say that he can remember a time where there were only a quarter as many trees. I want him to be able to say that this beautiful, fertile, forested land is indeed different from the way I remember it as a child. This is possible only when we move from rhetoric at Conferences to action with the poor and in God's creation.

It is my prayer that this Congress will inspire all those participating, and the Churches they represent, for more concrete action where action is most needed.

"Praise is due to you, O God, in Zion; O you who answer prayer! By awesome deeds you answer us with deliverance. The Mountains of Africa gird themselves with trees of every kind, the meadows of Europe clothe themselves with colorful flowers, and the Asian valleys deck themselves with an ever-flowing stream. The world you created and all its varied peoples shout and sing together for joy." Amen.

Walk with Love and Care on God's Earth

—Archdeacon Taimalelagi Fagamalama Tuatagaloa-Matalavea

Good morning. I am not going to preach because I am not licensed to preach! I also want to correct another myth. I am not an ordained Archdeacon. I am a lay Archdeacon, the first one in our part of the world and the first woman. I am a lay minister, though, and even my license says "Lay Minister," but this does not include preaching. You know how Anglicans are so strict about these things. So, I have said to myself that unless I have taken some theology, then I am not going to preach!

So, I will just share with you a few thoughts. Our journey this week has been so blessed. Do you agree? We have looked and marveled at the beauty of God's creation, and we have left our homes and families to come here because we are sincerely convinced about something. That is, we need to change. We need to look back and see how we can improve what has already been done by us; and then, we need to move forward to make this world a better world for our children.

About 200 years ago, some European Christians came to my country, Samoa, and called us "pagans." Many, many of the things they saw there were actually not accepted in their own European culture. In Cape Town, in 1993, during the ACC meeting—and the ACC is responsible for my being here and all of us being at this Congress—I was asked to speak on the changes I have witnessed in the Church since Christianity came to us in Samoa. So I tried to explain at the meeting that when the missionaries came, we were running around under coconut trees without wearing any-thing, because it was too hot! They came with their Bibles and all dressed, and they must have felt very hot! They said, "You go put something on, you look naked!" And now what happens? We are walking around with our Bibles, and praying, and people that come from other parts of the world feel so hot that they hardly have anything on. Now we are telling them, "Put something on!"

So, you see, I am like Paul. He seemed to understand that God made each of the peoples of the world, each nation, very different. Difference is good, and yet we are all one people, created by God. Certain ways of behavior and different styles of dress, established boundaries, may differ, but we are one people. But as I said, I am not going to interpret, because I am not licensed to interpret! Paul, though, actually understood, while the Europeans did not seem to understand. I think they did not read their Bibles!

What a wonderful thing that our God has said, as we heard on Monday from Denise Ackermann. Suffering also comes with lamenting and praises! The Book of Genesis portrays and conveys to us that there were sufferings at that time too. And the Psalms tell us to sing to the Lord, because we came out of the ark. Think about it—a lot of things came out of the ark, and, if all the animals and little insects were not in the ark, they would not be around. And we have to take care of the whole web of life that God made sure that Noah had with him in the ark.

Archdeacon Tai in a thoughtful moment.

In the Pacific, we say that we only wish Noah had swatted the mosquitoes. Some of our people cannot sleep because of the mosquitoes. Yet, they were put there for a reason so we have to make sure that they are still here with us.

Through the gospel, we are convinced about all the things we have spoken about here at the Congress. The problems that we have today are about hoarding—the hoarding of monetary and material wealth. That is what is happening in the world. It is because of this hoarding that we have the problems. As the gospel reading says, and this is almost word for word: "We should not be worrying about our clothes." I am wearing this, because I know I will be standing here, and that's the reason. In relation to food, we should not worry, because there is plenty. God actually provides this, and we are not supposed to hoard. If we do not have that *real wealth* within us, to share as much as we have of the godliness in us, then we have problems.

Yesterday, we dealt with the wealth within us; that is, the real wealth. To share what we have. Not to keep it for ourselves. We are a kind of Noah's ark in our own selves. He took care of creation, but he did not hoard it; and so, it was preserved. The web of life survived. We have everything, including the beauty, and so we must think a lot about these things, and our Bible has it all. Our Bible gives us all the directions that we need.

So what is the message for us from what we have heard, "Walk with love and care on God's earth." Walk with vital awareness of God's comprehensive mission and purpose in creation. Walk with awe and gratitude. The birds, the beasts, the trees and the rivers, the person next to you is not without purpose and meaning in God's scheme of things. The one who truly receives this cannot be alone, or powerless, or godless towards God's created world. As we said today, Christ will always give us hope and reveal what we need to do.

And I know that you will go with a lot of commitments to be blessed by the Archbishop tomorrow. Again, I think of my favorite part of Proverbs 16, where it says, and I better read from this, because I am not supposed to be saying anything without looking at the right text: "The plans of the mind belong to mortals, but the answer of the tongue is from the LORD." Then, in the third and seventh verses, "Commit your work to the LORD, and your plans will be established," and "When the ways of people please the LORD, he causes even their enemies to be at peace with them."

The human mind plans the way, but the Lord directs the steps.

Closing Homily and Blessing
of the Participants' Commitments

—THE MOST REVD. NJONGONKULU W. H. NDUNGANE

On behalf of our Province of Southern Africa, I greet you in the precious name of Our Lord and Savior Jesus Christ. I am greatly overjoyed that I can be with you at this closing Eucharist. I have come to say welcome and good-bye!

I have just returned, last night, from our AIDS ministry board meeting that was held in Nairobi, where we are continuing the process of looking at how to address this pandemic that has so tragically visited our continent.

There has been significant progress since we last met here in Johannesburg, when we convened the first All Africa AIDS Consultation to look at how we can confront this pandemic. We gave each of our Provinces and Dioceses a kind of a tool kit to deal with this pandemic at a local level. Reports that we have had from the various Provinces of our Church in Africa are very encouraging indeed. There is a report that will be presented at ACC-12, which I'm sure you will have access to, and also a statement that will be released, which in the electronic media you will be able to pick up. What's so encouraging to me is the fact that we are able to give a better capacity to the local churches to deal with this pandemic.

I'm sure that during this week, as I have listened to your deliberations here, that you will have an impact, a significant impact on the UN's agenda on sustainable development. And I just want to say to you that despite all the negative things that sometimes you may hear in the media, or whatever is said about the Anglican Communion, it is so encouraging to know the good that so many people are doing. People like yourselves, who are concerned about the well-being of humanity, people who are prepared to make a difference in other people's lives.

We need to continue to find so much of the talent and brains that we have in our Anglican Communion, and bring together all these different strands of people who are doing the good work, as in the Environmental Network that you are creating here. I recall from the days when I was at ACC, when I first met Archdeacon Matalavea, the thing that we used to notice about her was all the different kinds of colorful hats that she puts on! I was made in charge of the Anglican Networks and I used to say that I wonder whether one day I'll be entangled in these Networks and not know how to escape!

I think it's important that we not just say there is a resolution to ACC or some conference, and ask ourselves whatever we have some mechanism to make sure that things happen. I am the kind of person who likes ideas to have legs. I think that we need to be creative and strategic in dealing with these issues.

Let me share a few brief remarks. The first thing I want to say is that we are God's family, and we are inhabiting what has come to be called a "global village". On the one hand, the tragic events of September 11 have demonstrated most vividly the vulnerability of the human community in our world today. And on the other hand, it has shown us how interdependent and interconnected we are. These events have posed a single most important challenge to all us, which we have ignored at our peril, which is that we must work together for the common good of all.

Secondly, our faith teaches us how to live together in harmony in our global village. There are so many wonderful stories in the scriptures about this, but it's that beautiful vision of a new heaven and a new earth that we are told about in the Book of Revelation. This vision has already been realized in Jesus Christ who came and lived among us and who has promised that those who open their hearts to him, God the Father, God the Son, God the Holy Spirit, will come and make his home in them.

God has made us stewards of his creation with his vast and rich resources. While the work of the creative order is for our enjoyment, we must live in a balance that will guarantee the future for our children and our children's children. There is a saying that we have not inherited this world from our parents, but we've borrowed it from our children.

We should always be reminded that God has provided for our needs and not for our greed. Sustainability is not about the triumph of greed by some over the others. Sustainability means this: To each according to need and to each the gratitude to embrace life with respect and hope. Finally, we hear the God of our ancestors reminding us that we always have choice. I put before you this day life and death, so choose life, as recorded in Deuteronomy. Let us choose to move forward together, as we strive for a better world in which everyone has access to the basic resources necessary for living.

Let us choose life by making choices that do not uphold economic systems that consume our dignity. Let us journey together to create a more just world. Let us make a choice to be filled with God's grace. I'm often encouraged by the words of one Nobel Laureate who said, "We are the first generation in history, where ordinary people like you and me are taking responsibility for the well-being and the future of others". And our Lord Jesus said, "I came that you may have life and have it more abundantly." Today, let us claim; let us lay a claim to that life. AMEN.

The Blessing of the Commitments

Lord God the Almighty, we bring before you these commitments, these commitments of your children gathered here, and we ask you Lord to bless what they've committed themselves to do. Give us your grace Lord to do what is good in this world. We know that you've created us; we are your works of art, and you've created us for the good, enabling us, Lord, by your spirit and by your grace to do what is good in this world, and to forever champion making a difference. Make a difference in other people's lives, this we ask in and through the name of our Lord and Savior Jesus Christ. AMEN.

Lord God, you are the light of your world. May we stand in your light and reflect your light in this world. AMEN.

Commitment Statements from Anglican Congress Participants

As I'm the only delegate from the Diocese I am committed to give the report to my Bishop and the Mothers Union Executive Council. I will propose and encourage the different groups to take part in initiating environmental groups, which can work hand in hand with food security, which we have just started.

I will also have to invite the relevant people especially those in the Eastern Cape like Katie Davies to come and address different issues.

I will go back home, and work with the congregation, clergy and the NGO's, who have already started doing something about the whole issue of Stewardship of Creation. I will try my level best to be a good Steward of Creation. For me this Congress was and is an eye opener. I thank God that I was one of the persons to be invited to this Congress.

My commitment is to go back to Ethiopia and ensure that the building we place in Gambella uses solar power, collects rainfall and uses bio-gas for cooking. Also that the complex will include income-generation opportunities for the local population as well as training facilities for refugees in the campus. That the training will include stewardship of creation as well as Bible training and skills training.

Commitment to Act

1. To provide explicit Christian witness when dealing with environmental issues.

2. To strengthen ethical values education with which I am involved.

3. To adopt a personal lifestyle on a less consumptive level.

I commit myself to:

a. Personally doing something for a better environment through recycling, and solar energy.

b. Educating others about sustainable development.

c. Keeping issues about the environment on the agenda of committees I am involved with.

To light a candle here in South Africa at the end of the Congress and the start of the Summit, to take that candle to all dioceses in England and elsewhere in the World if possible and light it at workshops for those in the church working for the environment and others in partnership.

To search for more people-based solutions and creating opportunities for and support between people around the world.

I commit myself to a ministry of environmental justice and a sincere examination of lifestyle in light of simplicity compassion, sustainability and love.

Resolution: To continue to give enthusiastic and well-informed leadership to the Church of England, and as far as possible to work ecumenically with other Christian Churches.

In my personal life, to try to live more simply, more sustainably: to reduce my use of fossil fuels: to continue to grow my own organic vegetables and fruit: to campaign for a transformation of the world economy in ways which will be more favorable to the poor.

Psalm: 116:12

What can I offer the Lord
For all his goodness to me?
I will bring a wine-offering to the Lord,
To thank him for saving me.
In the assembly of all the people
I will give him what I have promised.

Commitment to his people sharing all the good things that I have learnt from the Congress.

To encourage environmental awareness and action from a theological perspective through speaking to others, preaching and writing in my church, diocese, province, the Anglican Communion and the church at large.

To transform my life

To work hard in my Communion

To educate and encourage action in the individual churches and dioceses around the environment

To empower people in local communities to discover, articulate and act upon their stewardship and the well being of all in their communities and their local eco-systems as well as their oneness with all humanity and care for all Creation.

During one of the workshops we were asked to write down just "one commitment", one thing we believed and brought to the Congress. . . . What I wrote was "to care for God's world so that I can share it with my children and my grandchildren."

This still remains my commitment.

To learn to live with less.

To return to study water issues in my province and country.

I believe my vocation is to make provision for the future generations—not deprivation

- putting ecological matters on the Diocesan agenda

- informing Archdeaconry structures on specific areas of concern

- drawing a viable program in which will start running within 6 months at parish level

- preach a sermon on ecology at least once in 2 months

- begin to live sacrificially personally as well as within my family

I commit to continuing my engagement with global environmental issues, as a journalist, economist and environmentalist also active at the Maltese level.

As a novice of the Third Order of the Society of St. Francis, I hope to be professed in September 2003, and to work with other Franciscans, Anglicans, Christians of other churches and peoples of faith for the restoration of the stewardship of Creation.

Things which I will do:

> There is an environment desk with the Diocese of Lesotho. Therefore my note will be to see it to it that it functions well and I will help them to form environmental groups within the Diocese.

> To form network and links with other Dioceses within CPSA and abroad.

> To encourage other organizations, institutions and churches to work together with us to avoid duplication.

> To establish a direct link with the government of Lesotho.

To encourage communities to form small and effective groups which will do conservation activities.

With God's help to start small fund raising with those communities, which will be used for among others things, training.

Directly on my return I must submit a report on the Congress to my Bishop—I will also submit a report for our Diocesan newspaper and hope to have environmental columns for ongoing issues.

Those of us from the Eastern Cape will be networking with the delegates from the Western Cape.

From what I heard from the Greenbelt Movement it sort of inspired me in many ways. I really learned a lot during this week and met different people and I know God has a purpose for me. I want to help school kids during the holidays to do something in the community or even people who don't have a job, to do handcrafts work.

I will work with YONGE NAWE (Environmental Youth Group) in sensitizing Anglicans on nature conservation involving the greater community.

I commit myself and continue to seek ways to prevent the extinction of species, with particular emphasis on primates and the prevention of their extinction.

I also commit myself to developing a Church Environmental Network for the CPSA and supporting an Anglican Communion Environmental Network.

I commit myself to reducing my own ecological footprint by trying to use less non-renewable energy and, with my family, to live a more sustainable lifestyle.

This has been the most wonderful and moving Congress that I ever attended. I have made a commitment to make people aware and to preach on the stewardship of creation. I am going to preach about this in my parish, in the archdeaconry and in the leaders meeting coming up next month. I am sure my Bishop will help me with the assistance that I will need. I am quite optimistic about making the difference and I thank God that I was able to come.

I am committed to living my own life in an environmentally sensitive way.

I am committed to leading my Diocese in an environmental program.

I am committed to a voice of prophecy in the nation.

I pledge myself to promote environmental awareness and fight environmental destruction in my country.

Produce newsletter and further aims of the network for earthkeeping Christian communities in South Africa.

I commit myself to work for the poor of the world and all species of the world and to promote global justice and ecojustice in Ireland.

I commit myself to go back and report immediately to my Bishop and Diocesan Council and call for a Diocesan Congress on Sustainable Development and hopefully to report back to the CPSA as well as the ACC.

I believe that is my obligation to make myself part of Environmental Education as Steward of the Creation—God's Creation

What I will do first when I get back to my Diocese is a report to the Bishop; and with him convene the meeting with my fellow priests—first in my archdeaconry.

Now as a team, we shall take the matter to the clergy conference in October. From there, I think it would be wise to teach our congregations about development especially on "Sustainable Development" as I have learnt.

I would like to monitor this until I become convinced that the communities around my place are involved to the extent that the whole country gets involved.

This will be done continuously by holding workshops when and wherever possible. We (priests) of the Diocese will share this ministry with volunteers and some committees formed in local communities.

I am going back to Uganda with a great zeal to do something on the environment for our people.

I will prayerfully endeavor to understand the mission activity of ECUSA in light of environmental problems, and to be a voice for the greening of all our international projects.

1. I write a weekly article for the Daily Observer, so I will endeavor to use the medium to open the eyes of the readers on the Stewardship of Creation.

2. I will include in the Curriculum for the Supplemental Ministerial Programme, the Stewardship of Creation.

3. Since I am the Coordinator for the radio programme, "Issues in the News"—Jamaica Council of Churches; I will place the theology of Creation on the topic of discussion.

4. I will include the "Stewardship of Creation" in the St. Mary's Radio programme.

5. Because I am a postulant in the third order of St. Francis who is for creation, my spiritual formation will be enhanced.

6. I will become more active in the community education programme that is linked to the National Environmental Protection Agency (NEPA), Jamaica.

7. I have been asked to lecture on "Creation Spirituality" in the Diocese of Jamaica, and the Cayman Islands and I intend to intensify the awareness of the Stewardship of Creation not only in the Anglican Communion but also in the Ecumenical circles.

8. The Catechism does include the awareness of creation and so the local churches must be conscientisied in the Stewardship of Creation.

9. The Jamaican government has passed laws to protect all endangered species (animals, birds, etc.) and the penalties which have been linked to any person who does an illegal act. The church will support this work of the government.

I have no idea, as yet, to what is God's plan for me, so I can't commit into my future life other than to say that where possible I will stand up and represent my church on issues of the environment. Furthermore, I will support any programmes especially involving the environment which occur in my diocese. Hopefully we may come from here as environmental evangelists, preaching God within creation and the importance of our environment even within our faith.

Working for a just society with special focus on grassroots communities. Eco and Gender justice are special interest areas.

In August 2002 I will be one of the leaders at a workshop to begin developing an environmental policy for the Church in Wales. I will be reporting on the Congress to this workshop and to a meeting of the Provincial governing body in September 2002. In both occasions I will be pressing for more action on the Stewardship of the natural environment by all Christians and the important part to be played in this field by Christian values.

In a moving spirit, I commit myself as a Steward of God's Creation to bring in new awareness of sacredness of one environment at home, at chapel, at church parish and community.

1. To teach and guide the children and women in rural areas.

2. To assist the congregations in South India to be the stewards of creation.

3. To establish an Environment Resource Centre in each Diocese in South India.

4. To network with others for Global, National and Regional input.

- To make a sustained effort to improve the common people in our country, teaching the people to obtain the basic needs of life, like education, health and nutrition, clothing etc. and to establish fundamental rights in society.

- To encourage the spirit of self-reliance among the disadvantaged, under privileged and deprived people of society.

- To improve human dignity to create awareness and social justice in society and to motivate the common people in practicing and sharing and joys of the common people.

- To preserve a pure and healthy environment and ensure the proper use of natural and human resources.

- To practice a participatory development ideology throughout the organisation and preserve the values and dignity of all walks of people.

My commitment to following up on the Global Anglican Congress is to:

1. Write articles about this event that will help tell the story of the Congress to tens of thousands of Anglicans in North America, and other parts of the world.

2. Help publish articles by Congress participants on our web site—www.thewitness.org—to highlight different perspectives on the Congress and the WSSD.

3. Participate in educational forums, activist events, and follow-up networks over the coming months to keep the focus of the people of faith in the US religious community on the issues of the WSSD.

This Anglican Congress on the Stewardship of Creation has strengthened my commitment and inspired me to do more action in the area of environmental regeneration, especially awareness creation.

Plenary Panelists discussing food and agriculture.

Participants on a nature walk at the reserve.

Leaving the Pleanary for worship at the retreat center chapel.

SECTION III

Provincial and Country Reports Submitted by Provincial Delegates

Church of Aotearoa, New Zealand and Polynesia
Church of Bangladesh
Church of Burundi
Church of Canada
Church of England
Church of Ireland
Church of North India
Church of Scotland
Church of the Province of Southern Africa (CPSA)
Church in Wales
Church of the West Indies
Episcopal Church in the United States of America

Provincial and Country Reports

Church of Aotearoa, New Zealand and Polynesia

Submitted by Gerald Billings

In Fiji, the well-being of indigenous coastal communities is directly dependent upon the health of coral reef ecosystems.

Coral reefs are vital providers of protein-rich food for island communities while providing needed income in the form of fisheries and tourism-related resources. Unfortunately, there has been an increasing decline in our coral reefs and its resources, brought about by human activities and increasing development pressures.

Fiji is currently the source of 81% of the global trade in corals, with Fijian villages removing over 293,000 kg of live coral per year from what was pristine reef. Live rocks (reef rocks) for use in the aquarium trade are also being exported at the rate of 1,500,000 kg/year.

Deforestation is another problem that is contributing to the destruction of the marine environment. Mud from deforestation has been smothering corals and marine life when brought down by heavy rains and flooding.

A common fishing practice here in Fiji is the use of dynamite for fishing. This practice is a serious problem. The region not only kills and crushes corals, but also leaves behind extensive areas of unstable rubble that does not favor natural coral reef recovery processes.

As a result of these non-sustainable activities and other negative environmental impacts, the Natural Oceanic and Atmospheric Administration (NOAA) recently stated that, the social, cultural, and economic prosperity of the Pacific Islands region is at risk of collapsing as a result of the decline of coral reefs. The Governments of Fiji and neighboring Pacific Island countries are aware of the negative environmental impacts occurring in the region and are now looking at addressing these problems through the promotion of sustainable livelihoods for communities facing these problems. Much effort is now being directed to local communities to assist them in drawing up of management plans for their respective fishing right areas. These plans include the establishment of marine protected areas (MPAs), the re-stocking of important marine resources, waste-management measures, and economic incentives such as eco-tourism.

Church of Bangladesh

Submitted by Davis Lalmohon Mazumder

Disaster and poverty are everywhere in Bangladesh. Over 120 million people live in this country, making it among the nations with the highest population densities. Most of her people are well below the poverty line. The average person earns US$260 per year. One in five people living in cities has no access to sanitation.

For every five children, there is too little food to grow healthily. Only 38 percent of the population can read and write. Over three quarters live in the rural areas, yet half own very little land (less than one fifth of an acre), and one fifth has no land at all. Some work as day laborers for rich people; most make up the bulk of "floating people", the poorest of the poor who sleep, eat and die on the railway platforms, street corners and in the slums. This is the scenario of Bangladesh. This is not a good statistic. It has many causes. Disaster is one of them.

Save nature to save the mankind—such a strong and convincing slogan to be carried out by both the Government and Non-Government agencies all over the world. It is true that humankind was brought up by nature. With intelligence and cleverness, humankind has grown up as the supreme living being in the world. It is well known and accepted that in the beginning God created heaven and earth. He made man the manager of the earth to keep it, maintain it, and get all his food from it. Anthropologists have proved that plants were the first existence of life on earth. Human lives have come much later. Soon they were misguided by their own interest. In search of a luxurious life, they started destroying nature; their greediness did not save the trees, birds and wildlife. The negative results soon started appearing with rapid urbanization, deforestation, and depletion of the ozone layer, mismanagement of water resources.

Mother Earth became hotter, and, at the same time, air became polluted and rainfall decreased. So-called material development at the expense of the environment had invited severe drought in many parts of the world. The inhabitants cried for a drop of fresh water and a cold shower of rain. Drought is not a natural calamity but a human-induced disaster, which is the negative result of a series of misuses and mismanagement of water.

The recently compiled environment sustainability index, propounded by international experts and discussed at the World Economic Forum meeting in Davos, has declared Bangladesh one of ten countries that rank as among the worst in environmental degradation. Air quality has seriously deteriorated.

Recently, an expert of the World Bank also labeled the quality of the air and water as the worst, while the quality of air is worsening. The other immediate vital necessity of life, water, is also causing many worries for us. Bangladesh is a land of rivers; the abundance of water has been an important resource. It is quite strange to think that with so much water that the lack of safe drinking water should become a major concern today.

Many people have already lost their lives. Worse still is the fact that the exact number of casualties will not be known for many years because arsenic contamination has long-drawn effects on the human body and it is widely known as a silent and slow killer.

The arsenic contamination in ground water is spreading in Bangladesh. This has been noted since 1996, when the first group of patients was identified as suffering from arsenic poisoning. The number of victims and the affected has been increasing every year. Arsenic contamination of tube well water is threatening the health of rural areas, propelling the trend of migration to urban areas.

One of the remedies for environmental imbalance is forestry, and in Bangladesh it is needed very much. The condition is dismal. We need at least 25 percent forest area for proper climate and atmospheric conditions. At present, we have only 18 percent of forestland, and the land area under the canopy of forests is comparatively very low. Economic growth and social development largely depend on maintaining the equilibrium of various environmental resources, such as air, water and forests in their proper quantity. Degradation of any of these is important and provides irreparable impact on sustainable human development. Management of these resources needs a practical approach that is related to their carrying capacities. Poor management and over-exploitation will certainly cause greater disaster.

In view of the above situation, the NGOs and the Government have undertaken a necessary and effective action plan on environmental programs. They want to achieve greater awareness and an education program to meet the silent crisis for its people, in both urban and rural areas at the grassroots level. We have to react to the situation surrounding us. It is our social responsibility to take necessary and effective action to fulfill the desired national objective as supplementary support.

Church of Bangladesh Social Development Programs (CBSDP)

The environmental development program is an integrated rural development intervention being implemented by the Church of Bangladesh Social Development Programs (CBSDP) in very underdeveloped and poor villages in respective parts of Bangladesh. CBSDP merged these programs with conventional development approaches to sustain other development initiatives. The environment promotion program is based on the acknowledgment of the symbiotic relationship between people and the environment. Through Eco-Agriculture and Social Forestry Programs of the CBSDP, rural communities are enabled to internalize these relationships and empowered to maintain the factors that immediately affect their quality of life. CBSDP has carefully revised and re-designed the programs with an emphasis on arsenic-free drinking water and sanitation, along with set-up nurseries and social forestry, to regain its ecological balance and sustainable development.

Church of Burundi

Submitted by The Rt. Rev. John Wesley Nduwayo

The National Context

Since 1993, Burundi has continued to experience one of its worst socio-political crises in which hundreds of thousands of innocent people have lost their lives. 500,000 people fled the country as refugees, and 730,000 are estimated to live in precarious conditions in displaced camps inside the country. These people will need to be repatriated and rehabilitated. Thousands of refugees from Tanzania have already started coming on their own.

Today most of the population suffers from a lack of sufficient food and other necessities of life. The gross domestic product has cumulatively decreased by almost 20% between 1993 and 1998. Income per capita has declined from $188 in 1993 to $123 in 1997, making Burundi the lowest ranking country in the world.

The humanitarian development indicator has declined from 38.21% in 1993 to 32.12% in 1999. The percentage of those living under the poverty line has increased from 39.64% in 1993 to 57.49% in 1999. External aid has gone down from US$228 million in 1993 to US$39 million in 1999.

The health indicators show a significant decline between 1993 and 1999. Life expectancy has been curtailed by two years. Immunization coverage dropped from 83% to 54%. The malnutrition rate among children under five years old rose from 6% to 20%. It should also be noted that even adults became the victims of malnutrition to the extent of losing their lives. Infant mortality increased by 25%, while HIV/AIDS prevalence is in rapid progression.

In the education sector, the gross rate of enrollment has gone down by nearly 40% in just over four years. Among the 1,485 schools, 105 were completely destroyed; 376 were damaged and pillaged. Available teachers are concentrated in eight out of sixteen provinces. In secondary and primary schools, almost 70% of teachers are not qualified. This crisis has resulted in massive illiteracy and infrastructure deterioration. Hence, because the government is unable to care for and look after all the schools, it is now handing back the church schools to the Church, despite the deteriorating situation those schools are in.

We have noted the effort of the government to try to overcome all those challenges and problems. It has initiated a politics of national reconciliation with the political situation. Prospects for peace do exist.

The peace and reconciliation agreement of August 2000 has hit major obstacles in implementation because of the lack of a cease-fire between the rebels and the government army. Without peace, good leadership in Burundi cannot bring about durable socioeconomic development.

We pray that God will restore peace in Burundi, in the Great Lakes Region, and in the whole world.

Ecological Situation in Burundi

The necessity of granting first place to production, and putting into place some infrastructure which support it, remains crucial to meeting the immediate needs of the population. Our first necessity should be to put production into place, with an infrastructure that supports it. This production and infrastructure will have an immediate positive effect on the population.

However, this imperative of the policy of development has a big impact on the environment. For instance, in the agro-sylvo-zootechnic sector, the population increase and the crisis, which began in Burundi in 1993, have handicapped the ecological balance because of an excessive clearing of trees. Because of the extension of the cultivated lands at the expense of the natural and artificial formations, these are over-consumed and erosion results.

Likewise, cash crops such as cotton and tea have contributed to the destruction of the natural reserves. For instance, the Euphorbia Dawei of Gatungura Forest has been destroyed in order to plant cotton. The forest of Kigwena has been damaged in order to plant palm trees. The Kibira forest has been partly destroyed for a tea plantation.

As a consequence, we now experience the erosion of soil, floods, the disappearance of bio-diversity. Local climate change, characterized by a long period of lack of rain, causes drought and desertification.

In the craftsman's trade industry sector, the uncontrolled use of raw materials such as clay, soil, and gravel has contributed to the deterioration of the soil. Although the industry sector in Burundi is not very developed, the concentration of factories near Lake Tanganyika could cause a risk of water pollution if appropriate decisions are not taken. Fortunately, a big action has been planned through regional organizations such as "Fight against pollution and other means for protection of the bio-diversity of the Lake Tanganyika." In the energy and mines sector, wood occupies a dominant place. However, its excessive usage is a threat to the ecological balance.

Putting in place infrastructures to produce electric energy has been also a cause a degradation of the environment. For instance, the dam of Rwegura has caused a decrease in oxygen in Gitenge River. The extraction of gold mines in some regions has been the cause of considerable environmental deterioration.

In the sector of roads and habitat, poor strategies and a lack of maintenance of infrastructures brings about negative effects on the environment. Erosion is due to the destabilization of slopes and mountains, along with the concentration of streaming water. In the domain of habitat, environmental problems are linked to those constructions. The extraction of clay, the consumption of wood for backing bricks and the effects of flowing water are also causes of erosion.

Current Situation in Burundi

Uncertainty and distress due to attacks of FDD and FNL rebels mark the current sociopolitical situation in Burundi. These days the FDD rebels have intensified their attacks in Burundi from the Republic of Tanzania. They kill innocent people with bombs, landmines, and bullets. They are destroying the public infrastructures such as hospitals, schools, factories, etc. throughout the country. National and artificial forests are burnt. The actual killings and war in Burundi have no justification after the Arusha peace agreement of August 2000. We appeal to those rebels to join other Burundians (Hutu and Tutsi) in restoring peace. The war itself is not a solution to our problems because it kills people and destroys their properties.

This situation is worsened by the social situation, characterized by poverty, diseases and many other life-threatening issues. We assist today the strike of teachers because of their low pay. Diseases like AIDS, cholera, meningitis and malaria are devastating the country. It is not easy to assist all the people who are suffering during the time of war.

We suggest that both sides cease fire and begin peace talks. We thank His Excellency Nelson Mandela for his tremendous effort to reconcile Burundians. We thank and strongly support the Vice-President of South Africa, Mr. Jacob Zuma, for his efforts to end the war in Burundi.

We also suggest an establishment of a neutral peacekeeping force between Tanzania and Burundi in order to avoid suspicion between the two countries.

We recommend an immediate cease-fire between the rebels and the Burundi government army, in order to begin the peace talks. People are suffering too much because of the atrocities caused by the fighters. Urgent aid is greatly needed in Burundi.

Church of Canada

Submitted by The Rev. Canon Kenneth J. Gray

Situated at the north end of the Americas, Canada is a land rich in natural resources. Our vast land encompasses coastal rain forests, Arctic tundra, prairies, mountain ranges, a polar icecap, huge and long bodies of inland water and for the most part, clean and life-giving air.

While most Canadians live within 100 km of the Canada-United States Border, our seemingly "empty" topography contributes wood for construction, power for consumption, food for the mouth, and water with wine for the stomach (1 Tim 5:23). For Canadians, if the earth is the Lord's and we are stewards, our stewardship is of plenty.

At a very basic level, we are called to share these resources with each other and with the global community. Increasing liberalization of trade laws—and the ever-growing presence of transnational corporations, which exert tremendous pressure on federal and provincial governments—means that any sharing must(!) include a profit component. The negotiation (or re-negotiation) of international trade agreements, in particular the North American Free Trade Agreement (NAFTA) and the General Agreement on Tariffs and Trade (GATT), means that more resources and services currently within the realm of Canada are becoming available for export or are subject to outside influence.

While there is much insecurity about such economic incursions, which may limit sovereignty, many middle-class Canadians demand a good return on their investments. They seek to balance personal gain against social responsibility. Indeed this struggle between the personal and the social is discovered time and again as the notion of the "commons" or the "common good" is all but absent in Canadian political and social discourse. We are a nation of autonomous individuals, or at least we act like it most of the time.

Resource sectors most vulnerable to rapid exploitation and exhaustion include: (1) water, where bulk export for human consumption or power generation results in depletion of aquifers and river habitat, (2) the bulk export of raw logs which further erodes ancient and newer growth forests—even when properly replanted the result is a loss of biodiversity, and (3) the continuing depletion of fish stocks on both East and West coasts.

Pollution in the industrialized south, especially in the Ontario-Quebec corridor, results in acid rain, smog, and haze. To some degree the government of Canada supports the Kyoto Protocol, but the federal environment minister has only limited influence at the Cabinet table and the government is slow to admit our own poor performance in relation to these meager standards.

The safety of Canadian drinking water has recently been called into question through crises at Wakerton, Ontario and N. Battleford, Saskatchewan and in other local communities. There is also increasing anxiety about food. The development of genetically modified organisms and their use in food production, the labeling of same, and support for the organic farming sector have become increasingly controversial.

Finally, the greatest victims of resource development are those who speak most profoundly and affectionately of the earth itself, our first nations. The most pressing issue for First Nations is justice in land issues. My own province of British Columbia resembles South Africa as we together face a complicated future in negotiating the just redistribution of the land.

Join with organizations in and outside the institutional church. Explain globalization, its advantages and potential exploitative tendencies to Canadians. We must live with globalization; it will not go away, but Canadians risk losing much in the name of profit. Economic research could reframe expectation and anticipation of profit by broadening terms of reference for global cooperation to include social consequence alongside corporate gain.

A new critique of technology could pose helpful questions about the appropriate use of technology. Just because we "can" do it does not mean we should. Issues such as the "precautionary principle" need more elucidation, especially in relation to the burgeoning biotech industry. The concept of "caution" itself seems absent in relation to conclusions about global warming and climate change. The twentieth century clearly showed that we could abuse our resources, sometimes irreversibly—for example, by depleting our forests. We now risk doing the same with water resources.

We could help the global community appreciate the wonder and God-given gift of the "global commons"; we would clearly show how access to the commons of air, water, and land affect the quality of life not only of the planet but also of its inhabitants. We have much to learn from our Mennonite brothers and sisters.

It is time to reconsider the history of our culture, noting especially its anthropocentric prejudices where humanity has thought more of itself than it ought. Indeed, the creation can live without us but we cannot live without the creation. A rethinking of spirituality incorporating the so-called "new cosmology" will greatly aid us in this regard.

Church of England

England contributes, like all industrialized countries, to problems of climate change, pollution, soil erosion threats to species and other harmful factors. However, because most of its citizens are protected from the consequences of these factors, there is little incentive to adopt a more restrained and measured lifestyles. We have had a share of natural and man-made disasters, including flooding, coastal erosion, depleted fish stocks, outbreaks of viral diseases amongst farm animals, to name a few. These events have been met with initial predictions of an impending apocalypse, followed by a collective amnesia. The suffering from these events is real, particularly amongst farmers; however, it tends to be local and in pockets, so the sense of a nationwide responsibility for harm is not maintained. Most people are enjoying higher economic standards than ever before, and they do enjoy their comfort, even though there is more and deeper poverty too. The Welfare State ameliorates the full harshness of the economic divide, allowing those who are really poor to survive, just about, and those who are rich to avoid too much guilt.

Our Prime Minister, Tony Blair, made an excellent speech about the environment in October 2000. He indicated that our present government understands exactly what the problems are and what needs to be done. It has introduced a number of measures to encourage people to reduce emissions, deal with waste, and save energy, as well as increase public understanding of the need to take these steps. However, the incentives are not great. The perpetrators do not feel the penalties for pollution and waste, and the attempts to educate the public seem only to be reaching those who are already converted. People in general are too comfortable to call upon their government to force them to change their lifestyles, and a democratically elected government cannot move too far ahead of public opinion, however much it might want to. Overall, one senses that there is no serious questioning of unrestrained growth.

For example, recently there have been proposals to build several new airports because the demand for air travel is growing exponentially. The demand creates the supply, and the average citizen of this country is still very demanding. Moreover, there is an economic incentive to feed the growth, on the grounds that if additional air space is not provided in this country, it will be elsewhere. The people feel they will lose an important market. International agreements, therefore, are crucial to reducing demand-led growth.

There are more nuanced problems with addressing environmental concerns as well. For example, attempts to introduce alternative energy sources through large windpower farms have produced one environmental good but two bads, namely the aesthetic ruin of landscapes and the disruption of eco-systems. Our experience with windpower indicates that alternative energy strategies would be more successful if they focused on solar power and photovoltaics.

Our lifestyle is not only determined by the desire to consume more. It is also governed by an economy, both individually and nationally, that serves the "bottom line", that is, profit earnings, dividends and the share price (which is the assessed present value of those dividends). The dramatic effect of this is accountancy fraud, to con the markets that profit exists where it doesn't. Even where profits do exist, getting those profits (which is unearned income) puts pressure on wages (which is earned income) leading to lower earnings with increased fear of redundancy and lower earnings. People who are employed find they have to work harder, and longer, than ever before. This has an effect on families, as parents find they cannot give the time and attention that is needed or they would like to give to their offspring. Individuals and families might have been happy to use public transport, not keep a car, walk rather than drive, buy or even grow local food, and generally live in a measured, steady and sustainable way. But the working environment is too fast and too furious, and time has become a precious commodity. Hence, although standards of living have never been higher for so many people, our quality of life is not good and people are showing the symptoms in contracting diseases that reflect this, such as: cancer, heart disease, obesity, diabetes, and ulcers. Meanwhile, those who are out of the economic loop have nothing to do. Any innate talents and skills go unrecognized and unused. They may have time to choose alternative lifestyles but will not, on the whole, be able to afford them.

Many, many individuals recognize that this situation is not sustainable, including many within the Churches and other faiths. Despite the economic chips being stacked against them, they do try to live more simply so that others may simply live. But this can become another time-consuming burden, and create disenchantment and resentment. If it is not economically rewarding to live a simple and undemanding lifestyle, it is not sustainable to do so. Nevertheless many try, and the Church has played its part in supporting such efforts, as well as engaging nationally and internationally with attempts to change minds and hearts towards sustainability. We have a number of Christian environment and development organizations working hard in these areas. In the Church of England, our bishops, notably the Bishop of Hereford, who is our spokesperson on the environment, engage with government and others to encourage change. In each diocese, there are officers dedicated to working on environment and development issues—not always together!—and at local level we have a number of parishes that have taken up some environment or development work, as a Parish Pump with the Conservation Foundation, with the Ecocongregation project, or in other programs.

Church of Ireland

Ireland is a part of the rich North and, as the recent WWF report shows, is living unsustainably, both economically and ecologically. Below is a series of snapshots to illustrate some of the problems of "sustainable development" in an affluent society, from the Irish experience. The "plastax" and the European Geoparks Network demonstrate that there is support for conservation and sustainable living, but economic growth undoes the good of such measures.

Economy and Society

Ireland has a total area of about 83,000 sq. kms. and a total population of 5.5 million, 3.8 million in the Irish Republic and 1.7 million in Northern Ireland, part of the United Kingdom. Both parts have experienced rapid economic growth in recent years. In the period of 1995 to 2000, Gross Domestic Product per capita in the Republic grew by 80 percent, earning the country the title "the Celtic Tiger". As a result, however, it now has the widest gap between rich and poor in the European Union. A by-product of prosperity in the Republic has been a reduction in emigration and an increase in immigration: racism is now part of the Irish picture. The "peace dividend" in the late 1990's brought similar prosperity to Northern Ireland. Average annual earnings in both jurisdictions are about US$27,000.

Agriculture

Although economic growth has reduced dependence on agriculture, this form of land use remains economically and socially important in both jurisdictions. Most important is the farming of beef cattle, dairy cattle and sheep. The rural economy has suffered in recent years from the indirect effects of animal diseases in Britain such as mad cow disease (BSE) and foot-and-mouth disease. Because both the United Kingdom and the Irish Republic are members of the European Union, the agricultural policy follows the European Common Agricultural Policy, which currently subsidizes food production rather than ecological conservation.

Energy

To reduce carbon emissions, small windfarms already exist. Larger ones are planned but face objections because of their "visual intrusiveness".

Transport

In the Republic, rapid economic growth has led to an expansion of car ownership and the road-building program. Fifty percent of people travel to work by car, of which 75 percent travel alone. Only 20 percent walk or use public transport.

Reuse and recycling of materials

Earlier this year the Irish government introduced the "plastax"—a tax on disposable plastic bags formerly given away in shops and supermarkets. This tax has led a 90 percent reduction in the use of these bags. Otherwise, the recycling of clothing, glass bottles, aluminum and steel cans, paper and plastics is voluntary at central locations. Half of house-holds claim to recycle something; many of those who do not claim it cite lack of facilities.

European Geoparks Network

EGN, similar to the World Heritage Site status, is designed to protect areas of special ecological or geological interest as well as to promote sus-tainable economic development. Recently, two areas were admitted to the EGN: in Northern Ireland: the Cuilcagh Mountain Park and the Marble Arch Caves Preserve, a rare blanket bog above part of a notable Karst region. Both are of international importance. The cave is open to the pub-lic and provides sustainable employment in a rural area. This is the first EGN designation in the United Kingdom. The first site in the Republic to receive EGN status was the "Copper Coast" of County Waterford.

Religion

The whole island has been predominantly Roman Catholic since the Reformation. The recent economic and social changes, combined with the exposure of several cases of pedophilia by Irish Roman Catholic priests, have seriously weakened religious adherence and belief, especially among the young. In Northern Ireland, the weakening of religion has fed political extremism in both communities. The (Anglican) Church of Ireland in both North and South continues to decline numerically but has a strong concern for global issue of social justice. Ecological issues do not yet figure on its agenda. Historically, all Irish churches have distinguished records of sending missionaries overseas and this continues.

Church of North India

Statement of the three-day National Seminar on "Dams and the People" held at The Ecumenical Christian Center, Bangalore, 15–17 March 2002

The National Seminar on "Dams and the People" was organized by the Ecumenical Christian Center in Bangalore, and attended by thirty-seven participants representing various Universities, NGOs, People's Movements, Colleges, Churches, Social Science Institutes and the Media. The delib-erations were on the following topics:

- Sharing of water

- Inter-state relations

- Problems of displaced people in the irrigated areas

- Large dams

- Impact on ecology and environment

- Alternatives to large dams, and rehabilitation issues; along with the dam seismic effect

According to official estimates, more than 100 million people have been displaced due to development projects around the world over the past decade. The international dam industry itself has displaced, over the last fifty years, over thirty million people. It is not well known that India has one of the highest rates of development-induced displacement in the world. During the last fifty years, some 3,330 big dams have been constructed in India. Many of them have led to the large-scale forced eviction of vulnerable groups. The situation of the tribal people is of special concern, as they constitute 40-50 percent of the displaced population. As a result of misguided policy, project-affected communities have been subject to sudden eviction, lack of information, failure to prepare rehabilitation plans, low compensation, loss of assets and livelihoods, traumatic relocation, destruction of community bonds, discrimination and impoverishment.

There are no official statistics on the numbers of people displaced by large projects since independence. According to official figures in 1994, there were about 15.5 million internally displaced people in India, and the government acknowledged that some 11.5 million were awaiting rehabilitation. However, calculations based on the number of dams constructed since independence indicate that as many as 21 to 33 million persons are likely to have been displaced. These estimates do not include persons displaced by canals or by the construction of colonies or other infrastructure. Neither do they include those who have been subjected to multiple displacements.

It is widely accepted that the forced displacement has adverse impact on the affected population. It creates a condition of homelessness, landlessness, joblessness and food insecurity, along with severe environmental imbalances and disruption of ecosystems. This miserable state of affairs is due to the present pattern of development that considers displacement as an inevitable part of development. Thus it is high time to think about alternatives.

Alternatives to major dams (namely minor irrigation projects, check dams, tank irrigation, ground water enrichment and use, rain water harvesting, drip irrigation contour bonding structures, sub-surface dyes and medium irrigation projects) should be worked out as strategies for better irrigation management. We can have hydro projects based on waves and solar energy that can be depended upon. We urge the following:

- The right to information regarding the projects at all the stages is ensured, as it raises issues concerning violation of human rights.

- The planning and implementation of dams should be in consultation with the people affected, as they are the would-be victims.

- Multiple displacement that further marginalizes the affected population should be avoided at any cost.

- Strict stage-wise monitoring of the projects is essential to avoid cost and time escalations.

- It is identified that women and children among the displaced families suffer the most. Hence their issues should be given special attention.

- Rehabilitation should be a right of the affected population and should be provided even before the beginning of the project.

- The affected population should be provided with adequate compensation to the assets lost.

- The affected population should be the first beneficiaries of the project. Providing the land in the command area itself can do this. Thus they can be "project benefited people", instead of project affected

- No reliable database is available regarding numbers of displaced, project-affected people, as well as details on rehabilitation. A strong and reliable database is required for policy implementation and for the use of people concerned.

- A National Policy on Resettlement and Rehabilitation of people displaced by dams should be formulated. A National Commission on Dams is also suggested, comprising representatives from affected populations, NGOs, social scientists, and Government officials.

- Ensuring accountability to the affected people should legitimately authorize the irrigation works.

- The ecological issues raised in the construction of big dams can be addressed to the global community. They are now committed to sustainable development.

- The question of the transfer of technology from the developed countries, through the umbrella of the multinational corporations (MNCs), is an important one. The developing/underdeveloped countries are also a matter of concern as transfer of technology also involves the transfer of culture. The host country will have to pay the price because it supports neo-colonialism at an ideological level and technical know-how.

We cannot fail to take steps to protect and assist the displaced and prevent others from doing so.

Statement Committee

Dr. M. S. Dhadave (Chairman), Dr. B. C. Barik, Mr. Anil Thomas, Mr. R. S. Mangaleker, Mr. Prakash Pillai, Mr. Siby Tharakan (Convener)

Church of Scotland

The Condition of Life in Scotland: Political, Socio-Economic, Spiritual and Environmental

In global terms, Scotland is a wealthy nation supporting a population of five million who are generally well-educated, enjoy a high standard of living and live in an environment which contains many areas of outstanding natural beauty. However, that statement masks great regional and local contrasts in wealth, education, quality of life and physical setting. Those contrasts have become sharper over the last twenty years.

Politics and Governance

The single most important development in the life of the Scottish people in recent years has been the restoration of the Scottish Parliament in 1999 and the experience of devolved government. For the first time since 1707, MPs sitting in Edinburgh determine how the nation is governed in terms of its education, health, housing, transports, the environment, planning and economic development. This is a bold constitutional experiment (unique in recent British history) in which each nation making up the United Kingdom is incrementally being allowed to govern itself in terms of "home affairs". Already there are changes in key areas such as care for the elderly and student support at the universities. Scotland is moving in a different direction from the rest of the United Kingdom. In part, this reflects a greater emphasis on collective responsibility, which has tended to undermine social and economic policy in Scotland. Whether this constitutional experiment will succeed is still unclear, but three years on there is still a palpable sense of pride in having the nation's Parliament restored.

Socio-Economic Conditions, Health and Standards of Living

One of the key challenges facing the new Parliament is to reduce the great inequalities that still exist across much of Scotland. Within the last ten years, all four major cities (Edinburgh, Glasgow, Aberdeen and Dundee) have witnessed major building programs revitalizing the city centers (especially as places of conspicuous consumption) and extending the wealthy suburbs. Over the same period, heavy industry has virtually vanished from these cities leaving behind pockets of poor-quality housing, ill health, poverty, low educational levels and high unemployment. While numerous government initiatives seek to promote new jobs, improve the housing stock and provide opportunities for work and training, the gap between the wealthiest 10 percent and the poorest 10 percent is only slowly being reduced.

This issue is not exclusive to the cities. Many rural areas also experience social deprivation due to low wages, isolation, poor public transport, and lack of communal facilities. Some of the most impoverished people in Scotland live in landscapes that rich tourists travel half the world to see.

Another area where the gap between rich and poor is acute is health. Working-class areas within Glasgow report some of the worst dental health in the developed world and exceptionally high death rates from heart disease and lung cancer. By contrast, the life expectancy of the wealthy middle classes continues to rise, reflecting their investment in a better diet, better medical services and education. Alcohol and drug abuse, traditionally associated with poverty and deprivation, is increasingly linked with the hedonistic lifestyles of the young and affluent. Both rich and poor suffer the health impacts of such excesses.

Government policy over the last five years has stressed the need for social inclusion and narrowing the gap between "the haves" and the "have-nots". Some successes have been registered in improved public housing, reduced levels of unemployment and over half of all 18-year-olds going on to higher education. Social Inclusion Partnerships in urban areas have also enabled community groups to draw upon government money to resource locally. Identified priorities are in areas such as childcare, nutrition, and family support, training opportunities and community development. Success is scattered and piecemeal, but communities and individuals are displaying increased self-esteem and confidence as a result of these initiatives. The challenge for the future is to build on these successes.

Conspicuous Consumption, Material Wealth and Spirituality

The majority of Scots are now materially better off than they have ever been. Much of this is based on a lengthy consumer boom during the 1990's in which material needs were readily met in terms of household appliances, videos, DVDs and mobile phones. Disposable income is increasingly used to support conspicuous consumption: keeping up with the latest fashions in clothing (especially amongst 15-25-year-olds) and satisfying leisure needs with costly holidays, entertaining and drinking. This is strongly linked with the cult of the individual and the promotion of celebrity by the popular media. By contrast, the traditional values of solidarity in the work place, communal identity and the importance of social occasions where one lives are being eroded.

Surveys often point to a continued belief in God, coupled with increasing indifference to the role of the churches. Over the last twenty years all the major denominations, have seen a steady decline, especially severe for the Church of Scotland (the established church) and the Roman

Catholics. The Scottish Episcopal Church has experienced a lesser decline in absolute terms (now around 40,000 members) but is increasingly absent from inner city areas and is declining in many thinly populated rural areas. Ecumenism is still viewed with suspicion (largely due to embedded historical stereotypes) but a United Church in Scotland could emerge within the next decade or so. House Churches and theologically conservative denominations appear to be reversing this trend with informal worship coupled with "biblically-based" teaching. This is proving very attractive especially to the young and affluent. The retreat from Orthodox Christianity has also been paralleled by a spiritual yearning, which often takes the form of "new age mysticism".

The State of the Environment

In comparison with many other parts of the world, environment threats are modest and rarely figure in most people's priorities. Environmental quality in the cities has steadily improved (especially in terms of landscaping and open water) although locally increasing traffic levels are reducing air quality. More generally, Scotland's rivers are cleaner than they have been for over a century, and beaches are showing a similar improvement. Large areas of the Scottish countryside are protected in terms of their landscape quality and importance for wild plants, animals or birds. But global climate change is already leaving its mark. Flooding is on the increase and some plants and animals are threatened with extinction from the UK due to global warming. The use of resources such as natural gas is not sustainable and insufficient regard is paid to energy efficiency and the equitable use of resources. Waste management and recycling are only at the very early stages of development. Agriculture is highly subsidized by the European Union and the recent experience of BSE and foot-and-mouth disease has identified major threats to agricultural supplies. These threats are variously being addressed by GM crops on the one hand and a shift to organic production on the other. Scots, like so many other peoples, are ambivalent about such issues, wanting food that is both cheap and safe.

Church of the Province of Southern Africa (CPSA)

Like her people, southern Africa's landscape is one of immense beauty, diversity and agony.

We have the splendor of the Cape floral kingdom, the majesty of the Drakensberg-Ukuhlamba mountain range that runs across Lesotho, the magnificent dunes of Namibia and the beauty of our long coast. The "good" weather enables people to appreciate and enjoy the celebration the diversity of God's handiwork in this part of the world.

There have been significant efforts to cherish our fragile environment, through the work of governments and environmental organizations, in preserving the World Heritage Sites and other places of ecological and cultural significance, and in undertaking development that respects the integrity of all creation.

However, the region has been plagued by bouts of drought and flooding, and little food security exists for many. And our history has bequeathed us a dubious legacy. Our landscape has been scarred through selfishness, greed, war and poverty. Under Apartheid the oppression of people also contributed towards the destruction of the natural environment. People were forcibly removed from the land of their birth and dumped in "homelands" which deteriorated through overcrowding, overgrazing and consequent soil erosion. Environmental racism persists. Poorer communities continue to suffer from the negative health effects of having polluting industries situated near them.

The civil wars in Mozambique and Angola have had a devastating effect both on people's lives and on the natural terrain. Many in our region do not have access to clean drinking water or adequate sanitation. This has contributed to the spread of preventable diseases and exacerbated the spread of HIV/AIDS, which is decimating our population.

Yet there are signs of hope. In South Africa, provision for strong environmental protection has been legislated by our democratic government. Environmental impact assessments have become a necessity for those embarking on any significant development projects. Amongst ordinary people, including people of faith, there has been a growing concern in recent years about the environmental problems that face us and the need to act swiftly and decisively in attending to them. The Anglican Church has taken a number of actions to show their commitment to caring for the earth community. An outstanding example of this is the work being carried out in the Diocese of Umzimvubu under the encouragement and guidance of Bishop Geoff Davis, which has impacted the whole church in our region.

Church in Wales

Wales is one of the nations that make up the United Kingdom. As a Celtic nation, 25 percent of the 3 million people speak Welsh, while everyone can speak English. Christianity came to Wales around 100 AD, and the Celtic Church continued through the Dark Ages when England was invaded by pagan tribes. In 1920 the Church in Wales was disestablished from the State and became a separate Province. Following a referendum, an elected National Assembly for Wales was established in 1997, with a degree in autonomy from the United Kingdom Government. Already this is improving conditions of life for the people.

Wales is a country of hills and mountains with smaller areas of lowland around its edges. Located on the northwestern edge of Europe, it has an average temperature of 5EC in winter and 14EC in summer. Annual rainfall in excess of 1200mm supports a lush green countryside in the 80 percent of Wales devoted to agriculture.

Since 1960, the economy has been restructured. There has been a continual decline of the coal mining and metal industries that previously dominated the industrial areas and in the number of farms. At the same time, diversified manufacturing has grown, tourism has become more important and employment in services is now overwhelmingly dominant. By the year 2000, 80 percent of national employment was in service activities, 18 percent in manufacturing and less than 2 percent in agriculture and mining. Average farm size has increased and the need for labor has fallen. Tourism has come to dominate some rural areas, especially around the coasts and near the National Parks which cover 20 percent of Wales. Economic and population growth has concentrated in the lowlands bordering England, particularly in the Northeast, and in the Southeast around the capital city of Cardiff.

There is a strong sense of place, accompanied by a tradition of voluntary activity. Mutuality, self-help and a rich cultural inheritance are reflected in a passion for sport, the arts and music. The annual National Eisteddfod is unique. Wales has many internationally known people including Anthony Hopkins, Catherine Zeta-Jones, Bryn Terfel and Shirley Bassey. In the Anglican Communion many know the name of our Archbishop, Rowan Williams.

Today Wales is still struggling to emerge from the decline and loss of primary economic activities. The worst affected areas are the valleys of the South Wales coalfield, and the rural areas of the West and North. The major challenges in these areas are low rates of economic participation by people of working age and particularly by women, high disability rates, poor health, low levels of education and skills, and too few entrepreneurs in economic and social enterprises. There is a legacy of poor housing in places and of inappropriate infrastructure. These parts of Wales are so poor that they have qualified for a major European Community economic development and investment program (Objective One) for the period 2002–2006. This is concentrated on community and individual capacity building, the provision of community facilities and assistance, improving the infrastructure and stimulating innovative activity and entrepreneurship. In addition, the Welsh Assembly is implementing policies to tackle the social and economic challenges. It is providing special funds to the 100 most deprived communities (of the communities in Wales), subject to those communities participating producing their own plans for development. There are also distinctive policies for education and reorganization for health services to achieve greater local responsibility and involvement. It is greatly encouraging that the Welsh Assembly has adopted a policy of sustainable development in all aspects of its work.

Church of the West Indies

As one who is representing the Province of the West Indies at the Anglican Congress, I would like to share with the Anglican fraternity the peculiar concerns of the Caribbean. As members of the Anglican Communion, we have a rich heritage in Creation.

What I mean by our rich heritage:

- Our Celtic theological foundations

- The positive manifestations with regard to the creation, as expressed by St. Francis of Assisi

- New provincial books of common prayer that reflect creation spiritually

- Our Catholic theological authenticity and credibility

How is the Caribbean Reacting to the Stewardship of Creation?

In a recent speech delivered by the Hon. K. D. Knight, Minister of Foreign Affairs and Foreign Trade, delivered at the National Council on Ocean and Coastal Zone Management, Jamaica, August 2002, he made the following remarks:

> At the regional level, Caribbean states have been working towards establishing a regime for the wide protection of the Caribbean Sea within the form of a Caricom and The Association of Caribbean States (ACS). So we have managed to persuade the international community to recognize the need for promoting an integrated approach to the Caribbean Sea in the context of sustainable development. In a resolution adopted two years ago, the United Nations, among other things, called for the international community to assist Caribbean countries and regional organizations in our efforts to ensure the protection of the Caribbean Sea from degradation. In this context, I wish to give special recognition to the UNEP regional seas program active since 1974, which has been doing invaluable work in carrying out its mandate, which includes the promotion of integrated management and sustainable development of coastal areas, associated river basins and their living aquatic resources.

The Caribbean states have been an integral part of the Law of the Sea agenda. We are committed to protecting, preserving and managing marine, coastal and freshwater resources. The Convention of the International Maritime Organization (IMO) is strictly against dumping at sea. These issues are of particular concern for the Caribbean, because of the impact on our tourism product.

The National Council on Ocean and Coastal Zone Management (Jamaica) is concerned with many issues. At the forefront is coastal pollution, but keeping our rivers, lakes and springs from solid waste is of utmost and equal concern.

The Barbadan and Guyanese Governments have rejected the request from the US to dump its waste in their coastal waters. Two years ago an American company approached the Jamaican government to dump solid waste in their coastal waters and the offer was rejected.

There is a move to object to Japanese vessels carrying nuclear waste through the Panama Canal. The entire Caribbean basin is subject to hurricanes from July to the end of November and if a ship is sunk in the Caribbean Sea, our waters will be polluted.

The Jamaican Government has formed a National Council on Ocean and Coastal Zone Management. In addition, there is the formation of a national environment and planning agency, which is a citizens' charter. Its mission is to promote sustainable development by ensuring protection of the environment and orderly development in Jamaica through a highly motivated staff performing at the highest standard.

This agency would be responsible for enforcing the laws and regulations prescribed under the following acts:

- The Natural Resources Conversation Authority Act

- The Land Development and Utilization Act

- The Town and Country Planning Act

- The Beach Control Act

- The Wild Life Protection Act

- The Watershed Protection Act

- The Endangered Species (Protection, Conservation, & Regulation of Trade) Act

In 2001, the Government of Jamaica through the Forestry Department has documented a National Management and Conservation Plan for Jamaica in March 2001. The functions are twenty-first-century oriented and included the following goals:

- To promote private forestry and argo forestry

- To promote forestry recreation and Eco-tourism

- To create research facilities

- To promote watershed management

- To promote community participation social forestry

- To promote public education and awareness

- To promote the conservation and sustainable management of forests.

The Menacing Drug Culture

One of the dangers to sustainable development in the Caribbean is the drug culture, which has Colombian connections and has infiltrated the judiciary system, the police force, and big business. It has also polluted the psyche of many Jamaican people. The "salvation syndrome" of getting rich quickly and a sense of the loss of meaning of life can fuel the need for drugs, especially cocaine. Violence at an alarming rate is rampant and all the security personnel in the Caribbean met recently to coordinate strategies. It can reach a stage where the drug culture undermines sovereignty and the self-reliance of Jamaican people. The "Drug Don" has replaced political patronage in many inner cities and within urban sub-cultures. A treaty of cooperation has been signed between the Colombian government and the Jamaican government to coordinate efforts in fighting this threat.

The Debt Burden

The Anglican Communion has been part of the culture of some countries in the Commonwealth for over 300 years. The Communion should understand the effect the debt burden has on sustainable development in all the developing countries of the South. This raises the theological discussion in terms of the Global Mission and the Church. The theological understanding of the stewardship of global resources must take into consideration the universality of creation and the intention of God towards humankind. The Church has to question the stewardship of the World Bank, the IMF, and the WTO, which together form the axis of cosmic principalities and powers that undermine the quality of life in developing world in repudiating the debt. The debt burden prevents developing countries in the South from having adequate resources to counter the AIDS epidemic. The English-speaking Caribbean has the second highest number of cases of HIV-AIDS in the world. The Church cannot relinquish the stewardship of creation to the WTO, the IMF or the World Bank.

The twenty-first-century Church needs to urgently return to a "creation centered theological tradition" that will face the ecological crisis and will help to facilitate the Church in coming to terms with its Celtic and Catholic heritage. The stewardship of creation is integral to the mission of the Church. Creation-centered theology examines the contribution of science which helps to fashion a new paradigm, and links with global ecumenism, justice and liberation movements, feminist movements, and fosters the vision of hope, religious transformation a new type of adventure and a keen sense of community.

The Anglican Communion must, without apology, go for a creation-based theological tradition that will certainly undergird the stewardship of creation. The Western emphasis on fall/redemption theology has not propelled twentieth-century people to be agents of the stewardship of creation. Instead it has been a dominating force and not one that guided a responsible thought process.

Some ideas concerning mission and ministry have been addressed by the Bishop of the Windward Islands, the Rt. Rev. Dr. Sehon Goodridge at the Anglican Congress 2000, held in Kingston, Jamaica:

1. Promote a lively sense of the connection between worship and mission with our cultural heritage, symbols and styles.

2. Foster genuine partnership with follow Christians in the Anglican Communion and with those in our ecumenical relations.

3. Seek transformation of relationships with people of other faiths.

4. Seek social transformation in our societies by supporting efforts to relieve poverty, alienation, substance abuse and violence, so that our people may attain wholeness and fulfillment.

5. Preserve our environment so that our region will reflect the beauty and integrity of creation.

6. Encourage stewardship, especially the sharing of resources in pursuit of our mission.

We need an explorative theology of mission for the Caribbean in order to address critically the stewardship of creation. The stewardship of creation must not only be concerned with the mission of the church, but with what is the mission of the World Bank, the IMF and the WTO, in facilitating a life that is attainable and sustainable.

A theology of engagement recognizes our peculiar context and also our universality and is sensitive to the structural forces ("principalities and powers" Ephesians 6:12) which retard and stultify the development and transformation of a people, who are still journeying from the Exodus.

Episcopal Church in the United States of America

In 1991, the Episcopal Church USA, at its General Convention, adopted Stewardship of Creation as a major program area for the Church. Several environmental resolutions have been adopted by General Convention at its meetings every three years which help determine what the Church's policy is regarding public policy issues, as well as guide congregation and individual lifestyle choices.

Many of the almost 100 dioceses of the Episcopal Church have environmental committees which provide educational and advocacy opportunities. Many of these committees work ecumenically and interfaith in their communities and states—for example, several are part of the growing number of state interfaith climate change campaigns. On a national level, the Episcopal Church works ecumenically with almost twenty denominations in the National Council of Churches' Eco-Justice Working Group, and interfaith with the Interfaith Climate Change Campaign as part of the National Religious Partnership for the Environment.

Some of the issues of concern are:

Water

In 1992, Congress passed the Clean Water Act, which had the goal of eliminating pollution from all of our nation's rivers, lakes and coastal waters. This Act has been responsible for significant improvements in the quality of our lakes and rivers. However, we are a long way from the goal of cleaning up all of our nation's waterways.

Several dioceses, along with the national Church, will be focusing on the issue of water in the years ahead. Working with the National Council of Churches' Eco-Justice Working Group, a large water campaign is being developed, dealing with issues of quality, accessibility, privatization and more.

Energy

Clean, renewable energy from sun and wind offer nonpolluting, economical and sustainable alternatives for generating energy. However, our country is heavily dependent on coal, oil and nuclear power; efforts are continually underway by the government to open up wilderness areas to oil and gas drilling; billions of dollars of subsidies are given to these polluting and dangerous sources of energy, and measures to cut global warming pollution are ignored. Uniform fuel energy standards for automobiles, SUVs (Sport Utility Vehicles) and trucks need to be raised, which will result in the cutting of carbon dioxide pollution and the savings of billions of dollars for consumers at the gas pumps. Subsidies need to be given to the development of alternative energy sources instead of the fossil fuel industries.

A focus of the religious community over the past several years has been around global warming. A major organizer has been Episcopal Power and Light. Thanks to the advance in energy efficiency technology, the deregulation of the energy industry and the development of renewable resources, Episcopalians have the historic opportunity to put their faith into action and play a critical role in the decline of global warming.

Clean Air

The Clean Air Act was passed by Congress in 1970. Unfortunately, efforts are underway to weaken the clean air protections by letting thousands of our biggest polluting facilities (including old, dirty power plants, oil refineries and chemical plants) to escape rules that require them to install sufficient pollution controls which would cut down on smog, soot and toxins released into the air.

Forests

Less than 5 percent of America's old growth forests remain, and there are efforts by the environmental community to protect the remaining undeveloped and roadless wilderness forests by preventing commercial logging and road construction in the national forests.

Environmental Justice

Sometimes known as Environmental Racism, this term refers to the fact that low-income neighborhoods and communities of color bear disproportionate environmental burdens in our society. These communities are more frequently chosen as sites for polluting facilities, oil refineries and incinerators over wealthier, predominately white communities that have more political power. As a result, the rates of cancer, asthma and other respiratory diseases are much higher in these low-income communities and communities of color.

Sprawl

Poorly planned development threatens the environment, health and quality of life. Increased traffic and the reduction, if not elimination, of open space are often the result of sprawl. As a result, environmental groups are working with housing groups, urban planners, etc. to plan development more appropriately.

Food Production

A more recent focus has been on food production, in light of the development of genetic-modification technologies. At the 2003 General Convention, a resolution will be debated which asks for the support of public policy and actions that foster research and development in the types of science and technology that preserve biodiversity in food production; that is, the maintenance of a healthy relationship among varieties of food crops and species on which they depend, awareness of trade conditions and intellectual property practices that exacerbate the tendency of genetic modification technologies to reduce biodiversity in food production; and the support and participation in programs that protect farming and farmlands and promote intentional purchases of food produced locally.

Participants continue the discussions at the coffee breaks.

A view of the Plenary.

SECTION IV

Biographical Sketches of Congress Speakers and Organizers

Biographical Sketches of Congress Speakers and Organizers

Denise M. Ackermann is a feminist theologian from Cape Town, South Africa, where she was Professor of Practical Theology at the University of the Western Cape. Presently she is a visiting professor at the Faculty of Theology of the University of Stellenbosch, teaching a course on Christian Spirituality and Gender, Culture and Religion. She has held visiting fellowships at Harvard Divinity School and the Center for Theological Inquiry in Princeton, New Jersey. She accompanied Archbishop Njongonkulu Ndungane to the 1998 Lambeth Conference as a theological consultant, served as a Trustee on the Desmond Tutu Peace Trust, and participates in the Circle of Concerned African Women Theologians.

Chantal Nicole Andrianarivo is a member of the Anglican Parish of Avaratranjoma, Antananarivo, Madagascar, where she is Head of Research and Biodiversity at the National Association of Protected Areas Management. Chantal is responsible for the Coordination of Researches and Biodiversity of the National Protected Areas Network (and also on the national level for biodiversity) and of Marine Protected Areas in Madagascar (from site identification to implementation of the MPA). She is the National Coordinator of UNEP's National Biosafety Framework implementation. She works also at national and regional levels in Environmental Impact Assessment. Her postgraduate qualifications include a Diplome d'Etudes Approfondies at the University of Antananarivo.

David Beetge was born in Witbank, South Africa, in 1948. He grew up in Krugersdorp on the West Rand where he completed his schooling. He worked in commerce for a time, completing his Chartered Institute of Secretaries and Administrators examination and being Company Secretary of ICI (South Africa) Limited. His theological education was at St. Paul's Theological College in Grahamstown, and subsequently, he completed both his Bachelors and Honours Degrees in theology through the University of South Africa. He has a Masters Degree from the University of Natal. Bishop Beetge is the first Bishop of the Diocese of the Highveld which was inaugurated in January, 1990. He is the liaison bishop for finance in the Church of the Province of Southern Africa and is Vice-Chairperson of the Pension Trust Board. He is a former spokesperson for the Province on arms and defence matters. He is also the Anglican Co-chair of the International Anglican Roman Catholic Commission for Unity and Mission.

Eric Beresford is consultant for ethics and interfaith relations for the General Synod of the Anglican Church of Canada, where he is a priest. For the last two years he has been seconded part time as consultant for ethics for the Anglican Consultative Council, working mostly on issues related to emerging biotechnologies and environmental issues. He is also convener of the Anglican Environmental Network. Before beginning his current work he was on the faculty of McGill University in Montreal where he taught ethics in the Faculty of Religious Studies. He can be reached c/o The Anglican Church of Canada, 600 Jarvis Street, Toronto, ON M4Y 2J6.

Sally Grover Bingham is a priest in the Diocese of California currently serving as the Environmental Minister at Grace Cathedral in San Francisco. She is the founder and executive director of The Regeneration Project, an internationally known nonprofit ministry working on a religious response to global climate change. Among The Regeneration Project's core programs is Episcopal Power and Light, which seeks to help the Episcopal Church become a zero emission community. Sally has been active in the environmental community for twenty years, and has brought widespread attention to the linkage between ecological issues and the Christian Faith. She has been the chair of the Episcopal Diocesan Commission for the Environment in California for the last eight years, and serves on the national board of Environmental Defense.

George Browning is Bishop of Canberra and Goulburn, Australia, a Diocese which encompasses the national capital and surrounding district, a position he has held since 1993. At the 1998 Lambeth Conference he chaired the section on the environment and with other members of his group was responsible for drafting the Lambeth resolutions on this subject. George has been Vice Principal of one theological College and Principal of another. His Diocese is the first in Australia to develop a Commission for the Environment by resolution of synod.

Simon E. Chiwanga is Bishop of the Diocese of Mpwapwa in the Anglican Church of the Province of Tanzania. Dr. Chiwanga was educated at St. Paul's Theological College, Limuru, Kenya; the University of Dar es Salaam, Tanzania; and the University of London. He completed his Doctor of Ministry at the Episcopal Divinity School in 1999. Dr. Chiwanga has been a member of the Anglican Consultative Council for over a decade as both a priest and bishop representative from Tanzania. Until recently, he was Chairman of the Anglican Consultative Council. He preached at the central Eucharist of the 1998 Lambeth Conference of Bishops.

Geoff Davies is the Bishop of the Anglican Diocese of Umzimvubu, which covers the northern half of the former Transkei, between the Drakensberg Mountains and the Transkei Wild Coast. Born in Cape

Town, Bishop Davies studied theology at Cambridge (Emmanuel College) and was ordained in St. Paul's Cathedral, London. Returning to Africa, he looked after the Parish of Serowe, on the edge of the Kalahari in Botswana. After a lifetime of ministry in Africa, he is increasingly aware of the incredible beauty but fragility of African landscapes. He has responsibility for environmental affairs for the Bishops of the Church of the Province of Southern Africa and has produced a booklet entitled "Save Our Future," and a number of other resources on the Church's care for the environment.

Claire Foster holds the portfolio for science, medicine, technology and environmental issues in the Board for Social Responsibility of the Church of England. Her background is in theology and moral philosophy and she has published widely in the area of medical ethics. She is working on developing the Church of England's agenda on environmental and sustainable development issues.

Richard Fuggle is Shell Professor of Environmental Studies in the Department of Environmental and Geographical Science at the University of Cape Town. Born in Zululand, South Africa in 1941, he has been involved in pursuits pertaining to environmental management since 1966. His primary activity has been university based research and teaching, but he has also led an active environmental consultancy that has undertaken environmental impact assessments throughout southern Africa. He served as deputy chair of the Council for the Environment (the sixteen-person body which advised the South African Government on Environmental Policy) and also as Chair of the Board of the South African Institute of Ecologists and Environmental Scientists. Richard serves on the Board of Directors for the Network for Environment and Development in Africa (NESDA—based in Côte d'Ivoire) and for several years was on the core faculty of the LEAD (Leadership Environment and Development in Africa) initiative. He has received recognition for his contributions to the field of Environmental Impact Assessment from a variety of sources. These include the Cape Tercentenary Medal as well as a citation from the Ministry of Environmental Affairs for his contributions to the conservation of the South African natural environment; the Premium Award of the Environmental Planning Professions of South Africa for his contribution to training in environmental management; and the prestigious Rose Hulman Award for his contribution to Integrated Environmental Management both in South Africa and internationally. Recently, he has been contributing expert advice and case studies to the African Environmental Outlook Report. This 400+-page document (available at www.unep.org/aeo/) is the basis for the African Ministers Submissions and position on environmental matters at the World Summit on Sustainable Development. He has been most involved with the "Human Vulnerability" chapter of the document as well as with case studies. A synopsis of his work on the Lake Victoria situation appears in Global Environment Report 3 (www.unep.org/geo/). He has also been involved with the inspection of World Bank Projects that have been challenged in China, India and Africa.

Jeff Golliher is Program Representative for the Environment and Sustainable Development with the Anglican Observer at the United Nations and is a parish priest at Saint John's Episcopal Church in Ellenville, the Diocese of New York. He has a doctorate in cultural anthropology based on fieldwork with indigenous peoples in the Talamanca Rainforest of Costa Rica and among modern religious pilgrims on the Isle of Iona, Scotland. He co-edited and contributed to "Crisis and the Renewal of Creation: Church and World in the Age of Ecology," and "Cultural and Spiritual Values of Biodiversity" (published by the United Nations Environmental Program), and contributed an article on environmental ministry in "Beyond Colonial Anglicanism: The Anglican Communion in the Twenty-First Century" (I. Douglas and K. Pui-Lan, eds.). He is a member of the Third Order of the Society of Saint Francis.

Jessie Jeyakaran, a biology teacher, trainer and organizer for the environment and sustainable development in South India. She participated in the National Environmental Education Programmes for school children, sponsored by the Ministry of Environment and Forests of India from 1991–1998. She translated and adapted "Essential Learning in Environmental Education" through the Ministry of Human Resource Development. Since 1992, Mrs. Jeyakaran has served as Eco-Missioner of the Diocese of Madurai-Ramnad, and since 1996 on the Synod Ecological Concerns Committee of the Church of South India. Using her platform as a teacher to launch young children on the path of environmental awareness and action, Mrs. Jeyakaran is a noted organizer, educator, and author in the area of sustainable development and environmental protection.

Jan Loubser is a Canadian citizen with thirty-eight years of professional experience, including twenty-three years in international development in both management and professional roles, mainly with the Canadian International Development Agency and the United Nations Development Programme. Dr. Loubser was educated at Harvard University and the University of Stellenbosch, South Africa. Since 1994 he has been working as a consultant with the UNDP and other UN agencies in promoting, planning and implementing holistic people-centred development strategies and programmes, focusing on the empowerment of local communities as the fundamental building blocks for sound governance and participatory management of development. He has assisted with the development of such strategies and plans in Thailand, Trinidad and Tobago, India, The Gambia, Chad, Mongolia, South Africa and Uganda. Recently, he has contributed to the development of strategies for promoting and implementing human rights based development policies and programmes with a focus on a holistic approach of all human rights for all. He has assisted with the implementation strategy for UNDP for the World Summit for Social Development Programme of Action and a global health sector strategy for HIV/AIDS for the World Health Organization. He is currently assisting UNDP with the development of support programmes for the African Union and NEPAD (The New Partnership for African Development).

Peter Mann is international coordinator for the New York based organization WHY (World Hunger Year and editor of "WNY Speaks" www.worldhungeryear.org>. A major focus of his work is the movement in the U.S. and internationally to build up local and regional food systems in order to achieve food security. Peter has been actively involved in the Sustainable Agriculture and Rural Development (SARD) aspects of WSSD that is developing partnerships between consumers, farmers and fisherfolk, farmworkers and unions, UN agencies and governments. A lifelong concern of Peter's is the sacredness of food, and the work of faith-based communities for economic justice.

Wangari Muta Maathai was born in Nyeri, Kenya (Africa) in 1940. She was trained in Biological Sciences in the United States, Germany, and the University of Nairobi. She obtained a Ph.D. (1971) from the University of Nairobi where she also taught. She became department chair and an associate professor in 1976 and 1977, respectively. In both cases she was the first woman to attain those positions in the region. She was active in the National Council of Women of Kenya from 1976-87 and was its chairperson from 1981-87. It was while she served the National Council of Women that she introduced the idea of planting trees with the people in 1976. She developed this idea further into a broad-based, grassroots organisation—the Green Belt Movement—whose main focus is the planting of trees with women's groups in order to conserve the environment and improve their quality of life. Through the Green Belt Movement, Wangari has assisted women in planting more than 20 million trees on farms and on school and church compounds. She is internationally recognized for her persistent work for democracy, human rights and environmental issues. She has addressed the UN on several occasions and spoke on behalf of women at special sessions of the General Assembly for the five-year review of the Earth Summit. Wangari has served on the commission for Global Governance and Commission on the Future. She has received numerous awards, such as Woman of the Year Award (1983), the Right Livelihood Award (1984), the Better World Society Award (1986), the Windstar Award for the Environment (1988), the Woman of the World Award (1989), Honorary Doctor of Law, Williams College, USA (1990), the Goldman Environmental Prize (1991), UN's Africa Prize for Leadership (1991), the Edinburgh Medal (1993), the Jane Addams Conference Leadership Award (1993), and the Golden Ark Award (1994). She was also listed on UNEP's Global 500 Hall of Fame. In 1997, Wangari was elected by the Earth Times as one of 100 persons in the world who have made a difference in the environmental arena. In 1986 the Movement established a Pan African Green Belt Network and has exposed over 40 individuals from other African countries to the approach. Some of these individuals have established tree planting initiatives in their own countries or they use some of the Green Belt Movement methods to improve their efforts. So far, Tanzania, Uganda, Malawi, Lesotho, Ethiopia, and Zimbabwe have successfully launched such initiatives in Africa. More recently, she has embarked on new challenges, playing a leading global role as a co-chair of the Jubilee 2000 Afrika Campaign, which seeks cancellation of unpayable backlog debts of the poor countries in Afrika by the year 2000. Currently, it has been her campaign against land grabbing and rapacious allocation of forest land that has caught the limelight.

Joe and Katie McGervey are serving as volunteers for mission from the Episcopal Church of the United States, Diocese of Washington, DC, St. Columba's Parish, to the Church of the Province of Southern Africa. They spent their first year exploring the relationship between the church's social development work and energy usage, specifically looking at opportunities for using renewable energy. They have provided recommendations to the CPSA on their findings. In this their second year, they are working in the Diocese of Umzimvubu with Bishop Geoff Davies. They are helping one parish, St. Andrew's, explore ways of using renewable energy in their three on-going development projects; they are also supporting Bishop Geoff in his preparation for the Anglican Congress and WSSD. Joe is a mechanical engineer who studied air pollution derived from large energy producers in the USA before coming to SA. Katie is a public administrator on leave from the US Department of Energy where she promoted renewable energy and energy efficient technologies for use in US government facilities.

The Rt. Rev. John Oliver was a parish priest for nearly twenty-five years in England before serving for thirteen years as Bishop of Hereford, a post from which he has now retired. As Bishop, he chaired the local Unity Committee and for five years chaired the Advisory Board of Ministry which oversaw the selection and training of ordained and lay ministers. He took his seat in the House of Lords from 1996 to 2003 as Lead Bishop of the Environment, speaking on environmental issues on behalf of the Church and representing Bishops on rural matters. This included discussions on genetically-modified crops, transportation and agriculture, and rural distress particularly during the outbreak of "foot and mouth disease" in 2001. Currently he is living in Wales.

William Rukirande, Retired Bishop of the Diocese of Kigezi, holds an honorary doctorate from the Virginia Episcopal Seminary (USA) and is now the Coordinator of Solar Light for Churches in Africa. Solar Light for Churches in Africa is a project started by Bishop Alden Hathaway,

Retired Bishop of Pittsburgh, together with John M. Semanda and Bishop Rukirande, to help church officers and church facilities, schools, clinics, convents and ordinary churchgoers access some light at night to extend their day. The programme has subsidised 1,256 solar systems of approximately 64 watts for many people in East Africa. The subsidy is 50% of the cost of such a system. This has been achieved through aggressive fund raising by the three gentlemen mentioned above. Requests for this gospel of light have been overwhelming. Every summer, he also leads a group of American high school students to Africa, where they choose a programme of their own (perhaps an orphanage or old people's home) and donate a solar system to that project and install it together with Ugandan high school students. The Programme is called "The American Youth Mission," an ecumenical programme involving teaching young people to identify with a need, and then to solve the need themselves.

David Shreeve co-founded The Conservation Foundation with the internationally renowned environmentalist Prof. David Bellamy in 1982. Their aim was to provide a means for interested parties in the public, private and non-profit sections to collaborate on environmental causes by creating and managing a wide range of projects and programmes. In its twenty years, the Foundation has worked with a wide range of partners and has endeavoured through a variety of initiatives throughout the UK and around the world to network positive environmental news.

Taimalelagi Fagamalama Tuatagaloa-Matalavea (Mrs.) is the Anglican Observer at the United Nations. The Archdeacon Emeritus from the Anglican Province of Aotearoa, New Zealand and Polynesia was Archdeacon for the Samoa Archdeaconry for eight years before taking up her present appointment in August 2001. She was a member of the Anglican Consultative Council from 1987 to 1993; was a president of the National Council of Churches Women of Samoa after being Treasurer for the same organization for five years. She was a member of the Board of Oversight for St. John's Theological College for nine years until June 2001. She worked for the United Nations Development Programme for twenty-five years, first in programme-related duties and later as Operations Manager of the Samoa Field Office.

Anthony Turton, a political scientist by training, currently heads the African Water Issues Research Unit (AWIRU) at the University of Pretoria. In his former life he was a senior officer in the South African Security Forces responsible for various issues. His main role was working at the strategic level to end hostilities in Southern Africa including the negotiations surrounding the Cuban troop withdrawal from Angola, Namibian independence, the release of Nelson Mandela and the normalization of the political process in South Africa, CODESA, and finally bringing RENAMO to the negotiating table, thereby ending the Mozambique civil war. He is thus a deeply committed peacenik. His current work centres on water as a fundamental driver of social, economic and political stability in Southern Africa. He has worked as a consultant to the British Overseas Development Institute (ODI), the Swedish Foreign Ministry, the South African Government, and Shell International in London etc. He has published a number of articles, book chapters, etc., and has edited two books, one of which will be launched at the World Summit on Sustainable Development by Mikhail Gorbachev, who wrote the foreword.

Alan Werritty is Professor of Physical Geography at the University of Dundee, Scotland. He is also Convenor of the Mission Board of the Diocese of St Andrews, Dunkeld and Dunblane, and a member of the General Synod of the Scottish Episcopal Church. His academic research includes work on floods, water resources and climate change. He is especially interested in how vulnerable communities and landscapes adjust to environmental change. His teaching covers issues such as global water resources, river basin management, big dams and hydropolitics.

Rosina Wiltshire holds the position of United Nations Development Program Resident Representative and UN Resident Coordinator for Barbados and the Organization of Eastern Caribbean States (OECS). Prior to joining the Barbados Sub-regional Office, she was Chief of the Learning Resource Centre/Office of Human Resources at UNDP, 1999–2001. She was Deputy Director of the UNDP Social Development and Poverty Elimination Division and Manager of Gender in Development from 1994–99. Prior to joining UNDP, Rosina worked in Ottawa, Canada where she was a Professor at the University of Ottawa and Head of the Gender and Sustainable Development Programme at the International Development Research Centre. She was Senior Programme Office of Caribbean Conservation and coordinated the Development Alternatives with Women for a New Era (DAWN) initiative for the United Nations Conference on Environment and Development (UNCED) in 1992. She participated in both the NGO and official UNCED meetings in Rio. Dr Wiltshire was also a member of the UNDP delegation to WSSD in Copenhagen in 1995 and the Fourth World Conference on Women in Beijing in 1995. Rosina holds a Ph.D. in Political Science (International Relations) from the University of Michigan, Ann Arbor, USA. She taught at universities in Canada and the Caribbean for twenty years and has published and lectured widely on issues of sustainable human development. Rosina is dedicated to the protection of the environment and to health and human well-being.